GRANTA

JAMES FENTON
THE FALL OF SAIGON

15

Editor: William Buford
Assistant Editor: Graham Coster
Managing Editor: Tracy Shaw
Executive Editor: Pete de Bolla
Design: Chris Hyde
Editorial and Office Assistant: Emily Dening
Editorial Assistants: Michael Comeau, Margaret Costa, Eric Burns, Piers Spence
Editorial Board: Malcolm Bradbury, Elaine Feinstein, Ian Hamilton, Leonard Michaels
US Editor: Jonathan Levi, 325 Riverside Drive, Apartment 81, New York, New York 10025

Editorial and Subscription Correspondence: Granta, 44a Hobson Street, Cambridge CB1 1NL. (0223) 315290.

All manuscripts are welcome but must be accompanied by a stamped, self-addressed envelope or they cannot be returned.

Subscriptions: £12.00 for four issues.

Back Issues: £3.50 each. *Granta* 1, 2, 3, 4 and 9 are no longer available. All prices include postage.

Granta is photoset by Hobson Street Studio Ltd, Cambridge, and is printed by Hazell Watson and Viney Ltd, Aylesbury, Bucks.

Granta is published by Granta Publications Ltd and distributed by Penguin Books Ltd, Harmondsworth, Middlesex, England; Viking Penguin Inc., 40 West 23rd St, New York, New York, USA; Penguin Books Australia Ltd, Ringwood, Victoria, Australia; Penguin Books Canada Ltd, 2801 John Street, Markham, Ontario, Canada L3R 1B4; Penguin Books (NZ) Ltd, 182–90 Wairau Road, Auckland 10, New Zealand. This selection copyright © 1985 by Granta Publications Ltd. Each work published in *Granta* is copyright of the author.

Cover by Chris Hyde

Granta 15, Spring 1985, Reprinted 1986

ISSN 0017-3231
ISBN 014-00-7581-X

Published with the assistance of the Eastern Arts Association

CONTENTS

Observations

Richard Ford On Harley-Davidson 12

Philip Norman Grandma Norman and the Queen 18

James Fenton The Fall of Saigon 27

Ten Years On

Frank Snepp Toothpaste 120

Norman Podhoretz Impotence 125

Noam Chomsky Dominoes 129

Nadine Gordimer The Essential Gesture: Writers and Responsibility 135

Nadine Gordimer What were You dreaming? 153

George Steiner A Conversation Piece 177

Salman Rushdie On Günter Grass 179

Günter Grass *The Tin Drum* in Retrospect 187

John Berger Go ask the Time 195

Ryszard Kapuściński Warsaw Diary 213

Marilynne Robinson The Waste Land 227

Michael Crick Reporting the Strike 243

Peter Greig Revelations 251

Notes from Abroad

Ted Solotaroff The Young Writer in America 263

Letters **Timothy Garton Ash and others** 281

Notes on Contributors 287

Editorial 5

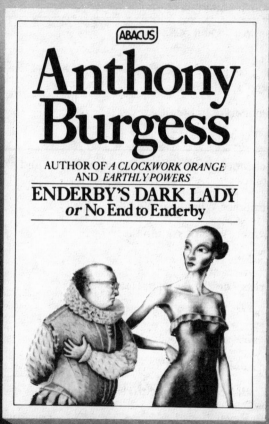

Editorial

The twentieth century has tolerated a number of mythologies about the role of the writer, and one of the most commonplace is the writer as inspired genius. The inspired genius theory of literary creation has given licence to all sorts of abuses of what we normally regard as civilized conduct: heavy drinking, running around with women or men or both, beating up your friends, excesses of every description, and, in general, acting in a pretty obnoxious way. There is, however, another, much less recognized category of deviant behaviour, and one that explains a great deal about the literature and literary reportage that this century has witnessed: the writer as lunatic.

The writer as lunatic differs from the inspired genius in a number of ways. Most importantly, perhaps, lunatic writers tend not to abuse those around them: the abuse is directed squarely at themselves. In thinking this exceptional, I should note that I'm assuming most of us go out of our way not to get killed: we look both ways before crossing the street, and if we're ever unfortunate enough to face a man with a gun (or, for that matter, a tank) we know that we want to get *very* far out of his way. This is not true of the writer as lunatic. For example, ten years ago, James Fenton went to Indochina to see the fall of Saigon. Just days before the North launched its invasion in the South, James Fenton could be seen strolling casually into an area occupied by Vietcong soldiers, sharing a coconut with them while noting the sound of approaching South Vietnamese army vehicles on patrol. And when Saigon did eventually fall, he not only joined in the looting of the US Embassy, but, on hearing that the first North Vietnamese tank had appeared in the city, rushed out of his hotel, flagged it down, and hopped on the back. This I regard as lunatic conduct. Another example is Ryszard Kapuściński, one of the most gifted writers of reportage today. Ryszard Kapuściński has not only spent most of his adult life looking for national disasters, but he also has the uncanny knack— unintended, I trust—of bringing them with him. When he arrived in Zanzibar, the revolution broke out; fleeing to what was then called Tanganyika, he encountered a coup. He was in Angola when it was attacked by South Africa, in Burundi where he was meant to be executed by a firing squad, in El Salvador during the war with Honduras, in Uganda witnessing Idi Amin's maddest moments, and in Iran when the Shah finally decided that it was time to go abroad.

5

Fearing that an army might descend on my doorstep, I'd think twice before inviting a man like this over for dinner. For it's obvious that Kapuściński, too, is a lunatic. And it's equally obvious that there are other writers like him, each sharing a common feature: the compulsion to seek out political crises.

L iterature and politics are meant to be incompatible partners, but consistently writers keep getting involved in political issues. This is in part, as Nadine Gordimer describes in her essay 'The Essential Gesture', because they have no choice: there are certain demands society makes on the author that, regardless of the difficulties they occasion, have to be met. But a writer who jumps on tanks, or one who travels thousands of miles to stand before a firing squad, has certainly sought his difficulties more than they have sought him. There is, I suspect, something else at work.

Fenton mentions that his journey started on the day Auden died, and the coincidence offers some interesting comparisons. For Auden's generation, Spain was more a cause than a country, and the Civil War itself a crusade in which the political issues were urgent, unambiguous and defined. But Auden accounts for his going to Spain mainly because, as he says in a letter cited in Humphrey Carpenter's biography, 'The poet must have direct knowledge of major political events.' He never mentions the Spanish cause. He went to Spain because he felt it was essential, as a writer, to be there.

The value of literature is not merely in its worth as an imaginative construct, but in its relationship to the political event, to history, to what's out there. Nadine Gordimer cites Camus—'It is from the moment when I shall no longer be more than a writer that I shall cease to write'—and the aphorism can apply equally to virtually every contributor in this issue: from Salman Rushdie's creed—'Keep grinning. Be bloody-minded. Argue with the world'—to George Steiner's terrifying 'Conversation Piece'. And it also applies to James Fenton, determined to find out what happens after a communist victory: a literary lunatic who visited places he wasn't meant to, but returned able to satisfy a need for a narrative answerable to the world.

William Buford

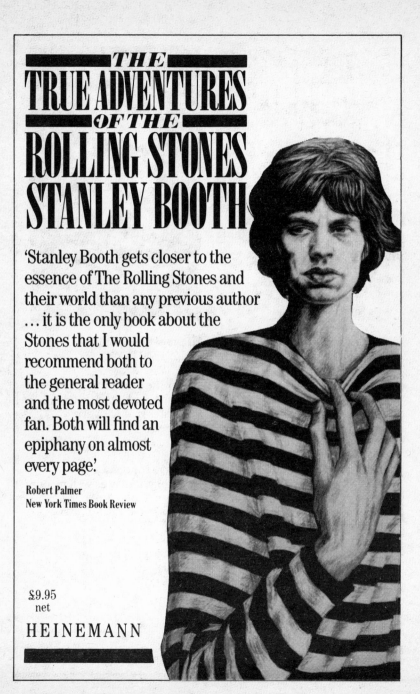

THE TRUE ADVENTURES OF THE ROLLING STONES
STANLEY BOOTH

'Stanley Booth gets closer to the essence of The Rolling Stones and their world than any previous author … it is the only book about the Stones that I would recommend both to the general reader and the most devoted fan. Both will find an epiphany on almost every page.'

Robert Palmer
New York Times Book Review

£9.95
net

HEINEMANN

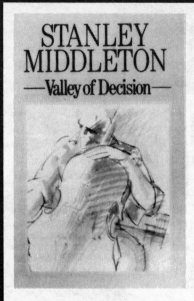

OBSERVATIONS

Richard Ford
On Harley-Davidson

There is no use getting sentimental over a motorcycle. *Especially* a motorcycle. Even if it is the motorcycle I and ten million other American men have coveted all our lives, the last big-bore, honest-to-God *motorcycle* motorcycle made in America, and the epitome of what the motorcycle dream means. Harley-Davidson.

I am not certain if it is in my very soul to have wanted such a bike. Some people come to their adulthoods already equipped with nice understandings of just what it is they're not. And maybe I just lack that certainty—my 'location in the world' seeming always more iffy—so I am willing to give more things a try. That is as close to my soul as a motorcycle needs to get—something admired, then tried.

I don't love it. There is no use loving a thing not fully alive—animals or landscapes or particular vistas or things to eat or drink. I wouldn't, for instance, want HARLEY-DAVIDSON tattooed on my biceps. (In fact, I'm not quite sure what would be worth a tattoo anymore. If my wife left me, maybe: LOSER). I may have passed now that young man's reckless season for tattoos.

But not for motorcycles. At least not this one, not yet. Though now that I own a Harley-Davidson, my feelings for it are only a notch above what they were before: I still covet it, and ownership has simply amplified that into a kind of prideless self-satisfaction.

It is a standard Super Glide—a big bike—a '79, one of the ones made by AMF, and a repo. It is rose red, with fat bobbed tanks, a minimum of chrome, an eighty-cubic-inch 'shovel head' motor vaguely the size of a Volkswagen Beetle, which torques the bike up as sudden as a jack hammer, runs it at 130 miles per hour, and produces such a gratifying systoltic *Ba-doom, Ba-doom* that it is recognizable as a Harley two streets away. Jack Nicholson, I've heard, used to own one. And I understand why.

Speed, to me, is an unmagical, linear business—just more of everything, harder. Wind, rain, insects. I've never craved it, or danger either. I wouldn't, for instance, jump out of an airplane not already on the ground. But there is a fierce, thriving elation in going up through the gears, feeling the wind stiffen, the motor reach down, and the big frame grow airy as it takes on movement. There is a sensation when this happens of being transformed—even though you aren't—a sweet slippage off dead centre, a self-cancelling association with the size and literalness of this particular bike. It is unprofound. But not many things, other than the imagination, can routinely induce such a feeling. Not fly fishing, or bird hunting over a finished dog. None of the other things I like. Which is not to rhapsodize; only to describe an express appeal. I suppose it is the experience of sport: a brief, earth-tethered freeing. A pleasure. A small thing.

Though a Harley does not seem to be a 'sporting machine'. Its ancestry is more everyday-industrial-mechanical, a midwesterner's version of the idea: motorcycle.

Neither have I met, in what one could call the 'Harley Riding Community', many I'd call sportsmen. Not among the staunch burgher-looking fellows—the touristes—who plunk down fifteen thousand for a fancy 'dresser' (padded fairing, Marantz, matching trailer, intercom and a swanky-plush jump suit for the wife), a bike in the spirit of a motorhome; nor among the other ranks, those fellows who ride their 'scooters' *inside* motel rooms and bars, call themselves names like 'Sleaze', and 'Luger,' and 'Amana', and have 'I'D RATHER BE EATING PUSSY' tattooed on *their* biceps. Fate-tempters. But not sportsmen; no more, say, than Bobo Brazil and the Terror Twins could be thought of as gifted athletes.

Harleys have always appealed to that incumbency in us to let something else do the talking. They are the most public of bikes, the most Republican of gestures. Rakish, yet grave. Untranscendant.

One-dimensional. Meaning, logically, brought down to a name: Harley-Davidson.

For those who have never ridden a Harley-Davidson, and for some reason may never, I will admit the one fact salient and interesting to all: it is a cinch to ride, inexcusable as that might seem for a machine so difficult-appearing. You just need to touch ground with your feet when you sit on it, and be able to keep balanced so that it doesn't fall over at a stop light (a grave public embarrassment). A small woman could ride mine. And in truth the first Harley I ever sat on was the first one I ever rode. And, as it happened, it was the one I bought.

It *is* dangerous, of course. And that fact, coupled with the ease of riding, makes up part of its appeal: the thrill that requires no expertise. A circus thrill. But at 700 pounds my Super Glide handles ungracefully at slow speeds, tends to wallow (its front wheel becoming a doughnut) and when it falls over on you it is difficult to dislodge. (My neighbour once mistook me for a Hell's Angel, tailgated me all the way up the muddy road to my house and when I slowed to a creep to take the turn in my drive safe as possible, my bike schlumped down on top of me and almost got me killed.)

Speed, though, is the more pertinent and poignant matter, since it is part of the bike's destiny with its rider. (No one buys a Harley dreaming of going slowly). But by being both heavy and very powerful, a Harley-Davidson underway with speed takes on an enormous inertia, and because it is sleeker than an automobile and only on two wheels, prefers to go as straight as possible. The Mississippi Delta, with its long, dog-less roads, is an ideal place to ride fast. Vermont is a bad place. The proof of this is that in exactly the time it takes you to check your digital watch, a Harley will bring you straight up and over the top of the gentlest curve, take sudden flight and break you to pieces. A Shriner I once knew told me you could fall off a Harley-Davidson—his was one of the old '74s, with police lights and a siren—and it would run on down the road without you. Which may be true. He also said the bike would eventually turn round by itself, come back and run you over. Which is not.

But other horror stories are almost certainly true. Hitting a chicken and being thrown off. Hitting a pocket of invisible cold (or hot) air and being thrown off. Hitting nothing you ever know about, and being thrown off. 'Kiss the pavement,' this is called, and you would always want to be careful.

Though most of us who ride Harleys *are* careful—inwardly vigilant types, after the manner of our motorcycle, which portrays within itself a kind of gravity; that discourages cut-ups. This is true even for Sleaze and Luger, whose aboriginal attitudes towards most things shouldn't be misread as unconventional. When, indeed, we *are* hurt it's usually because we've been run *into*—as with my neighbour up the hill bearing down my tailpipe. Often we don't even know what's hit us and are blameless—a disconsoling fact to a fellow like me who dislikes danger and whose meanest injuries have merely been temperamental.

I am not one to work on my Harley. To me, there is absolutely no Zen in it. A gasoline tank that passes too close to a hot cylinder head would never catch my eye. I am uncertain adjusting the chain. As with my own private illnesses I am quick to put my bike in expert hands.

As a consequence, though, when I look at my bike what I see is—mystery: founded, as mystery always is, on ignorance. It is rash, I suppose, to buy a complicated machine you know absolutely nothing about, can't fix, can't take apart—can only gas up, start and ride away on. But that is all I have interest for. If I am a dilettante because of it, I am at least one who has satisfied a fond wish. We all of us do it all the time, with our cars, our weed-eaters, our rototillers; the only difference being that my Harley-Davidson is purely *optional*, and so seems to incur a duty.

But I am, after all, my father's son.

I remember when we moved into our first and only suburban house in Mississippi in 1955. My father, a big, sweet-natured man, dedicated a shadowy part of his new utility room behind the carport as his 'tool bench'. He didn't have any tools, and was too busy working to buy and learn how to use them, so it was eventually ignored—its only use coming when he built me a punching bag out of a kit from Monkey Ward's, and attached it to the wall. It was his only carpentry. Though when I whacked the bag good and hard its first time, it fell on the floor. Every bit of it. And even though we picked it up and put it back on the wall, in the end it stayed down, my boxing career shortened by his lack of know-how.

He was not a problem-solver. Nor am I. He had other things to do, things he already knew about and took pride in; and I am like him. What would it be like to look at my bike and see a thing whose *every* part and movement and mundane principle I understood? What boredom. What a useful mystery lost, what spark of innocence—the first principle of my father's goodness—would I extinguish in myself once and for all just for the privilege of being *handy*?

These days I tend to stand at the window and look out at my wonderful red bike and wonder what will go wrong, what suspicious noise I'll hear and know nothing about as I ride up into desolate Idaho, bent on earth-tethered freedom, where there are no Harley shops between Boise and Coeur d'Alene, and where you'd need to know something if something went wrong. I even wake at night and think about that. It is a small and acute and—it seems—uniquely post-industrial agony. But still one I will resist. I bought my bike to ride, not fix. That is its pleasure. That is all I really want from it.

I can say plainly enough why I bought a Harley-Davidson.
I liked its looks.
Nothing more complicated than that. Especially I liked the figure cut by the bike and rider together, a 'line' that on a Harley makes the rider seem to sit in the 'basement' of the motorcycle. Low-bellied, semi-recumbent, centred. Precisely as it should be. No

other bike looks that way. And that is reasoning enough to buy a motorcycle: a shape gives pleasure, exhausts its own small aesthetic, and provokes desire.

A nd indeed that is the way of my desires now: towards the finite, the tangible—what can be acquired. The limited ultimate. Such reasoning doesn't even seem so bad, considering it's hard, sometimes, to know exactly what we want; hard to take the precise measure of our desires. We all want our pleasures to have a future—to be like love. And I admit it is not clear what kind of future one can have with a motorcycle. Particularly a Harley-Davidson, a thing so immediate and complete. So much itself. And taking into account as well the limits of my own pleasure.

Not long ago I asked my wife to take my picture 'with my bike'. I stood out on the gravel drive beside it, in my chinos and my deck shoes, a red pullover, a blue blazer and a smile. *My* clothes, in other words. What I wear.

And when the picture came back I was surprised at how superfluous I looked. All wrong. I've seen pictures of grown men standing alongside great ocean fish they'd caught, and with which they hoped to strike a brief, self-proving intimacy—only to have those very hopes disappointed by the unsympathetic literalness of that breathless thing beside them. For me, it was as if I had brought to heel a bright red *motorcycle*, a big one, and wanted to make it, somehow, 'one with me'—an impossibility, I now know, since neither I nor anyone can ever 'be with' a thing that won't 'be with' us.

And still, when I am off and going, whirling along some street in the town I live in, and for an instant can catch a splashy glimpse of myself in a store front or a car window—man, moment, motion all one effect—then I am proved well enough, located certainly, in terms as absolute and complete and futureless as my machine's— this Harley-Davidson, most certain of motorcycles. And I am not disappointed then. And that, after all, is the most it has been worth to me from the beginning.

Grandma Norman and the Queen
Philip Norman

Like every English child of the early fifties, I grew up close to the Royal Family. We met almost every week—I at the Scala or Theatre Royal cinema, they on the Movietone newsreel, waving from their usual balcony. There was King George VI, always in Naval uniform, always a little drawn and tired, as if weighed down by the gold rings on his sleeve. There was his wife, the then Queen Elizabeth, smiling hard enough for both of them. There was old Queen Mary in her Edwardian toque, and Princess Elizabeth with the dashing young husband whose name was the same as mine. I knew them as beings of immense importance yet infinite kindliness, employing their incalculable power for my welfare and somehow, among all their vast preoccupations, willing to take a personal interest in me.

My knowledge of them derived chiefly from my father's mother, Grandma Norman, a tall, loving gipsy rogue of a woman, born six years before Queen Victoria's Diamond Jubilee, whose chief pleasure, apart from Guinness and Craven-A cigarettes, was peering through the railings of Buckingham Palace, hoping to see the Guard change or a Royal limousine glide out. Grandma Norman's love of royalty transcended time. To her the death of Queen Victoria's husband, Prince Albert, in 1861 was still a cause for keen regret. Edward VII was spoken of with a twinkle, acknowledging his racy life, but also as the last bulwark of pre-1914 Europe. 'The Kaiser was his cousin, you know; if old King Teddy had lived, there would have been no World War.' Bound up with that story was the tragedy of Edward's nephew, Tsar Nicholas II of Russia, and 'the poor Tsarina' and what had been done to them by the Bolsheviks at Ekatrinburg. The cruelty of it still reverberated near Clapham Common in 1952, now that all such violent death seemed to occur only in history books.

Each morning in her steamy back kitchen, Grandma Norman would give me my puffed wheat in a porridge bowl produced in 1936 for the aborted Coronation of Edward VIII. She had cups, saucers and mugs, too, all embossed with the same pointed, slightly petulant face, set about with standards and imperial lions of an Empire shortly to be renounced. As I ate puffed wheat, Grandma Norman would tell me yet again how a brilliant Prince of Wales had turned into this melancholy temporary King. It all went back to Albert the Prince Consort and his cold aloofness with his son, the future Edward VII, who had reacted by being warm and affectionate with his children, even allowing them to race slices of buttered toast down the front of his evening trousers. But Edward's son, the future George V, though kind, had been formal and withdrawn like Prince Albert, and unable to communicate affection to his son, the doomed eighth Edward. Grandma Norman, at the time, would instantly have joined the 'King's Party', unsuccessfully proposed to allow him to marry a divorced woman and still remain sovereign. 'He's the poor Duke of Windsor now,' she said, still indignantly as that familiar, half-royal countenance surfaced yet again through the clouds of my cereal milk. 'It was all that Stanley Baldwin's fault, plotting the way he did with that Cosmo Lang....'

The King I knew was Edward's successor, a shy, stammering naval officer who, when told he must follow his brother, threw himself down on a sofa and wept. 'George the Good' Grandma Norman called him, as did the whole country, for his simple, indomitable determination to share the wartime discomforts of his subjects. He had insisted on having a food ration book like everyone else, and taking only three inches of water in his bath. In drab postwar years, when I was small, the struggle for national reconstruction seemed written on his worried face. He was so concerned, and the Queen so very kind, one felt the whole world—even fierce Maoris and Zulus—being soothed into amity and harmony by their Royal Tours. In 1951, when the King inaugurated the Festival of Britain, marking the centenary of Prince Albert's Great Exhibition, it truly seemed that the past was over: that Grandma Norman, the Royal family and I should all live happily ever after.

I remember the freckled nose of the boy who turned to me in our junior school singing lesson and casually told me that the King was dead. The rumour skittered back and forth along rows of us like a terrible joke until old Mr Monk the singing teacher leaned on the top of his battered piano and, enunciating each word almost with nausea, told us, 'The *King...is...dead.'*

We were plunged into a period of blackest Victorian mourning. All entertainment programmes on the radio were cancelled. The Movietone newsreel showed only flag-draped coffins and slow-marching Guardsmen, with a sound of eerie, squealing naval pipes that seemed to come direct from the grave. There in endless flashback were the last official duties, the heavily-striped sleeve, the face—one could see now—growing greyer and more haggard. 'For all these months...,' a solemn voice intoned, 'the King walked with Death....' No one could say, of course, that he'd been suffering from cancer.

We glimpsed royalty then in its age-old form of self-renewing miracle. 'The King is dead, long live the Queen.' When national grief dissolved at last, it was into the sunshiny thrill of Coronation Year. I thought it might go on forever with its strawberry teas, its commemoration spoons, calypsos, bunting, the fleets of all nations drawn up for review off our seaside town like hazy fish, twinkling into a maritime city after dark. Then the unseasonable downpour on Coronation Day itself when we gathered round a neighbour's TV set: the Queen, so frail in her top-heavy crown, peering shyly round the encrustations of the State Coach; the rain-blurred hours of liveried postillions and marching troops; the Queen of Tonga, waving from her open landau. Grandma Norman told me the Queen of Tonga used to be a cannibal and Noel Coward, at another vantage-point, said the little man with her in the coach was 'probably her lunch.' Mount Everest had been conquered by Britons only days before. British children like me were told we were 'New Elizabethans', standing like Drake and Ralegh on the threshold of our brilliant heritage.

*T*hen, as we know, Elizabeth II ruled for thirty-two years. And nothing she did or said ever spoiled the good opinion of her formed on her Coronation Day.

Harold Nicolson, in his various masterly studies of the Windsor dynasty, marvels repeatedly at their ability to pass through social tempests that have swept most other European Royal houses into extinction, and to emerge not merely intact but mysteriously strengthened in the British people's goodwill. The great example was George V, whose twenty-five year reign encompassed world war, a general strike—almost automatically the prelude to revolution anywhere else—and, finally, a Depression even more cruel than Britain's present one. Throughout the latter period, as Nicolson himself records, the King did virtually nothing but slaughter pheasants and tend his stamp album. His value was that he did not change. His constancy, through cold, gloomy ages, gave the comfort of some slow-burning night light. Half a century after his death, a pang of sadness still lingers in that final Palace gate bulletin: 'The King's life is moving peacefully towards its close.'

Elizabeth II has reached back past her troubled father to her grandfather to attain this same quiet constancy. For her first two and a half decades, indeed, she was so constant as to become almost invisible. The smile, the hats, the corgi dogs, all dwelt in the national retina as elementally as Christmas or Test cricket. It took her impending Silver Jubilee, in 1977, to remind one that she had ruled for as long as George V and that, after twenty-five years spanning social and political upheaval of every kind, the dynasty looked as healthy as ever. From the fifties to the seventies the Queen hadn't put a foot wrong.

It is the first thing you notice: how carefully she advances from the royal car or the royal train, not walking, rather floating on two identical tiny State cushions of air. The clothes are garish perhaps for obvious reasons of visibility: a cherry red coat, emphatic hat—scarlet, it may be, festooned with black objects like African leeches—a shy little hand floated forth towards those forewarned they may shake it.

Grown up as I consider myself in every other way, 'The Queen' is, for me, still a phrase full of vague comfort and reassurance. No matter that all the more disagreeable things in Britain are done in the Queen's name: that 'Her Majesty's Service' encompasses policemen, punitive taxes, a dreadful postal system and prisons currently deteriorating towards nineteenth-century overcrowding and squalor. When I hear of some prisoner detained 'At Her Majesty's Pleasure'—that is, indefinitely—the effect is still maternal benignity. One feels sure that, when she hears of it, the Queen will let him off.

It is a shock to remember how that little cherry red figure is steeped in the art and single-minded practice of hanging on to power. The Royal Family is a chief instrument of our fatal complacency—the belief that the world's rules don't apply to us, that things are always different in Britain. How we laugh, for instance, at foreign dictators who remain in office only for as long as they can appease and cultivate the army. Few British people, I'm sure, find it at all significant that the Queen spends her official birthday reviewing troops, that each of her sons automatically enlists in one or more armed service, that even the cuddly Queen Mother is 'Colonel in Chief' of certain crack regiments. We say it is all for tradition and ceremony and the benefit of tourists. Isn't it also to banish from those crack regiments' minds any notion that they might one day surround Buckingham Palace with a ring of tanks?

*R*evolution threatens modern monarchs somewhat less than press scandal. That the Queen has ruled Britain for thirty-two years without a speck of notoriety attaching itself to her is indisputably miraculous.

It's more miraculous considering the number of potential trouble-makers in her family. One thinks of Princess Margaret, a pleasure-loving, erratic person rather like a female Edward VIII, whose misfortunes, time and again, have illustrated how inflexible is her elder sister's belief that happiness must always be sacrificed to constitutional propriety. It was so in 1956 when Princess Margaret could not marry the war hero Group-Captain Peter Townsend because (shades of 1936) he had been married before. It remained so in the late seventies, during her estrangement from Lord Snowdon, when everyone seemed to feel most sorry for the Queen. I remember seeing Princess Margaret at the height of her press torment, at an army camp in the West Country, miserably inspecting a line of eight identical army tanks and their identical crews. Her profile is the Queen's but without a smile: as if all those coins and stamps and postal orders looked sad and ill at ease and a bit worried about tomorrow.

Prince Philip, too, has sometimes seemed like a decoy for bad publicity with his outbursts of temper, his sardonic *faux pas* and other manifestations, over the years, of a talented but profoundly under-exploited man. Strange it is to remember how glamorous Prince Philip used to be, putting on an Indian head-dress at the Calgary Stampede and resolutely 'taking the controls' of whichever aircraft the Royal party happened to be using.

For fifteen years that pilot's prowess, along with Lord Snowdon's photographs and Princess Margaret's fondness for the Beatles, represented the sum total of Royal glamour. *En masse*, 'Royals' were the antithesis of smart. They were, like archbishops and the BBC, a standing British joke, uttered without malice. This was the era of young satirists, of radicalism and classlessness, of *Private Eye*'s naughty anti-Royal pantheon, 'Buck House', 'Brenda' and 'Phil the Greek'. The press covered them incessantly but perfunctorily. Gossip columns had become extinct, it was thought for good. Elsewhere the subject was deemed inimical to sensible prose. Dire memories still lingered of 'Crawfie', a nanny to the two princesses in the thirties, whose serialized memoirs in the fifties remained synonymous with a rising of the collective gorge. That death knell name 'Crawfie' would be sufficient to discourage any proposed article or book on any Royal subject save, perhaps, the abstract principles of monarchy. As a journalistic commodity, the Queen just did not sell.

Such was the 'serious' media's indifference that in 1969, just before Prince Charles's State investiture as Prince of Wales, half a dozen senior journalists were invited to Buckingham Palace for the unprecedented experience of taking morning coffee with the twenty-one year-old Prince. My editor being otherwise occupied, I was sent along in his place. The six of us were taken in through the Privy Purse Door, shown to a room overlooking The Mall and served with milky coffee and chocolate biscuits wrapped in shiny gold paper. The Prince came from the far end of the room, approaci.ing with great, long, nervous strides as if he was playing Granny's Footsteps. I remember his shiny old-fashioned ox-blood shoes, and the oddly pale blue Windsor eyes in the weatherbeaten young face—eyes watchful even then, for the ink squirt in the official bouquet. 'Hello...,' he said apologetically. 'Did you all get away from your offices all right?' We chatted with him for about an hour. He told us about his passion for digging up Roman remains in Cambridgeshire, and how he disliked putting on his prince's crown for the investiture rehearsals because it was all bent and dirty. I did not write a word about the encounter; nor, I think, did anyone else present.

The Silver Jubilee altered everything. People were genuinely astonished to realize that twenty-five years had passed since the Coronation; that, in the charmless world of 1977, one found the selfsame petal-hatted, well-corgied, ever dependable little sovereign. The Jubilee celebrations, conceived as a fairly mercenary exercise for the tourist trade, turned into something quite different. Travelling in the Queen's wake as I did on the Jubilee visits to Scotland and Northern Ireland felt like stepping back into postcards of the 1896 Jubilee—the streets skeined with ribbons, the tossing fields of flags, the bewildered delight on tough Celtic faces when the petal hat stopped close to them. I remember how, in Ulster, outside the rings of tanks, sharp-shooters and guard-dogs, people climbed spiked railings, clung to bus-corners, made themselves stick somehow to sheer surfaces, all for the merest glimpse of that cherry-red coat.

This sudden rediscovery of something agreeable and spontaneous in British public life came too late, alas, to benefit the incumbent socialist government. Shortly after the Silver Jubilee there was a general election, producing momentous results. Our fifth female sovereign ratified the administration of our first female Prime Minister. Britain was now headed—in Germaine Greer's phrase—by 'a woman who can't tell a joke, and a woman who can't understand one.' We know what has happened to Britain and to the Royal Family since then.

ARENA

Masks FUMIKO ENCHI

Fumiko Enchi is one of Japan's most prestigious writers. **Masks** is an eerily evocative, beautifully written tale of seduction and manipulation on the classic Japanese theme of the immutable force of feminine jealousy. **£2.25**

Clancy's Bulba

MICHAEL O'GORMAN

Set in Ireland in 1928 this is an old fashioned story of four men and their simple dreams — and of Taurus Bulba, the finest fighting cock to come out of County Mayo. Warm, sparkling and irrepressibly humorous, myth and reality combine with extraordinary, free-wheeling dialogue. It won a special mention from the judges of the **David Higham First Novel Award.** **£2.25**

The Notebook of Gismondo Cavaletti

R.M. LAMMING
The winner of the **1983 David Higham First Novel Award.** Set in the Florence of Buonarroti and da Vinci, it records the tragedy and comedy of a man whose reality cannot match the dreams of perfection of the glorious age in which he lives. 'An acute and sympathetic imagination. **Observer** **£3.95**

The best in International Writing

James Fenton
The Fall of
Saigon

In the summer of 1973 I had a dream in which, to my great distress, I died. I was alone in a friend's house at the time and, not knowing what to do, I hid the body in her deep freeze. When everyone returned, I explained to them what had taken place: 'Something terrible happened when you were out. I—I died.'

My friends were very sympathetic. 'But what did you do with the body?' they asked.

I was ashamed to tell them. 'I don't know where it is,' I said, and we all set out to search the house for my corpse. Upstairs and downstairs we looked, until finally, unable to bear the deception any longer, I took my hostess aside and confessed. 'There wasn't anything else in the compartment,' I said, 'and I just didn't know what to do.' We went to the deep freeze and opened it. As the curled and frozen shape was revealed, I woke up.

I was glad to be going off on a journey. I had been awarded a bursary for the purpose of travelling and writing poetry; I intended to stay out of England a long time. Looking at what the world had to offer, I thought either Africa or Indochina would be the place to go. I chose Indochina partly on a whim, and partly because, after the Paris Peace Agreement in February of that same year, it looked as if it was in for some very big changes. The essence of the agreement was that it removed American military personnel from Indochina and stopped the B-52 bombing raids. The question was how long could the American-backed regime last without that accustomed support. I wanted to see Vietnam for myself. I wanted to see a war, and I wanted to see a communist victory, which I presumed to be inevitable. I wanted to see the fall of a city.

I wanted to see a communist victory because, in common with many people, I believed that the Americans had not the slightest justification for their interference in Indochina. I admired the Vietcong and, by extension, the Khmer Rouge, but I subscribed to a philosophy that prided itself on taking a cool, critical look at the liberation movements of the Third World. I, and many others like me, supported these movements against the ambitions of American foreign policy. We supported them as nationalist movements. We did not support their political character, which we perceived as Stalinist in the case of the Vietnamese, and in the case of the Cambodians . . . I don't know. The theory was, and is, that when a genuine movement of national liberation was fighting against imperialism it received our unconditional support. When such a movement had won, then it might well take its place among the governments we execrated—those who ruled by sophisticated tyranny in the name of socialism.

There was also an argument that Stalinism was not a simple equivalent of Fascism, that it contained what was called a partial negation of capitalism. Further, under certain conditions it might even lay down the foundations of a socialist organization of society. In the Third World, Stalinism might do the job which the bourgeois revolutions had done in Europe. Even Stalinism had its progressive features.

Our attitudes may have looked cynical in the extreme. In fact they were the formulation of a dilemma. After all, we had not invented the Indochina War, and it was not for us to conjure out of thin air a movement that would match up to our own aspirations for Britain. To remain neutral over Vietnam was to support the Americans. To argue for an end to all US involvement, and leave the matter at that, was to ignore the consequences of one's own argument. If there was a conflict on which one had to choose sides, then it was only right to choose sides honestly, and say: 'Stalinists they may be, but we support them.' The slogans of the Vietnam movement were crude stuff indeed—'One side right, one side wrong, victory to . . . Vi-et-cong!'—but the justice of the cause was deeply felt.

This feeling was shared by many people who were not socialists or communists by any stretch of the imagination, and who did not have any other political axe to grind. Such people had merely to look at what was being done to Vietnam in the name of the Free World to know that the Free World was in the wrong. The broadest support for the anti-war movement was engendered by a disgust at what the Americans were doing. In Britain, the Communist Party made precious few gains in this period. The tradition to which the students looked was broadly or narrowly Trotskyist, a fact that no doubt intrigued the Vietnamese communists, who had taken care to bump off their own Trotskyists a long time before. But the Trotskyist emphasis, like the general emphasis, was again on opposition to American imperialism. Very few people idolized the

Vietcong, or the North Vietnamese, or Uncle Ho, in quite the same way that, for instance, the French Left did. Indeed, it might be fairly said that the Left in Britain was not terribly curious about or enamoured of the Vietnamese movement it was supporting.

By the time I was about to go to Indochina, the issue had fallen from prominence. When the Indochina Solidarity Conference was held in London that year, my own group, the International Socialists, did not bother to send a delegation. There were other, more important campaigns: against the Tories, against the Industrial Relations Act, against racism. Our movement had grown up: it was to be working class in character; it had graduated from what it thought of as student issues. It had not abandoned Vietnam, but it had other fish to fry. At the conference itself, I remember two speeches of interest. One was by I. F. Stone, who was hissed by the audience (which included an unusually large number of Maoists) when he attacked Chairman Mao for shaking hands with a murderer like Nixon. The other was by Noam Chomsky, who warned against the assumption that the war was over, and that direct US intervention in Vietnam would cease. Chomsky argued that the Left were wrong to dismiss the 'Domino Theory' out of hand. As stated by the Cold Warriors it might not measure up to the facts, but there was another formulaton which did indeed make sense; it was US foreign policy, rather than Russian expansionism, which knocked over the dominoes: countries might be forced into positions where the only alternative to accepting American domination was to go over to the opposite camp and would thus be drawn into the power struggle whether they liked it or not.

I mention such arguments because I do not wish to give the impression that I was completely wide-eyed about the Vietnamese communists when I set out. I considered myself a revolutionary socialist, of the kind who believes in no Fatherland of the Revolution, and has no cult hero. My political beliefs were fairly broadly based and instinctively grasped, but they were not, I hope, religiously held.

But I wanted very much to see a communist victory. Although I had a few journalist commissions, I was not going primarily as a journalist. I wanted to see a war and the fall of a city because—because I wanted to see what such things were like. I had once seen a man dying, from natural causes, and my first reaction, as I realized what was taking place, was that I was glad to be *there*. This is what happens, I thought, so watch it carefully, don't miss a detail. The first time I saw a surgical operation (it was in Cambodia) I experienced the same sensation, and no doubt when I see a child born it will be even more powerful. The point is simply in being there and seeing it. The experience has no essential value beyond itself.

I spent a long time on my preparations and, as my dream of dying might indicate, I had developed some fairly morbid apprehensions. The journey itself was to be utterly selfish. I was going to do exactly as I pleased. As far as political beliefs were concerned, they were going to remain 'on the table'. Everything was negotiable. But the fear of death, which had begun for the first time to enter my calculations, followed me on my journey. As I went through the passport check at Heathrow, I glanced at the Sunday papers and saw that the poet I most admired, W. H. Auden, had just died in Vienna. People were talking about him in the passenger lounge, or rather they weren't talking about him, they were talking about his face.

I kept seeing the face, on the plane, in the transit lounges, on the empty seat next to mine, and I kept remembering Auden. From the start he had willed himself into old age, and it was not surprising that he had not lived longer. He had courted death, cultivated first eccentricity and then what looked to the world very much like senility. It was not senility, but it was a useful cover for his despair of living, the deep unhappiness which he kept concealed. He had held the world very much at arm's length, and had paid a heavy price for doing so.

Between sleeping and reading, I found myself passing through a depression compounded of one part loneliness, one part uneager anticipation, one part fright and two parts obscure self-pity. In Bombay the depression began to lift: I slept all morning at the Sea Palace Hotel, then, surrendering to the good offices of a driver and guide, set off to see the sights. The evening light was first a muddy yellow; next it turned green. On the Malabar Hill, I paid my respects to the spectacular view, the vultures picking the bones on thⁿ Parsee tower, the lights along the waterfront ('Queen Victoria's Necklace') and the couples sitting on the lawns of the Hanging Gardens, in attitudes reminiscent of a Mogul miniature. The most impressive sight was a vast open-air laundry, a yard full of boiling vats between which, through the dark and steam, one could scarcely make out the moving figures of the workers. There was a steamy warmth everywhere, which I liked immediately. Waking the next morning, I looked down on a wide meandering river, either the Salween or the Irrewaddy, whose muddy waters spread out for miles into the sea. Seen from the plane, the landscape of the Far East was dazzling, silver and blue. You could tell you had arrived in Indochina when you saw the rows and rows of yellow circles, where muddy water had filled the bomb craters.

Fear of Madness: November 1973

'I know not whether others share my feelings on this point,' wrote De Quincey, 'but I have often thought that if I were compelled to forego England, and to live in China, and among Chinese manners and modes of life and scenery, I should go mad.' I read this sentence the other day, for the first time, and as I came to the last clause I was struck once again with the full nausea of my first trip to Vietnam. 'The causes of my horror lie deep,' De Quincey went on. But he set them forth beautifully:

> No man can pretend that the wild, barbarous, and capricious superstitions of Africa, or of savage tribes elsewhere, affect him in the way that he is affected by the ancient, monumental, cruel, and elaborate religions of Indostan, etc. The mere antiquity of Asiatic things, of their institutions, histories, modes of faith, etc is so impressive, that to me the vast age of the race and name overpowers the sense of youth in the individual. A young Chinese seems to me an antediluvian renewed . . . . Man is a weed in those regions.

I was impressed, overawed, by the scale and age of the subject: a war that had been going on for longer than I had been alive, a people about whose history and traditions I knew so little. I had read some books in preparation, but the effect of doing so was only to make the country recede further. So much had been written about Vietnam. I hadn't even had the application to finish Frances Fitzgerald's *The Fire in the Lake*. The purpose of the book seemed to be to warn you off the subject.

I could well have believed that somebody was trying to tell me something when I came out of my room on the first morning in Saigon and stepped over the decapitated corpse of a rat. I was staying, as most British journalists did, in the Hotel Royale, but even there I felt something of an intruder. I had to find work, I had to sell some stories, but I was afraid of trespassing on somebody else's patch. There was an epidemic of infectious neurosis at the time: as soon as one journalist had shaken it off, another would succumb. It would attack without warning—in the middle of an otherwise amiable meal, in the bars, in your room. And it could be recurrent, like malaria.

The reason for the neurosis was not far to seek; indeed it sought you out, and pursued you throughout the day: Saigon was an addicted city, and we were the drug; the corruption of children, the mutilation of young men, the prostitution of women, the humiliation of the old, the division of the family, the division of the country—it had all been done in our name. People looked back to the French Saigon with a sentimental warmth, as if the problem had begun with the Americans. But the French city, the Saigon of the Piastre as Lucien Bodard called it, had represented the opium stage of the addiction. With the Americans had begun the heroin phase, and what I was seeing now was the first symptoms of withdrawal. There was a desperate edge to life. It was impossible to relax for a moment. The last of the American troops had left at the end of March, six months before I arrived, and what I saw now was what they left behind: a vast service industry clamouring for the attention of a dwindling number of customers: Hey you! American! Change money, buy *Time* magazine, give me back *Time* magazine I sell you yesterday, buy *Stars and Stripes*, give me back *Stars and Stripes*, you number one, you number ten, you number ten thousand Yankee, you want number one fuck, you want *Quiet American,* you want *Ugly American,* you give me money I shine shoes, number one, no sweat . . . on and on, the passionate pursuit of money.

The bar at the Royale was half open to the street. The coffee at breakfast tasted of diarrhoea. You washed it down with Bireley's orangeade ('Refreshing . . . and no carbonation!'). Through the windows peered the shoe-shine boys—Hey! You! It was starting up again. One morning I was ignoring a particularly revolting specimen when he picked up a handful of sand which he pretended to eat: 'You! You no give me money, you want I eat shit!' His expression, as he brought the dirt to his mouth, was most horrible. It was impossible to imagine how a boy of that age had acquired such features: he was about ten, but his face contained at least thirty years of degeneration and misery. A few days later I did give him my boots to clean. He sat down in the corner of the bar and set to work, first with a matchstick and a little water, meticulously removing all the mud and dust from the welt, then with the polish. The whole process took about half an hour, and the barman and I watched him throughout, in fascination. He was determined to show his superiority to all other contestants in the trade. I was amused, and gave him a large sum. He was furious; it wasn't nearly enough. We haggled for a while, but I finally gave in. I gave him about a pound. The next day, at the same time, he came into the bar; his eyes were rolling back in their sockets and he staggered helplessly around the tables and chairs. I do not know what he had taken, but I knew how he had bought it.

O f all the ingenious and desperate forms of raising money, the practice of drugging your baby and laying the thing on the pavement in front of the visitor seemed to me the most repulsive. It did not take long to see that none of these children was ever awake during the day, or that, if asleep, something was amiss. Among the foreigners, stories circulated about the same baby being seen in the arms of five different mothers in one week, but the beggar who regularly sat outside the Royale always had the same child, a girl of eighteen months or so. I never gave any money either to the girl and her 'mother', or to any of the other teams.

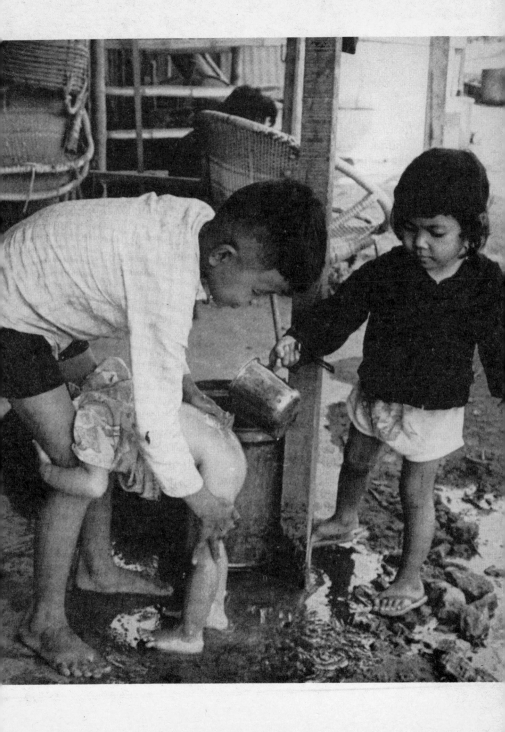

One day, however, I was returning from a good lunch when I saw that a crowd had formed around the old woman, who was wailing and gesticulating. The child was more than usually grey, and there were traces of vomit around her face. People were turning her over, slapping her, trying to force her eyes open. At one point she and the old woman were bundled into a taxi. Then they were taken out again and the slapping was repeated. I went into the hotel and told the girl at reception to call a doctor.

'No,' she replied.

'But the child is sick.'

'If baby go to hospital or doctor'—and here she imitated an injection—'then baby die.'

'No,' I replied, 'if baby *don't* go to hospital maybe baby die.'

'No.'

I took the girl out into the street, where the scene had become grotesque. All the beggars I had ever seen in Saigon seemed to have gathered, and from their filthy garments they were producing pins and sticking them under the child's toenails. 'You see,' I said to the girl, 'no good, number ten. Baby need number one hospital.'

'No, my grandmother had same-same thing. She need this— number one.' And the receptionist produced a small phial of eucalyptus oil.

'That's not number one,' I said, 'that's number ten. Number ten thousand,' I added for emphasis. But it was no good insisting or appealing to other members of the crowd. Everybody was adamant that if the child was taken to hospital, the doctor would kill it with an injection. While I correspondingly became convinced that a moment's delay would cost the child's life.

Finally, after a long eucalyptus massage and repeated pricking of the fingers and toes had produced no visible results, I seemed to win. If I would pay for taxi and hospital, the woman would come. I pushed my way through the crowd and dragged her towards the taxi—a battered old Renault tied together with string. The baby was wrapped in tarpaulin and her face covered with a red handkerchief. Every time I tried to remove the handkerchief, from which came the most ominous dry gaspings, the woman replaced it. I directed the taxi-man to take us to number one hospital and we set off.

From the start everything went wrong. Within a hundred yards we had to stop for petrol. Then a van stalled in front of us, trapping the taxi. Next, to my amazement, we came to what must have been, I thought, the only level-crossing in Saigon, where as it happened a train was expected in the near future. And around here we were hit by the side-effects of Typhoon Sarah, which at the time was causing havoc in the northern provinces. We also split a tyre, though this was not noticed till later. Driving on through the cloudburst, the taxi-man seemed strangely unwilling to hurry. So I sat in the back seat keeping one hand on the horn and with the other attempting to ease the baby's breathing by loosening the tarpaulin around her neck. I also recall from time to time producing a third arm with which to comfort the old woman, and I remember that her shoulder, when my hand rested on it, was very small and very hard. Everything, I said, was going to be number one, okay: number one hospital, number one doctor, babysan okay. We were travelling through Cholon, the Chinese quarter, on an errand of Western mercy.

All things considered, it took a long time for it to dawn on me that we were not going to a hospital at all. We even passed a first-aid post without the taxi-man giving it a glance. In my mind there was an image of the sort of thing required: a large cool building dating from French times, recently refurbished by American aid and charity, with some of the best equipment in the East. I could even imagine the sententious plaques on the walls. Perhaps there would be a ward named after the former US Ambassador. It would be called the Bunker Ward.

It was when the old woman began giving directions that I saw I had been duped. We were threading our way through some modern slums, which looked like the Chinese equivalent of the Isle of Dogs. 'Where is the hospital? This is no hospital,' I said.

'Yes, yes,' the taxi-man replied, 'we are going to hospital, number one doctor.'

We stopped by a row of shops and the taxi-man got out. I jumped from the car and seized him by the arm, shouting: 'I said number one hopsital. You lie. You cheap charlie. You number ten thousand Saigon.' We were surrounded by children, in the pouring rain, the taxi-man tugging himself free, and me gripping him by the arm. It was left to the woman, carrying the little bundle of tarpaulin, to find out exactly where the doctor lived. Finally I gave in, and followed her up some steps, then along an open corridor lined with tailors and merchants. At least, I thought, when the baby dies I can't be blamed. And once I had had that thought, it turned into a wish: a little cough would have done it, a pathetic gurgle, then silence, and my point about Western medicine would have been proved to my own satisfaction. I should have behaved very well, and would have paid for the funeral.

In retrospect it was easy to see how the establishment would command confidence: the dark main room with its traditional furnishings, the walls lined with photographs of ancestors in traditional Vietnamese robes, a framed jigsaw of the Italian lakes. And in the back room (it would, of course, have to be a back room) a plump, middle-aged lady was massaging the back of another plump, middle-aged lady. They paid hardly any attention when we came in. There was not the slightest element of drama. Indeed, I began to see that I was now the only person who was panicking. When she had finished the massage, the doctor turned her attention to the baby. First she took some ointment from a dirty bowl at her elbow, and rubbed it all over the little grey body. Then from another bowl she produced some pink substance resembling Euthymol toothpaste, with which she proceeded to line the mouth. In a matter of minutes, the child was slightly sick, began to cry, and recovered. I had never been more furious in my life. To complete my humiliation, the doctor refused any payment. She provided the old woman with a prescription wrapped in newspaper, and we left.

We drove to the miserable shelter in which the old woman lived.

'Sit down,' she said, indicating the wooden bed which was the only feature of her home apart from the roof (there were no walls).

In any other mood I might have been moved by the fact that the only English she knew beyond the terrible pidgin currency of the beggars was a phrase of hospitality. But I so deeply hated her at that moment that I could only give her a couple of pounds, plus some useless advice about keeping the baby warm and off the pavements, and go.

I left the taxi-man at a garage not far from the Royale, where I also gave him some money towards repairing the split tyre.

'You number one, Saigon,' he said, with a slight note of terror in his voice.

The weather had cleared up, and I left him, strolling along past the market stalls. Here, you could buy US army foot-powder in bulk, K-rations, lurp-rations (for Long Range Reconnaissance Patrols), souvenir Zippo lighters (engraved 'Yea though I walk through the valley of the shadow of death I shall fear no evil, for I am the evilest sonofabitch in the valley'), khaki toothbrushes and flannels, and model helicopters constructed out of used hypodermics. You could also buy jackets brightly embroidered with the words 'When I die I shall go to heaven, for I have spent my time in hell—Saigon,' and a collection of GI cartoons and jokes called *Sorry 'bout that, Vietnam*. Five years ago, there had been over 500,000 American GIs. Now there were none.

As I approached the hotel people began asking how the baby was, and smiling when I replied, 'Okay.' I began to think: Supposing they were all in it together? Suppose the old woman, the taxi-driver, the man whose van stalled, the engine-driver—suppose they were all now dividing the proceeds and having a good laugh at my expense, congratulating the child on the way it had played its role? That evening I would be telling the story to some old Saigon hand when a strange pitying smile would come over his face. 'You went to Cholon, did you? Describe the doctor ... . uhuh . . . .Was there a jigsaw puzzle of the Italian Lakes? Well, well, well. So they even used the toothpaste trick. Funny how the oldest gags are still the best . . . .'

Indeed I did have rather that conversation a few days later, with an American girl, a weaver. It began: 'You realize, of course, first of all that the taxi-driver was the husband of the old woman....' But I do not think there was a conspiracy. Worse, I should rather conclude that the principals involved were quite right not to trust the hospital doctors with a beggar's child. It was for this reason that the hotel receptionist had countermanded my orders to the taxi-man, I learned afterwards, and many people agreed with her.

When the old woman came back on the streets, I hardly recognized either her or the child, who for the first time looked conscious and well. 'Babysan okay now, no sick,' she said, gazing at me with an awful adoring expression, though the hand was not stretched out for money. And when I didn't reply she turned to the child and told it something in the same unctuous tones. This performance went on for the rest of my stay: whenever I was around the child would be made to look at the kind foreigner who had saved its life. I had indeed wanted to save the child's life, but not in *that* way, not on the old woman's terms.

I was disgusted, not just at what I saw around me, but at what I saw in myself. I saw how perilously thin was the line between the charitable and the murderous impulse, how strong the force of righteous indignation. I could well imagine that most of those who came to Vietnam to fight were not the evilest sons-of-bitches in the valley. It was just that, beyond the bright circle illuminated by their intelligence, in which everything was under their control and every person a compliant object, they came across a second person—a being or a nation with a will of its own, with its own medicine, whether Fishing Pills or pink toothpaste, and its own ideas for the future. And in the ensuing encounter everything had turned to justifiable ashes. It was impossible in Saigon to be the passive observer. Saigon cast you, inevitably, into the role of the American.

Elsewhere it was possible to breathe more freely, but I was conscious always of following in somebody else's footsteps. On a trip to Quang Tri, the northernmost city in South Vietnam, I asked my driver how far away was the town. 'This is the main street,' he said, indicating the overgrown rubble. We stopped and walked to the edge of the river, looking across to the liberated zone and the still figures of the soldiers on the Other Side. I had heard endless stories of people's exploits in Quang Tri, but it meant nothing to me. There was no point in my being there. I was more at ease in Hué. I walked around the Imperial City in the rain, through the beautiful, shabby grounds that looked like the vegetable gardens of an English country house. But I was nothing more than a tourist. Once, I thought I was actually going to meet someone important when a Vietnamese took me to see a woman. But the woman was his girlfriend, whom he was hoping to marry. She worked in a chemist's shop, and when we arrived the drill was simply that I should go in, buy some aspirin or something, look at her, and tell her boyfriend what I thought. He waited outside for my opinion. I gave the girl a warm recommendation.

I went also to Dalat, a village in the Highlands that, because it was once a resort, had been spared from attack. I walked through the forests where the tall poinsettias were in flower: the Vietnamese called them the Man of Genius Tree. In my hotel room, there were poems scrawled in ballpoint on the walls:
I am a fairy from the moon.
You are my happiness.
When the sun sets
The river will be without water
And the rocks will scrape.
Our promises will be forever.
There was a war going on, but the nearest I got to it was in Gia Nghia, a former American base in the Quang Duc region. It had been a great feat of engineering: the wide roads of red earth cut through the jungle, the vast clearing. There were little signs of America everywhere, the half-caste children, even the dogs of the area were mongrels from the American trackers. There was a dog's footprint on a concrete floor, with the words 'Our Mascot (MACV)' scratched beside it. There were drunken Montagnards wandering round, and in the market-place, which sported two billiard saloons, a soldier was smoking marijuana through a waterpipe made out of an anti-tank shell. There was music and the sound of motorbikes from the Wall of Death, but when we went in the evening and asked them to open it up we found the family asleep on the track.

The USAID compound had a commanding view of the town. A Montagnard soldier, with huge stretched earlobes, stood on guard outside. Inside, leaning over a short-wave radio, was Ed Sprague, the local USAID official and the only American I ever met in the field. He was marking positions on a map. There was a rifle propped against the wall and a neatly polished revolver on the table. The rest of the room was magnificently equipped, with photos, souvenirs, stereo tape-recorder, cocktail bar, Montagnard girl, soft furnishings. Above the bar, engraved on copper and nicely framed, were the sayings of Sprague himself:
The Special Forces have done so much for nothing for so long that now we are expected to do everything for nothing for ever.

And:

> If you kick me once in the back when I'm not looking I'll
> kick you twice in the face when you are looking.
>
> —Sprague '71

He was very polite, but the USAID compound had no room to put us up, so we went to the local hotel in town. The South Vietnamese helicopter pilots were billeted there, and I spent the evening playing Co Tuong ('Kill the General'), the Chinese and Vietnamese version of chess. The round wooden pieces were engraved with Chinese characters, and the board was made of paper. A river flowed down the middle of the board, separating the two rows of GIs, who had to move forward, one square at a time, until they crossed the river, after which they might move in any direction. Just behind the GIs lay the two artillery pieces, which might fire in straight lines at any of the pieces, as long as there was some single obstruction in between. The horses made knights' moves, and could cross the river, as could the tanks, which were the equivalent of rooks. But the elephants, which always moved two squares at a time, diagonally, were unable to cross the river and were reserved for the defence. The general was protected by his officer escort. He lived in a compound of four squares. The red general must never 'see' the black general—that is, there must always be something in between.

'This is the black general,' said my teacher: 'He is Ho Chi Minh. This is the red general. He is Thieu.'

'But Ho Chi Minh is dead.'

'I know. I killed him in the last game.'

I also spent some time in the billiard saloons, collecting Vietnamese jokes from the pilots. The jokes were different in character from Cambodian jokes, which were all about sex. Here is a typical Cambodian joke. A mosquito is caught in a storm and takes shelter in an elephant's cunt. (Roars of laughter.) After the storm, the mosquito meets a friend.

'Did you know what that was you were sheltering in just then?' says the second mosquito.

'What?'

'It was an elephant's cunt.' (Further roars of laughter, particularly from the women.)

'Oh,' says the first mosquito, flexing his muscles, 'a pity I didn't know that. If I'd realized it was an elephant's cunt I might have done something about it!' (Hysterical laughter, old men clutch their sides, tears course down the faces of the women, food and wine are produced and the teller of the joke is asked for more.)

Vietnamese jokes were all about tactics. This is one: during the Tet Offensive in 1968, the Vietcong blew up the central span of the main bridge over the Perfume River, and for some time afterwards planks were put across, and the bridge was very dangerous. A young and beautiful girl was walking home from the school in which she taught (nods of interest, audience leans forward and is very quiet) when she fell into the water (smiles), which was most unfortunate because she could not swim (smiles disappear). So she started calling out, 'Help me, help me,' and a large crowd gathered on the river bank, but none of the young men wanted to help her (expressions completely disappear). So the girl called out: 'If anybody jumps in and saves me, I will marry him.' (Smiles.) At this point all the young men rushed forward, but every time one of them reached the edge of the water (smiles) another man pulled him back, because every one wanted to marry the young girl (smiles disappear, anxiety expressed on faces of young men). And so the girl was very near to drowning, when an old man succeeded in getting into the water and saving the girl.

At the wedding, he was asked by the press: 'How come a weak and ugly old man like you managed to win the girl, when all the young men were trying?'

And the old man replied: 'Every time a young man tried to get in, he was pulled back by another. But when an old and ugly man like me appeared on the scene, they didn't bother to pull me back. In fact they pushed me in.' (End of joke. Heads nod. There is a little laughter.)

Later when I was in the city Hué, I tried this joke out, and the effect at the end of the story was striking. First, there was a silence. Then I was asked to repeat the punchline. Then all hell broke loose, and I thought for a moment that I might be chucked into the Perfume River myself. After several minutes of animated conversation the company turned back to me. They had two comments: *Primo*, the young men were right in the first place not to jump in—after all, they might have been killed. *Secundo*, the story was not true.

While not collecting jokes or playing Chinese chess I was trying to find out about the war. This was difficult. Some of the small outposts that now represented the division between North and South and that were dotted around the mountains—they had names like Bu Prang and Bu Bong—were under attack. The helicopter squadron with which I was staying was here to give support to these outposts. There was a low-level campaign on the part of the Vietcong to wipe out these little impediments, which were used by the South Vietnamese as listening posts along the region of the Ho Chi Minh trail, and which had been set up largely by the Special Forces in which Sprague had served. Now the campaign was under the aegis of Saigon, and these outposts were beginning to fall. At one point my chess-master produced a hand-drawn map and started to show me what was happening, but he didn't get far before somebody came into the room, and he shoved the map quickly into his pocket.

We slept seven or eight to a room, and in the middle of the night I awoke to the sound of rifle fire. There was an extraordinary noise going on, and I suddenly thought—Good God! They're attacking Gia Nghia. They're coming into the camp and blowing whistles. Why are they all blowing whistles? They're blowing whistles in order to tell each other where they are, perhaps to create a panic in the camp . . . . Panic!

I got up and went to the window. One of the soldiers burst out laughing. There was no gunfire any more: a soldier had shot at a shadow, perhaps. The noise of whistles, though it continued, was nothing more than the noise of the jungle. Go back to bed, you idiot.

During this period, moving from one outpost to another, I often suffered from nightmares. It was as if some great spade was digging through my mind, turning over deep clods of loam. If Saigon was a nightmare by day, it was to Phnom Penh that my thoughts returned at night. In Saigon, I was shown some photographs that had come in from Cambodia, which Associated Press had decided were too horrible to use. In one, a smiling soldier was shown eating the liver of a Khmer Rouge, whom he had just killed; from the expression on his face, he could have been eating anything—the liver was obviously delicious. In the next photograph, a human head was being lowered by the hair into a pot of boiling water—but it was not going to be eaten. In the third photograph, decapitated corpses were being dragged along the road behind an armoured patrol carrier.

My nightmares were about war and torture and death. I remember one particularly vividly. We were standing, myself and a friend who was a poet, at the edge of a battle. The landscape was hilly, but belonged neither to Cambodia nor to Vietnam; it seemed to be northern European. The soldiers had taken several prisoners, and there were wounded and dead lying all around. Their features were Cambodian. As the prisoners were brought in, it became obvious that they were about to be beaten up and killed. The soldiers gathered round them. The poet began to shout out: 'No, no, this isn't happening. I'm not here, I'm not here.' When the beatings began, all the bodies of the dead and wounded rose into the air, and began to travel around the sky above the hill.

'Look,' I said, pointing to the hill, 'isn't that interesting? Those figures. They look just like the shepherds in that van der Goes altarpiece in the Uffizi.'

'I say,' said a journalist at my elbow, 'that's a rather good image. But I suppose you'll be using it in your story.'

'Oh no,' I replied, 'have it by all means. I'm not filing on this one.' Here the dream ended.

After a month, I returned to Saigon. I was due to go to Laos, and my visa was coming to an end. I paid up at my hotel, and by the time I was through immigration at the airport I had no currency left. I was badly in need of a coffee, and I was absolutely terrified that the plane would not come. Suppose I had to stay in Saigon any longer? The neurosis came back alarmingly. I got talking to a Chinese businessman, whom I had helped with his luggage. He bought me a coffee and began a lengthy chat about the virtues of South Vietnam as a source of raw materials. Raw materials were very much needed in Hong Kong. He dealt in anything he could find—here was his card—in timber, scrap iron, swatches . . . .

'What are swatches?' I asked.

'Rags,' he said, 'like these,' and indicated my clothes. Then he left for Hong Kong.

I just did not believe that my plane would go. As it taxied along the runway, a cockroach scuttled along the floor in front of me. I thought, This plane is hopeless, it'll never make the journey. We flew for some way along the Mekong, and the neurosis subsided. Then suddenly I looked out and—what! We were flying over the sea! Something's gone wrong, I thought, the pilot's got lost, he's going to turn back and go to Saigon. It's all going to happen over again. But then I looked down and saw that the sea effect was a mirage. We were indeed flying over Laos, and we were beginning to lose height.

South Vietnam as It was:
December 1974

'Ask him why he paints his little fingernails.' And it wasn't just the fingernails. It was the little toenails as well—carefully pedicured and varnished a deep shade of red. This seemed most inappropriate in a professional soldier. What would his officers say on parade? In the British army, I reflected patriotically, the offending nails would have been ceremonially torn out.

As the question was asked, I watched his face. A slow and secret smile came over it. He looked down at the table and mumbled inaudibly. The face was like a baby's, quite unmarked by the experience of war. It went, in a way, with the painted nails, but not with the Ranger's uniform. In any event, he didn't want to answer, so I asked him what he thought of the war.

We were sitting in a café in Go Da Hau, a small town near the Cambodian border, on the Saigon-Phnom Penh road. He desperately wanted to talk, but found it difficult. Finally, he said that the war was like a guttering candle. Occasionally it would flare up, but before long it would be entirely extinguished.

And what did he think of that?

There was nothing now that he could do. He would become a monk, he said. He would never marry. There was no job he could do, and little possibility of earning money except by soldiering. If the war ended, that was that.

He was an orphan. His father had died in Dien Bien Phu, and his mother soon afterwards. He had been educated at military school and served in the army ever since. No wonder he was still prepared to fight. No wonder, despite what people said, the Saigon army was still prepared to fight. For many of the soldiers there was simply nothing else they could do.

The Ranger talked sadly until late into the night. For the most part, he did not know how to express himself. His features strained with the burden of something very important that he wanted to say. Finally, a couple of Vietcong were sighted just outside town. Gunfire burst out all around us. The family who ran the café gave us shelter in the back. The Ranger straightened himself up, put on the look of a professional soldier, and disappeared into the blackness of the street.

Conversations in the dark, sad rambling discussions which always led back to the war, shy officers who told you one thing by night but begged you not to remember it the next day. Conducted to the accompaniment of Chinese chess, the tongues loosened by Vietnamese alcohol, which tasted like meths and probably was. Click, click went the chess-pieces, as the dead GIs lined up on either side of the board, the tanks crossed the river, and the officer escort moved around the compound—always diagonally—to protect the general. I developed a theory of journalism, on which I hoped to build a school. It was to be called the Crepuscular School and the rules were simple: believe nothing that you are told before dusk. Instead of diplomatic sources, or high-ranking sources, or 'usually reliable sources', the crepuscular journalists would refer to 'sources interviewed last night', 'sources at midnight', or best of all 'sources contacted a few hours before dawn'. It would be considered unprofessional to interview the general on the morning of the battle. You would wait till the evening, when he was reviewing the cost. Crepuscular stories would cut out the bravado. Their predominant colourings would be melancholy and gloom. In this they would reflect more accurately the mood of the times.

For the war was not guttering out yet by any means. It was a year since I had been in Vietnam, and, if anything, military activities had increased. In a matter of three weeks the equivalent of the population of a small town was killed or wounded, or went missing. District towns fell, remote outposts fell, enormous enemy losses were claimed—little of it was ever seen. If things were going badly, the military did not want you around. If well, no interest was shown. It was, again, difficult to locate the war, difficult to get to it. Indeed most of the journalists in Saigon had given up trying. The same editor who would have insisted on maximum-risk reporting when the Americans were fighting now considered such journalism a matter of minority interest. And so the idea grew up that ARVN, the Saigon army, was simply not fighting; an idea that as far as I know was never tested against the reality of the time, although later it received a sort of retrospective justification.

I really wanted to meet the Provisional Revolutionary Government, the PRG, but I was beginning to think that the chances of 'going across' into the areas it occupied were rather slim. The problem was simply the transition: in 'going across' you were likely to be fired at by the South Vietnamese troops both when you tried to go in and, of course, when you came out. The problem was not to locate the Vietcong areas. It was simply a question of accreditation and opportunity. In the end, I took a long short cut.

I had returned to Saigon where I was introduced to a man by the name of Jean-Claude. Jean-Claude had been to Vietcong areas several times before, spoke a bit of Vietnamese and was a sort of Vietcong groupie. He had been educated, he said, at an English borstal—and much admired the film of *The Loneliness of the Long-Distance Runner*—had been active in 1968 in *les événements*, was now a member of the French Communist Party and lived as a freelance photographer-cum-reporter-cum-entrepreneur. The emphasis was very much on the entrepreneur. I never knew how much of what he said was sheer fantasy and how much was true, but the fact remains that when he finally left Saigon it was in an official limousine provided by the People's Revolutionary Government of South Vietnam. He 'made things happen'.

Our intention was to hire a car and travel from Saigon to Quang Tri, taking in en route every major town and covering a large part of the Central Highlands. At points along the way, we were bound to come across the PRG; indeed we intended to go through areas they controlled, and to drop in on them as the occasion arose.

We left Saigon with great relief: the city was in a festive mood; the loudspeakers were blaring 'Angels from the Realms of Glory'; there were toy Christmas trees, Stars of Bethlehem, tanks and machine-guns on sale, and the street-vendors were being very insistent about the merits of the most hideous Christmas greetings cards.

The first village of interest we encountered was on the main road that had been napalmed a couple of days before. The Vietcong had come into the village to cut off the road, and had been trapped there along with many of the villagers by the Saigon troops. The village had then been destroyed by a force obviously capable of creating enormous heat. I noticed a pile of bananas that had been charred right through, although they preserved their original shape. They looked like something discovered and preserved in Pompeii.

We went on through landscapes as varied as their inhabitants—the coffee plantations near Djiring, for instance, which were worked by a Montagnard race whose language sounded curiously like Italian. We stayed the first night as the guest of an Italian missionary, who had married a Montagnard and was working in agriculture. He told us of the Montagnard resistance movement, *Fulro*—how it was growing, and how it maintained an uneasy, informal liaison with the Vietcong. We met a French planter, whose factor was Vietcong (there was an 'arrangement' as in all rural areas). And we gave a lift to a Frenchman known as Raquin, the Shark, who made his living by selling his own brands of French cheeses and Pernod, which he concocted in a small shack next door to the American Embassy in Saigon. Raquin was on the road distributing his wares to the various Frenchmen dotted around the country, so we dropped in with him to share a rum punch with an old Martiniquan soldier living just south of Dalat.

At Dalat, much less than halfway between Saigon and our destination, we hit the edge of a typhoon. Mist and pouring rain accompanied us as far as the coast and the seaside resort of Nha Trang, where we spent a gloomy Christmas Eve. It would be nice, would it not, to get to the PRG on Christmas Day?

'You know, my friend,' Jean-Claude would say, crossing his legs as he drove, steering with one hand, lighting a cigarette with the other, and giving me what appeared to be the full benefit of his attention, 'you know, my friend, we're going to see some great things, for sure. For sure. Yes, man.' And occasionally, looking out across the paddy-fields of the coastal strip, he would say, Yes, we were getting warm, and then, No, we were getting cold.

At one point we came upon what had been a large military base, one of those that disappeared overnight when the Americans left, torn down by a thousand tiny hands and carted away for building materials. There were large roads and runways beside the dunes, and at the edge of the sea a single standing arch marked '*Das Schloss*'. Beside it stood a village, surrounded by a thorn hedge, where our arrival caused something of a stir. 'This is it, my friend,' said Jean-Claude, 'they're here, for sure, I know it.' But of the group of elders who came out to meet us nobody seemed willing to talk, and they said there was no food to be had in the village. There were no government soldiers, no Vietcong to be seen, and no flags of any kind. The only notice in the village had come from the military base, and now formed the wall of a house: 'Rabies Suspected—No Unauthorized Personnel.' We left disappointed.

And continued up the coast, and through a steep valley which had been almost entirely defoliated. The mountains were strewn with huge boulders, and the white stumps of the dead trees pointed up out of the returning scrub. Several of the rocks had been decorated with the skull and crossbones, and under these sat groups of Saigon soldiers sheltering from the rain, high up the hillside. We drove until evening, when the light began to fade, and we were determined to get to Bong Son that night or fail in the attempt: a failure meaning that we would thus have come across a Vietcong checkpoint. But no such luck. We passed through several astonished and frightened groups of Saigon soldiers, bivouacked by the bridges, and the road was just closing up altogether for the night when we entered Bong Son. An officer in his jeep, *en tenue libre* for the evening, was chatting up the girls in the main street. He asked us what we were doing, explained there was no hotel and invited us to spend the night at his headquarters. He turned out to be the District Chief, a certain Major Bang.

The major, as his name so painfully suggests, was very keen on artillery. He explained to us at supper—shouting over the sound of his own weaponry outside—how scrupulously he was adhering to the Paris Peace Agreement: he was firing only defensively, and only at known targets. I concluded, by the end of an ear-splitting night, that he must have been very much on the defensive, and that his *deuxième bureau* must have been working round the clock to provide him with new co-ordinates for the known targets. Either that or, as in the majority of such camps meant to guard strategic bridges and bases, the tactic was simply to fire enough ordnance to give an impression of strength. We ourselves were not fired at once during the night. Major Bang also told us that the people of the area, after their experience of the Vietcong, loathed and despised the communists. We had an opportunity to check up on this statement the next day.

The soldiers told us that three bridges had been destroyed just up the road, and that the flood waters from the typhoon had rendered repairs impossible for some days. This meant that our plan of driving to Quang Tri—or indeed to Danang or Hué or anywhere else in the northern provinces—was spoiled. It was therefore in a mood of some frustration that we drove up to the first bridge to check the damage for ourselves.

There had been a small battle the night before between the Vietcong and the guards beside the bridge, and one of the Vietcong had been killed. His body lay there. The face had been completely stoved in and the whole corpse lacked blood. It looked as though it had been dragged through the water; round its waist there was still a length of rope. As we stood there, a battalion of soldiers arrived by truck, dismounted and began to climb along the broken bridge. They were about to begin an operation to flush out the Vietcong from the area, and they were in a rather bloodthirsty, hysterical mood. There was tension too among the large crowd of local villagers and travellers who had assembled by the bridge. One of the soldiers took a stick and prised open the mouth of the dead man.

'We go kill too many VC,' the soldier said. There was in the soldiers' manner a mixture of satisfaction and fright.

Jean-Claude was angry enough at the reversal in our plans, but the scene by the bridge roused him to furious action. 'You know, my friend,' he said, 'the VC are all around here, that's for sure.' If we weren't going to get as far north as Quang Tri, we might as well 'go across' at the earliest opportunity. We drove a little way back down the road, and came to a pathway where we could leave the car fairly inconspicuously. Then we simply started walking across the fields. We met a peasant, and Jean-Claude asked him the way to the 'Giai Phong' (liberators). He gave a vague indication with his hand. When we had crossed a couple of small fields, and were still only about a hundred yards from the road, we came to a small stream and a broken bridge. I was just wondering why the bridge had not been repaired when, looking up, I saw a soldier in green peering over the hedge. He beckoned to us to come quickly and pointed to the part where the stream was shallowest. We waded through, and found that we had crossed into the liberated zone.

The soldier carried an American M-79 grenade-launcher, and wore an American jacket with pouches for the grenades. From his lack of insignia or helmet we took him to be Vietcong, but there was no particular way of telling. He had a transistor radio slung from his belt. Behind where he stood there was a large pond, and beyond the pond another hedgerow. Behind the hedgerow, looking to see what on earth was happening, was a row of green pith helmets. The first soldier indicated that we should be careful as we could still be seen from the road. We hurried through the pond, avoiding the bomb craters that he pointed out to us, and emerged, dripping with mud and sweat and trembling with excitement, where the group in the pith helmets were waiting. During the whole process, nobody had pointed a gun at us and, although we had dropped in unannounced, nobody seemed at a loss as to what to do. They took us into a small hut and gave us a couple of coconuts to drink.

'Fuck me,' said Jean-Claude, 'we've made it, didn't I tell you we'd make it, my friend?'

It dawned on us that, although we had got so far, we were now in a considerable quandary. After all, we were only about a mile from where the operation to flush out the Vietcong was supposed to begin, and only about two miles or so from Major Bang.

'You know what, my friend,' said Jean-Claude, 'we're going to have to leave that car. They'll see it on the road in no time. But you know what, I don't care, man, I don't fucking care. If we have to walk to Hanoi I don't mind. We can't go back to Saigon now, my friend, that's for sure.' I was too elated by having actually got across to be much worried by this talk. It was as if we had just stepped through the looking-glass.

The first thing I noticed, with slight dismay, was how well-dressed and clean everyone was. Their clothes were for the most part of Chinese cloth, rather well-cut. Their watches came from Japan and were set to Hanoi time. The Northerners among them wore pith helmets and Ho Chi Minh badges, but otherwise they were in mufti. Most carried the regulation guerrilla rifle, the AK-47, but one had an American M-16. One man unzipped the embroidered pouch in which he kept his transistor, and turned on Radio Hanoi. A solemn voice, which I afterwards learned belonged to Miss Elizabeth Hodgkin, said: 'I'm a teacher. I-apostrophe-M. A. T-E-A-C-H-E-R. *You're* a student; Y-O-U-apostrophe . . . .' But the thing that struck me most was the number of ball-point pens they wore.

I mention the ball-point pens because they seemed a rather important part of everyday life. When they conversed with us, either in English or in Vietnamese (there were no French-speakers among them), they seemed much happier when committing their thoughts to paper. Jean-Claude said that the Vietnamese they wrote was highly elegant and classical. My conversation was rather less satisfactory. It showed, I thought, that their conception of education, or perhaps Miss Hodgkin's conception, might lean a little far on the rigid side. It went like this. First the soldier wrote: 'HOW ARE YOU?'

Then I wrote: 'VERY HAPPY TO BE HERE.'

The soldier looked mistrustfully at this for some time. He almost crossed it out, but then he wrote underneath: 'FINE THANKS, AND YOU?'

Clearly, as an English-speaker, I had failed at the first hurdle.

While we were thus conversing, a meal of chicken and rice was brought by the villagers, who crowded round to watch us eat. There was intense curiosity, but very little noise. Authority seemed to come very easily to the older soldiers, and the children responded to them at once. Several of those who had been at the bridge came back to tell the soldiers what was happening. One boy of about sixteen seemed particularly moved by what he had seen. He sat on the floor and talked about it for some time in a low voice. Everybody spoke quietly, almost as if they might be heard by the Saigon soldiers on the road. Apart from the odd rifle shot, the only noise was that of the military traffic going up to the bridge. One might have been lulled, by the confidence in everybody's manner, into a sense of total security, had not the political officer politely told us after lunch that it would be dangerous to stay any longer.

Thinking of Major Bang's pronouncement the night before, that the people of the area loathed the communists, I wondered whether I could be completely mistaken in thinking that it was quite false. Two things stayed in my mind. First, the Saigon troops that we had seen that morning were clearly frightened, conscious perhaps that they were in hostile territory. The second was the sight of a small child among the villagers who had crowded round us: he wore the uniform of the local school from where we had just come. Every day he must have had to cross the lines and would have been imbued with Saigon propaganda. Crossing the lines was obviously no problem, but did it not argue a certain political confidence on the part of the People's Revolutionary Government that the child was allowed to do so?

A little girl showed us an easy path back to the road and we made towards where we had left the car. There, to our horror, stood a couple of Saigon soldiers. We walked up as calmly as possible.

'You,' said one of the soldiers, 'why you not obey me? You go see VC.'

We had our excuses prepared. We had wandered innocently into the paddy to take photographs, we said, and we had been stopped by the VC. 'Beaucoup VC,' we said, spiritedly, 'with guns, same-same you.'

'I no VC.'

'No,' we said hurriedly, 'you no VC. Hey, we very scared. VC take us, not let us go. We have to talk, many hours.'

One of the soldiers, a warrant officer, was particularly angry because he had apparently been shouting at us, telling us not to go.

Finally we said to him, would he and his friend like a beer? Yes, he said angrily, so we took him to the nearest village, where he made a great scene about buying the drink. Then we took him and the beer back to his friend. I put some money in his hand.

'What's this?' he said.

'English custom,' I said, 'It's called Boxing Day, give beaucoup money to friends. Look, if you tell Major Bang we go VC, beaucoup trouble for us, maybe trouble for you. You no say nothing, okay?' And we left him standing by the roadside, suspiciously eyeing the money and the beer.

Driving as fast as we dared back towards Bong Son, we came again upon the body of the dead Vietcong. It had been dragged down the road and dumped near a small market, no doubt as a warning to the local populace. The rope was still around its waist, but the arms, which previously had been stretched out, were now bent into an embrace. I was surprised. I hadn't thought you could do that to a corpse once it was cold. Jean-Claude brought the car to a near-halt. 'For Christ's sake,' I said, 'let's just get out of here as quickly as possible.' Above all, I did not want to meet Major Bang again, after we had so shamefully abused his hospitality.

D oubling back on our tracks, we drove south and inland, up into the Central Highlands to Kontum—still almost 275 miles north of Saigon. The road was permanently blocked a few miles north. We stood on the hillside looking down into the valley, where a couple of burned-out trucks across the road indicated the front line. On our right was a strangely pleasant camp that looked like a fortified *Club Méditerranée*. There were straw huts and wooden tables and chairs set in the shade, and you hardly noticed the ingenious system of trenches and foxholes leading to the officers' bunkers. Painted faces with plucked eyebrows emerged from the trenches, while from the bunkers came the sound of female laughter and one or two other things. It was widely feared at the time that the Vietcong might attack Kontum. This camp would be their first obstacle.

'You must spend the night with us,' said the medical officer, 'in order to share something of the life of the soldier.' We were happy to accept.

Most of the officers had 'wives'. The major's wife prepared a meal, after which another one of the wives sang a mournful song. Then we all sang songs apart from the major, who produced a cassette radio and played us a medley of dreadful Vietnamese tangos. As it grew dark, the soldiers gathered round to watch us, from a respectable distance. You could see their cigarette ends glowing through the trees. Sometimes, as they began to get drunk on rice spirit, the soldiers would abruptly disappear from sight, falling into foxholes or disappearing into trenches. When the officers retired underground with their wives, we were invited to drink with the other ranks.

Their drunkenness had an edge of desperation. They shouted a lot and staggered blindly outside the perimeter fence, saying that they were about to go off on an ambush. Then they leaned forward and were quietly sick. On one occasion a gun went off by mistake, which didn't frighten me nearly so much as the thought that all this noise must be perfectly audible to the Vietcong in the valley below—the shouts, the laughter, the songs, my fearful rendition of *The Water is Wide* (in the Britten arrangment). Having been on the other side only the day before, I was more conscious than ever of the forces patiently biding their time. Suppose they suddenly decided that the time was ripe? Supposing they came down, or rather up, the mountain like a wolf on the fold—what would one, as it were, do?

The soldiers were also conscious of enormous preparations being made on the other side. On most nights, they said, they could hear the tanks and Molotova trucks of the North Vietnamese Army manoeuvring on the road that was being built in the mountains, the road that would link the Ho Chi Minh trail with the coast. But there were other things that made them depressed. Some of them had not seen their families for two years. They didn't get any leave. They didn't find it easy to live on twenty dollars a month. They didn't like having to go out on patrols, from which their comrades often did not return. They didn't like the fact that the local version of malaria can kill a man in two months, and they didn't like the bitterly cold nights. They slept in makeshift bivouacs, with a sack of rice as a pillow, protecting their food from the numerous rats. In contrast to the officers, they were not allowed 'wives', even if they could have afforded them at the going rate of three dollars a night.

The guard on the north gate was a Cambodian from the Delta. He had very much liked serving under the American officers in the Special Forces, but said that with the South Vietnamese Army everything was a fuck-up. I sat up with him most of the night, hoping to hear the movement of the tanks and trucks. From time to time an old man, also Cambodian, came round with a stick to make sure that the guard was awake. This man was in a good mood: in two weeks, after a service of twenty-five years, he was due to retire. As it happened, he came from one of the villages near Wat Champa, which I had visited on my earlier trip. So I was able to tell him that his home was now in a contested area and very likely to be taken over by the Vietcong. He didn't seem at all worried or surprised by this. He was going to retire—and that was that.

But the guard on the north gate was young and had no option to retire. He wanted to leave the army. There were so many things he wanted to do, he said, if only he wasn't a soldier. When I asked him exactly what it was he wanted to do, he was at a loss to say. We sat and shivered and talked. The quiet landscape was brilliantly lit by the moon. To our left we could see the mountains through which the Ho Chi Minh trail used to run, and ahead of us the site of the new road. Although there was no noise of tanks or trucks, there was no particular comfort from the silence.

'Sometimes,' said the guard, 'I think I will go AWOL —I did it before but the military police arrested me.'

I told him that I thought it would be a very good idea to go AWOL. Some days later, when I was leaving Saigon, I received a visit from him in my hotel room. I was packing. The guard had come to Saigon because he was about to be moved on to some new operation. He didn't know where he was going, and he asked if I had any civilian clothes to spare.

'I want you to write,' said the director of the Open Arms programme whom I saw the next morning in Kontum, 'that the people of Kontum are not afraid of attack by the VC.' The idea of an attack was very much in the air. In Saigon it was feared that the coming dry season—January to May—would see a renewal of hostilities in the Central Highlands, and that Kontum, a well-known city, difficult to defend, would be a tempting target. It is surrounded by mountains and forests. 'You see that mountain,' said the director, as we drove aimlessly around the city, 'you see that mountain? It belongs to us.' But precious little else in Kontum belonged to Saigon.

We drove on south from Kontum through Pleiku to Ban Me Thuot, on a road that was alive with possibilities: we were told to expect bandits, Vietcong, the North Vietnamese Army, Montagnard guerrillas or the South Vietnamese. As the road deteriorated, it rose through thick forests to a clearing that commanded a panoramic view of Laos and Cambodia, and the fields where the Montagnards cultivated their rice. The road was quite free of traffic except at one point when a military convoy of empty trucks appeared, guarded by a helicopter. We were at pains to keep our distance, not wishing to be ambushed. First we overtook it, then we had a puncture and it passed us by. By the time the wheel was changed, we were quite alone.

We were alone, but it did not feel as if we were. At regular intervals along the road there were checkpoints, but none of them, on this day, seemed to be manned. Who had built the checkpoints was a matter for conjecture, and it gave one an eerie feeling, to say the least, to wait around at each, in order to make sure it was possible to pass. The checkpoints were beautifully constructed bowers, woven out of the tall grasses that grew on the edge of the road, and the ground showed clearly that they had only recently been made and only recently abandoned. At one point, outside the checkpoint, a gleaming new B-41 rocket stood on its tripod. This suggested the presence of Vietcong—and yet it was uncharacteristic to leave good ammunition behind. Were they simply unwilling to show their faces? At another point, three stuffed mannikins of Saigon troops, with GI helmets, lay overturned on the road. This suggested magic, some terrible Montagnard curse perhaps.

'Fuck me, my friend,' said Jean-Claude, 'they're here somewhere, you know, that's for sure.' Sometimes, when it looked as if a checkpoint was very recent indeed, we would stop the car, get out and call into the forest—in French, in English, in Vietnamese. If the convoy had frightened them off, surely the convoy was now past. If they were listening in the bushes, they must have thought our behaviour was most singular.

Towards Ban Me Thuot—where some of the most recent battles had been fought—the road gradually improved. The sun began to sink and the villagers were returning from the fields in long columns, carrying sacks of rice on their shoulders. We saw one soldier marching in a column, but when he saw us he jumped off the road and scurried behind a hedge. Further on, we came to a Montagnard graveyard and stopped the car. On the other side of a small valley, there was a large fortified settlement. The cattle were being brought in for the night, and we could hear them lowing in the distance. It was a beautiful sight, in the sunset. One of the villagers recognized Jean-Claude from a year before, when he had been in military hospital. He told us that after being wounded, and after the South Vietnamese had disbanded the Montagnard units, he had decided to get out. We asked him whether we could spend the night in his settlement. He said no, it was not possible. He was a little shifty about his reasons, but I thought I understood them well enough.

Everything we had seen, everything we had been told, should have made it clear to us that something was about to happen. That night, in Ban Me Thuot itself we met an officer from the *deuxième bureau* who told us of the latest military disasters in Phuoc Long province. He said that he thought Ban Me Thuot would be attacked next, and that it might last at most three weeks. In Pleiku that morning, we had been told at length how reduced the ability of the South Vietnamese Army was, and how they would be unable to withstand any concerted attack. We were sceptical. We knew that South Vietnam was calling out urgently to America for more funds, and that it was therefore convenient to paint as gloomy a picture as possible. It also seemed highly improbable that with all those soldiers and all that material—the fourth largest air force in the world, the tanks, the trucks, the convoys we had seen, all that expensive equipment—well, it just seemed impossible that the whole show would be over in such a short space of time. In the *end*, yes—but if someone had come up to us and said, 'The Saigon regime has exactly four months left,' we should never have believed him.

As a matter of fact, someone did tell us just that, almost, on New Year's Eve, the last night of our journey together.

'**M**an proposes, God disposes,' he said, by way of opening the conversation. We were slightly taken aback. He was a cyclo-driver in Nha Trang, whom we had invited to join us at dinner to celebrate the New Year. 'Yes,' he had said, accepting our invitation, 'if you have the goodness,' and he took out his long trousers from under the seat, where, as was customary, they were kept ready pressed by the weight of customers. As he put on his trousers and joined us at the table, he seemed to grow in stature before our eyes. The servility left him, and he became garrulous in excellent French. It was as if everything he had ever learned during his French education and his period as a government employee in Tonkin had swelled up inside him and was now bursting out. He had a store of proverbs to meet every situation. When we asked him whether he resented being a *cyclopousse* after having been a *fonctionnaire*, he told us that every man must work in order to repay his debt to society, and that there was no such thing as stupid work, only stupid people.

The evening passed. He recited a poem about the poor in winter, and some verses about a princess weeping under a tree. After every line, he would give us a perfect paraphrase, in case the slightest shade of meaning had escaped us. Then he declaimed a poem by Lamartine, whom I vowed at once never to read. He sang a Boy Scout song (he was a keen Boy Scout, or had been) about the life of the matelot and its attendant dangers. Finally, with terrific flourish and style—you could almost hear the piano accompaniment—he sang a song called '*Tant qu'il y aura des étoiles*': though we are only beggars, the song went, and although our life is utterly wretched, as long as there are the stars, we shall be blissfully content with our lot. He seemed at this point to be the paragon of supine virtues. And he had, of course, a thing or two to say about communism: violence, deception and lying are the methods employed, he said, by those who wish to attain a classless society. When we asked him, however, what he *thought* about the possibility of a classless society, he affected not to understand. Finally, using a phrase of Ho Chi Minh's which had become a password for Vietnamese communism, Jean-Claude asked him: 'Don't you think that nothing is more precious than independence and liberty?'

At this point he underwent his second transformation of the evening. He looked down at the tablecloth and paused dramatically. Then, as he began to speak, his mouth twisted into the most extraordinary snarl. 'I think that Vietnam has been a prey,' he said, 'a prey to foreigners. We could not do anything about it in the past because we were too weak and feeble. But things are changing now. The future, the future will show you'—and here he raised his voice to the climax: '*L'avenir vous montrera. Je ne peux pas dire plus que ça.*'

The Fall of Saigon: April 1975

On my return to Saigon from this trip, I learned that the Khmer Rouge had launched their New Year offensive against Phnom Penh. Cambodia was my chief interest, and I went immediaely to report on the death-throes of the Lon Nol regime. During this time, the situation in Vietnam changed very fast. Ban Me Thuot was overrun by the North Vietnamese, and President Thieu decided to abandon the Central Highlands. His troops were decimated as they retreated, and the general collapse of the southern regime soon became inevitable. President Ford attempted to secure funds for both Vietnam and Cambodia, but in the end even he had to write off the Phnom Penh regime. The American Embassy left Phnom Penh the day after Ford made the announcement in which this was implied. The majority of the press corps went with them. We were helicoptered to the *USS Okinawa* in the Gulf of Siam, and from there I made my way to Bangkok. I was angry with myself for having left Cambodia, and wondered what to do next. The question was—whether or not to go to Saigon? I knew that if I went I would not want to be evacuated by the Americans yet again. I would want to see this story through. So I took all the advice I could, and then decided I would go to Saigon and stay.

On 24 April 1975, the day before my twenty-sixth birthday, I boarded the plane for Saigon. In the seat next to me was a man named Garth W. Hunt, the Field Secretary for Asia of Living Bibles International, who was on his way to get his team out of Vietnam. His team was a 'hard core' of ten to fifteen translators who produced the Vietnamese *Living Bible*, plus a 'broad base' of theological and stylistic reviewers. Then there were the consultants ('men of stature, recognized in their own field') including literary consultants, exegetical consultants, theological consultants, technical consultants and editorial consultants. Each of these had a family and dependants and most of them wanted out.

Living Bibles International is an evangelical organization with strong, unmistakeable political leanings. 'God loves the sinner but he hates the sin,' said Mr Hunt, and in this case the sin was communism, which God certainly despised. So did Living Bibles International: at the present moment, their powerful transmitters were broadcasting the Chinese translation of the *Living Bible* at *dictation speed* into the People's Republic. 'International boundaries', said Garth W. Hunt, 'can't keep out God's message.'

They'd had no luck in North Vietnam, although they had asked to work there. But in the south they had always had tremendous co-operation from the government. A translation of *The Gospel According to Saint Mark*, the only thing this vast organization had so far completed, had already sold 120,000 copies. It had been broadcast over the radio, and was distributed in camps and refugee centres. An earlier book, produced by a sister organization, had been distributed to every psychological warfare officer in the country, and also to every Vietnamese embassy and consulate throughout the world. 'This book,' said Mr Hunt, 'became the most influential book in Vietnam, apart from the word of God himself.' It was called *God Still Performs Miracles*.

My reading-matter for the journey, in addition to my complimentary copy of *The Living Bible*, was *Time* and *Newsweek*. *Newsweek* contained a story describing Khieu Samphan as he entered Phnom Penh: 'When he returned to Phnom Penh last week, Khieu Sampan [*sic*] was dressed in a simple black pajamas suit and *krama*. No one would have guessed from his peasant look that he had spent the last eight years plotting—and carrying out—the

overthrow of the Cambodian government.' The story was written by
Fay Willey in New York with *Newsweek*'s reporter-in-the-field,
'Paul Brinkley Rogers in Hong Kong', who may have written the
footnote explaining that Samphan's *krama* was a 'traditional
Cambodian cotton scarf that can be worn as a turban, a towel to
protect the neck or as a loin cloth.' The thing that puzzled me was
where this story came from. No correspondent or newsagency
had reported seeing Khieu Samphan entering the city, and there
was no evidence that he was even there. But somebody in New York
must have assumed that he had been, looked up his photo, and
written up the story nevertheless. This was an unusually vivid
example of a tendency in American magazine journalism to
embellish . . . ever so slightly. I think it was six weeks before that'
Newsweek described the Khmer Rouge as prowling through the
humid jungles around Phnom Penh. There are no jungles around
Phnom Penh. It is likely that, if there had been jungles, they would
have been humid, and it is possible that the Khmer Rouge, if
anybody had been able to watch them, would have been prowling.
So, given the jungles, everything else followed, more or less.
Without the jungles, things were a little different.

The two magazines were run in a manner similar to that
adopted by Living Bibles International: by committee. There was
an army of researchers and rewrite men, the key figures, who stayed
in the office. And given the fact that each magazine had its own
journalists on the spot, it was surprising how often the stories
originated in New York. Each week, someone in the office would
read all the papers and wire services, and each week he would send
out long lists of questions to the reporters and stringers. Steve
Heder, the Phnom Penh *Time* stringer, once received a
questionnaire for that week's story which included the thoughtful
query: 'Do the homeless, poor, maimed etc. of Phnom Penh huddle
under flimsy straw lean-tos. Know they have these in Saigon, but
are they also in Phnom Penh?' You could see the idea forming in the
guy's mind, and, being a scrupulous journalist, he wanted to make
quite sure that there were some flimsy lean-tos for his homeless,
poor, maimed etc. to huddle under. He was guarding against error,
but he'd overlooked one point. The weather was very hot, and no
one huddles under a lean-to when it is very hot.

Newsweek now makes it perfectly clear that the man on the spot is only *helping* someone in the office, whose name comes first. Occasionally, if a reporter does something rather spectacular, he is allowed to tell the story as he saw it. But this is a great honour. There was one such story in this same copy of *Newsweek*. It was about the fall of Xuan Loc, and pretty nasty stuff it was too. But the author, Nick Proffitt, told me that evening that even that story was touched up. He had had a pair of crutches lying in the road. Somebody in New York had decided it would read better as a *forlorn* pair of crutches. The chances that the crutches might have been anything other than forlorn—hilarious, for instance—were remote.

We landed in Saigon, and I got my tourist visa without any trouble—they seemed to be giving the things away. But the customs man confiscated my *Time* and *Newsweek*: it was at last impossible to allow too many Saigonese to see the wretched things. One of the covers had a photo of a Saigon soldier with a target drawn over his heart. It was headlined 'Target Saigon'. The customs man asked, 'Do you think . . .?' and made a sign as if to slit his throat. I told him not to worry. Everything was going to be okay, no sweat.

I checked in at the small hotel near the market where I had stayed before, and went off to dinner at the Continental. The garden was crowded—*tout le monde* was there. *Le Monde* was there. The famous Dr Hunter S. Thompson was there, surrounded by admirers, and was rumoured to have bought a gun. All the Indochina hands were back for the last act, which to the Americans meant the evacuation. The *Washington Post* staff had now been ordered, under pain of dismissal, to leave with the Embassy. The *New York Times* had also ordered its journalists not to say behind, and the American networks were planning to evacuate. Everyone was talking about the secret password, which would be broadcast when the time came: an announcement that the temperature was 105 and rising, followed by the song 'I'm Dreaming of a White Christmas'. It was all very jolly: I had a good meal, and sloughed off some of the misery of Bangkok.

I was woken the next morning by a sharp rap on the door. In came a rather beautiful Vietnamese girl, who plunged, without preliminaries, into a passionate speech: She had been a night-club dancer, and now she simply must leave Saigon, and I must help her. It was early in the morning and I was rather gruff. She redoubled her efforts. 'How can I live with the communists?' she wailed. 'I can't spend my money and I can't wear my clothes. I have to wear Vietcong clothes.' Then she kneeled on the floor beside my bed and pretended to cry—or gave what was, at best, a terrible imitation. 'Please help me,' she whined, 'please help me leave Saigon.' She was offering 300,000 *piastres*—a large sum for her, but with the soaring black market rate it amounted only to forty pounds. To earn this money I had only to say that she was my sister, then the Americans would give her papers. She would go to Hawaii, where she would automatically be given a US passport. She had a house in Singapore, which she could sell for $100,000. In addition, she already had $1,500 in greenbacks. The last figure she mouthed with respect and wonder. I decided that the house in Singapore was probably a fiction, and pointed out that the greenbacks would not last very long in the United States. But she had it worked out. She would live in Hawaii and set up a Vietnamese restaurant. There were so many Vietnamese going to Hawaii. She would be able to sell spring rolls and things like that. President Ford had said that two million Vietnamese could go to America. They could go this month, but after that it would be too late. I avoided giving her a definite answer, and she left the room in great distress.

300,000 *piastres*? people said scornfully. Oh *we*'ve been offered far more than that. Wherever you went, Saigon was using its most ingenious methods either to get out or to make money out of those who were leaving. It was said that the Americans were also running the rackets. Hopeful young girls would be relieved of their savings and then left stranded. The bars of Tu Do Street had been combed by the talent-spotters of the Phillipines. An enormous number of people were caught up in a craze for leaving. In a friend's hotel, I met a youth of about twenty rushing around asking for help. He had suddenly remembered something his father had given him—the torn end-paper of a book on which was written an American name and address. In his other hand, he carried the wording of a cable:

'Please send a cable to American Embassy Saigon accepting responsibility for . . . .' It seemed highly unlikely that the addressee would have any recollection of either father or son. Nevertheless we told the boy to send the cable with that wording. He didn't know how to send a cable. He did not know why he wanted to go; he knew only that he had to. He confessed that his head was in a spin. From his manner it seemed as if he had about five minutes to get out, or face the firing-squad.

This mad dash for the planes had begun about a week before when it was noticed that the Embassy had started rounding up the people they believed to be in danger when the communists took over. The calls had been carefully conducted under cover of darkness, in the manner of a Stalinist arrest. The criterion was broad. As one of the embassy personnel put it, 'The kind of people who know us are the kind of people who would be in trouble.' The Embassy was clearing out everyone in its address book, but to do so they also had to take their wives and families, and the families got larger and larger. The rich Vietnamese also wanted to take their maids. Sometimes this would be challenged at the airport: it was not customary in America to have maids. So the rich Vietnamese would then turn round and dismiss their maids with a wave of the hand. Then there was a flood of letters to the Embassy from Americans and Vietnamese living in America . . . . Discreet diplomats would pad up the stairs, knock quietly so as not to arouse the neighbours, and deliver the message: 'Your son-in-law says you must leave. Can you be ready this time tomorrow night?'

'I don't know. I haven't got a suitcase.'

'Couldn't you buy a suitcase?'

'Yes, I think so.'

'All right then?'

'What shall I wear?' And so on.

Sometimes these visits must have been welcome. At other times they shattered a few illusions. A man, living not far from my hotel, was a member of the local defence force. I sat up late one night with him and the other members of the force, drinking Vietnamese spirit and chatting about what was going to happen. They were clear about one thing: they would not lift a finger to defend the area from the Vietcong. They had seen the writing on the

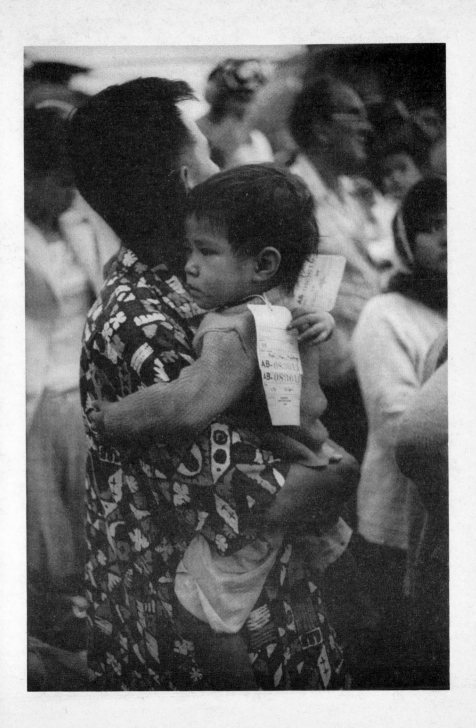

wall; when the Vietcong arrived, their duties ended. They all talked with admiration for the other side, and there was not a trace of the usual intransigence or panic of Saigon.

The exodus was continuing at a rate of about 10,000 a day. It was estimated at the time that out of each day's departures, 3,000 had Embassy connections, 1,000 were relatives of Americans and 1,000 were friends or contacts of Americans. What about all the rest? When I went to Tan Son Nhuot airport to watch the processing of the evacuees, I found very few who had a clear notion of why they were leaving. Some were North Vietnamese refugees from the 1950s, others were going because they had once worked in PX stores or as ancillary staff on American bases. One woman just did not know why she was going. Her husband had left the north as a young student. Her sister was married to an American, who had insisted that the family should leave. She did not want to do so at all. She was leaving so much behind. For instance, she had saved up for five years in order to buy her son a piano. It had only just arrived. Another man did know. He claimed to have led the National Revolutionary Movement in the days of Diem. 'Obviously,' he said, 'as a journalist you will know what it means to live under communism. No? Then you should not in that case be a journalist.'

There were snackstands at the entrace to Tan Son Nhuot, set up to cater for the waiting crowd of refugees, many of whom slipped past the guards without any papers. Processing was done in the Defence Attache's Office Compound, one of the last bits of pure America left in Vietnam. The last hurdle was in the gymnasium, under the basketball net. There were old notices reminding you not to bring in your pets, and not to put your hands on the walls. The forms were filled in by sour-looking GIs in olive drab, with daggers hanging from their belts. The prevailing atmosphere was of general menace.

While the American evacuation accelerated, the Vietcong, we later discovered, were filling the place up with their own troops. The operation was haphazard. The soldiers came in wearing Saigon uniforms, in military trucks that had been acquired during the last few months, as the Southern army had retreated in disarray. But the soldiers had no identity cards and must have lived continually on the verge of discovery. They took up positions near important

installations, in order to take control swiftly when the time came. The students' groups were also working out what to do in order to help in the takeover, and the Chinese, the shrewdest businessmen in Saigon, were already manufacturing the three-coloured flags of the National Liberation Front, in readiness for a quick sale. There must have been a tremendous run on the haberdashers. When red, blue and yellow cloth ran out, they used coloured plastic.

One night I was awakened by the sound of three large crashes, and I realized that the rocketing had begun. I went up to the top floor of my hotel (once a bar and billiard room for GIs) where I had a good view over the roofs. Already there was a large fire, fuelled no doubt by the petrol kept in the houses of the poor. Soon a whole block was ablaze, and the fire was spreading. I watched it with mixed feelings: the Vietcong had announced their proximity—the fire, though distant, spelled an immediate danger; nevertheless a city fire, far enough away, has a terrible splendour. The fire attracted me. The next day I walked around the burnt-out area, a huddled group of make-shift shacks built on an old Catholic graveyard. The fire brigade had refused to put out the blaze until massive bribes had been produced, and a large number of poor people's homes had consequently been destroyed. All this I might have guessed at the time, and yet I was excited by the fire. It seemed to be the curtain-raiser for the last act.

The next morning, 28 April, began dramatically enough. I went out to the edge of the city at about six-thirty, where I found that the Vietcong had come to the very outskirts of Saigon and had closed the road on the other side of the bridge. There were, it turned out, only a few of them, but they served their purpose, calling down a massive amount of firepower where they were ensconced. Saigon brought out all its weapons, and the helicopter gunships blasted away all day. It was not until evening that the road was cleared of a few brave men. After watching this scene for a time, I went back to my room and was reading a book when, without warning, the city became ablaze with rifle fire. I thought: that's it. The insurrection has begun.

Once again, I went up to the top floor, but this time there was nothing to see. There was simply a noise, a massive, unvaried, unstinting noise. It was too uniform. There was meant to be grenades, machine-guns, more variety. I asked a member of the hotel staff. Perhaps a coup d'état, he said, shrugging. That, again, was possible. But then, as suddenly as it had started, the firing ceased. I walked out into the deserted street. No dead bodies. Nobody much around. On the corner I met a soldier, and gave him a quizzical look. 'Sorry about that,' he said, and turned away.

President Minh, at this time, would have just finished his speech, calling on the Americans to leave, and on the other side to negotiate. The other side would have been answering that this was not enough—there had to be total unconditional surrender. For it was at the same time, for the first and last time in the war, that the Vietcong air force was brought into play. It had been a masterly piece of timing. These planes had been picked up in the previous months, having been left behind as the provinces north of Saigon had fallen in swift succession and in such disarray. Now these same South Vietnamese planes were used to bomb the Saigon air force. There was no other way in which the Vietcong could ever have used an air force except against an air base. To have done so at that moment was to announce imminent victory, and to make sure that the victory cost them as little blood as possible. As for the firing I heard outside my hotel, the troops had been told of enemy planes on the attack, but they were confused. The plane they were firing at was in fact civilian. It got away.

The incident unnerved people. It was a foretaste, we thought. From now on, anything could happen, and happen swiftly. And when something did happen, there would be nothing we could do about it.

The next morning I was woken by the ancient doorman of the hotel, who walked straight into my room carrying one loaf of French bread, two large chunks of palm sugar and a bottle of Coca-Cola. He returned a little later with ice, and insisted I get up and eat. I gathered from a rather complicated conversation that there was still a curfew, and that these were the siege rations. The bread was wrapped in what appeared to be an American Embassy report. As I attempted to eat the sugar and the bread, there was another knock. A young man came in, looking for an American who had promised to get him out of the country. He had been planning to leave from New Port the night before, but the place had been under attack. Now his father, a captain in the army, was waiting outside. We talked for a while. The young man had an infinitely sad face. He was not pushing. He probably knew already that he had missed his last chance. Anyway, he was unclear about why he wanted to leave Vietnam. I told him that he should not leave, since this was his country, and if he left it now he would never get back. He said wistfully, 'I like going to the country. My family always goes to the country for holidays. We go to Rach Gia and Ha Tien.' I said that Ha Tien was now in the hands of the Vietcong. He said: 'Do you think people are happy in Ha Tien?' I said I thought so. We discussed what would happen to his father, and I tried to reassure him. But he left as sadly as he had come in.

The curfew did not seem to be very strict, so I set out to find the other journalists and see what was happening. Saigon looked beautiful that morning, with its deserted streets. Everyone was smiling. There were families standing in the doorways, smiling. A group of soldiers passed, smiling. A beggar girl in a tattered silk blouse, to whom I gave some money, ran laughing along beside me. She was young, with an idiot look and no teeth. Clearly the curfew did not apply to idiots. There was a Sunday morning atmosphere. I felt very happy, as if I were in some English town, setting out to buy the Sunday papers. On the way I met one of my friends from the local defence force, who told me that the airport had been attacked during the night. I appeared to have slept through everything.

At the Continental all the journalists were talking about the previous night's fighting at the airport. They had seen planes shot down with Strela missiles and this, coupled with the previous day's panic when the airport had been bombed, convinced several people that they should leave. Others who had not intended to stay on were having difficulty making up their minds. I felt very excited, but did not consider going. The same principle that had taken me from Phnom Penh would keep me in Saigon. I had made my decision in advance. But I can't deny that I felt a certain superiority to those rushing around, paying their bills, gathering their stuff together, or dithering.

There was a strong move that all the British journalists remaining behind, one of whom was keen to acquire a gun, should stick together. The main worry for those staying on was that the 'friendlies' might get nasty. One of the calculations of those leaving was that the Vietcong would certainly be nasty. As a Beaverbrook reporter said to me, 'I wouldn't like to be interrogated by them. You know, they have methods. . . .'

'I doubt if it would come to that,' I said.

'Have you ever done any work with the Americans?' he asked.

'No, I was never here with the Americans.'

'Well, I can think of things I've done, places I've been and so on, that I'd find very difficult to explain away.'

I never found out exactly what he meant. As the hotel emptied I looked at the garden and was reminded of Coleridge: 'Well, they are gone and here I must remain, This Lime-tree bower my prison.' I said: 'Won't it be nice to have the place to ourselves.' This remark was considered incredibly irritating.

I had to get my possessions and bring them to the Continental. As I walked along the street people asked me why I had not left yet. 'Are you French or Australian?' they asked. One small restaurant was open, in which a group of lieutenants were sitting eating Chinese chicken and drinking Johnnie Walker Black Label. They invited me to join them, which I did with some diffidence since they were obviously out to get drunk, and might therefore become aggressive. They began by explaining that they would sit there until they were killed. I tried to say that I thought they were wrong, but when I explained why, I saw at once that I had gone too far. Ice formed over the conversation. 'How long did you spend with the communists?' they asked. I said I hadn't been with the communists. Hitherto we had been talking in English. Then we switched to French. They were amused, they said, that when I started speaking in French I began to tremble.

I was afraid that I had fallen into the hands of precisely those 'friendlies' who were supposed to turn nasty. I reached out for a piece of chicken and nonchalantly picked up the head. It was not the part I had had in mind, but I bit into the eyeballs with great gusto, and sucked out the brains. The ice was finally broken when one of the officers asked in Cambodian whether I spoke Khmer. A little, I said, and we exchanged a few phrases. These men belonged to a breed that was just on the verge of extinction—the nattily-dressed, well-groomed, gun-toting, sunglass-wearing, American-style, narcissistic junior officer. The weight of their impending extinction bore down upon them.

Inevitably, the conversation returned to the impending take-over. I asked them why they were afraid. They were well aware, they said, that in Phnom Penh the people had greeted the Khmer Rouge with open arms. But they said that that was just for appearances. Afterwards there would be a settling of accounts. They insisted again that they were going to die. I bade them farewell. They repeated that they were going to sit there drinking all day, until they died.

Some people get rich on others' misfortunes, and it appeared that I was one of them. I became, during the course of the day, acting bureau chief of the *Washington Post*. *I* had a bureau! The keys were waiting for me in the office, together with a charming farewell note from the staff. I had a pleasant young Vietnamese assistant, who was good enough to show me how to open the drawer to get at the office petty cash. The office was well equipped; I could have moved in to live. Nice bathroom, plenty of books, fridge, bottle of Polish vodka in the fridge. I settled down to work, assuming that the evacuation had begun, since there was now a fairly large amount of helicopter activity over the city. I had also assumed that the operation would be conducted as quickly as it had been in Phnom Penh. But this was not so. A few moments later I got a phone call from the *Washington Post*'s former Bureau Chief, David Greenway. He was at the US Embassy. They were stuck. Nobody had come yet, and Embassy staff were getting nervous that the place might be shelled. Oh, and did I want the car keys? They had left the Volkswagen by the Embassy gate.

I went round to the Embassy. The crowd outside had grown, but it had not yet reached the alarming proportions of later in the day. There were shady Koreans, a few stranded Americans and several hundred Vietnamese waiting around or attempting to argue with the Marines on the gate. South Vietnamese Army Officers in mufti would come up and, producing an Embassy visiting card, say,

'Excuse me, I'm a good friend of Mr So-and-so. Do you think I could get in?' Greenway appeared on one of the Embassy's turrets and threw down the *Washington Post* car keys. He had the look of a man convinced that he was about to be shelled, but was far too polite to mention the fact. I went to the car, and found that I lacked the knack of turning the key in the ignition. It had always been troublesome, and I had never driven the thing before. In fact, I had never, I remembered suddenly, learned how to drive. As I tried to start it I became nervous at being so close to the Embassy. There was a sound of rifle-fire nearby, and around the Embassy the police would occasionally shoot in the air when some angry man became too importunate. I decided to abandon the car.

Before too long the large helicopters, the Jolly Green Giants, began to appear, and as they did so the mood of the city suffered a terrible change. There was no way of disguising this evacuation by sleight-of-hand, or, it appeared, of getting it over quickly. The noise of the vast helicopters, as they corkscrewed out of the sky, was a fearful incentive to panic. The weather turned bad. It began to rain. And as the evening grew darker, it seemed as if the helicopters themselves were blotting out the light. It seemed as if the light had gone forever. All the conditions conspired against calm. All over Saigon there were people who had been promised an escape. There were others, like the officers of the morning, who thought that they would definitely die. And there were others still who for no definite reason went into a flat spin. Always the beating of the helicopter blades reminded them of what was happening. The accumulated weight of the years of propaganda came crashing down upon a terrified city.

The crowd around the Embassy swelled and its desperation increased. It became dangerous to go out on the streets. The looters were out and the cowboys were on their Hondas: who knew what grudge might be worked out on the white face of a passer-by? The first major looting took place at the Brinks building, which had served as a billet for American officers from the earliest days of US involvement in Indochina. It proved a rich source of booty. To add to the confusion of the city, the electricity cut out at around seven in the evening. It was then that I had to make my second move of the day, from the Continental to the Caravelle Hotel across the square, where it had finally been decided that we should all stay together for however long it took for order to be restored. A mere matter of lugging a few cases across a small square—but I remember finding it an arduous and frightening task, as the Honda boys drove by shouting 'Yankee, go home!' I cursed the Embassy for its bungled withdrawal, and began for the first time to admire John Gunther Dean, the American Ambassador in Phnom Penh who had evacuated at such speed. But here: always the sound of the helicopters, stirring the panic, making things worse.

Indoors it was all right. Finishing my work in my new office that evening, I came across a note from my nice Vietnamese assistant. It informed me that the office was most likely to be looted by the soldiers, and that the assistant had therefore taken home the petty cash. This was the last time I saw the man. Well, easy come, easy go, I thought. I went to the fridge, and broached the Polish vodka. It turned out to be water.

The power cut turned out to be a godsend, since by the time light was restored the majority of the crowd had gone home and the police had regained control of the streets. As the lights went on in the Caravelle Hotel, they found our gallant press corps in the best of spirits. We didn't know how long we would be holed up in the hotel, or in what manner the city would fall. Most people I think were envisaging a rather slow and bloody take-over, but this did not spoil the brave mood of the evening. We had a distant view of the war. Towards the airport it appeared that an ammunition dump was exploding. Great flames rose up and slowly subsided. It went on for hours, like some hellish furnace from Hieronymus Bosch. If you went up on to the roof itself you could hear the war from every direction. But the city centre had calmed down.

I had one more story to send out. In the foyer of the hotel I found a policeman in mufti, and arranged to walk with him to the Reuters office. It was okay at first, but as we approached the dark area around the cathedral we both became more and more apprehensive. Turning left, we walked down the middle of the road, hand in hand, to keep up each other's spirits. We exhibited all the heroism of children in the dark. To any Vietcong agent, watching us from the top branches of the trees, I should say we must have looked too touching to kill.

E arly on the morning of 30 April, I went out of my hotel room to be greeted by a group of hysterical Koreans. 'The Americans have called off the evacuation!' said one. The group had been unable to get into the Embassy, had waited the whole night and had now given up. Of all the nationalities to fear being stranded in Saigon, the Koreans had most reason. I went up to breakfast in the top-floor restaurant, and saw that there were still a few Jolly Green Giants landing on the Embassy, but that the group on the Alliance Française building appeared to have been abandoned. They were still standing there on the roof, packed tight on a set of steps. Looking up at the sky, they seemed to be taking part in some kind of religious ritual, waiting for a sign. In the Brinks Building, the looting continued. A lone mattress fell silently from a top floor balcony.

There was one other group at breakfast—an eccentric Frenchman with some Vietnamese children. The Frenchman was explaining to the waiter that there had been some binoculars available the night before, and he wanted to use them again. The waiter explained that the binoculars belonged to one of the hotel guests.

'That doesn't matter,' said the Frenchman, 'bring them to me.'

The waiter explained that the binoculars were probably in the guest's room.

'Well go and get them then!' said the Frenchman. It seemed extraordinary that the Frenchman could be so adamant, and the waiter so patient, under the circumstances. I had orange juice and coffee, and noted that the croissants were not fresh.

Then I went to the American Embassy, where the looting had just begun. The typewriters were already on the streets outside, there was a stink of urine from where the crowd had spent the night, and several cars had been ripped apart. I did not bother to check what had happened to mine, but went straight into the Embassy with the looters.

The place was packed, and in chaos. Papers, files, brochures and reports were strewn around. I picked up one letter of application from a young Vietnamese student, who wished to become an Embassy interpreter. Some people gave me suspicious looks, as if I might be a member of the Embassy staff—I was, after all, the only one there with a white face—so I began to do a little looting myself, to show that I was entering into the spirit of the thing. Somebody had found a package of razor blades, and removed them all from their plastic wrappers. One man called me over to a wall-safe, and seemed to be asking if I knew the number of the combination. Another was hacking away at an air-conditioner, another dismantling a fridge.

On the first floor there was more room to move, and it was here I came across the Embassy library. I collected the following items: one copy of *Peace is not at Hand* by Sir Robert Thompson, one of the many available copies of *The Road from War* by Robert Shaplen, Barrington Moore's *Social Origins of Dictatorship and Democracy* (I had been meaning to read it for some time), a copy of a pacification report from 1972 and some Embassy notepaper. Two things I could not take (by now I was not just pretending to loot—I had become quite involved): a reproduction of an 1873 map of Hanoi, and a framed quotation from Lawrence of Arabia, which read, 'Better to let them do it imperfectly than to do it perfectly yourself, for it is their country, their way, and your time is short.' Nearby I found a smashed portrait of President Ford, and a Stars and Stripes, mangled in the dirt.

I found one room which had not yet been touched. There were white chairs around a white table, and on the table the ashtrays were full. I was just thinking how eerie it looked, how recently vacated, when the lights went out. At once, a set of emergency lights, photo-sensitively operated, turned themselves on above each doorway. The building was still partly working; even while it was being torn to pieces, it had a few reflexes left.

From this room, I turned into a small kitchen, where a group of old crones were helping themselves to jars of Pream powdered milk. When they looked up and saw me, they panicked, dropped the powdered milk and ran. I decided that it would be better to leave the building. It was filling up so much that it might soon become impossible to get out. I did not know that there were still some marines on the roof. As I forced my way out of the building, they threw tear-gas down on the crowd, and I found myself running hard, in floods of tears.

Although the last helicopter was just now leaving, people still thought there were other chances of getting out. One man came up to me and asked confidentially if I knew of the alternative evacuation site. He had several plausible reasons why he was entitled to leave. Another man, I remember, could only shout, 'I'm a professor, I'm a professor, I'm a professor,' as if the fact of his academic status would cause the Jolly Green Giants to swoop down out of the sky and whisk him away.

There was by now a good deal of activity on the streets. Military trucks went to and fro across town, bearing loads of rice, and family groups trudged along, bearing their possessions. As I finished writing my Embassy story, the sirens wailed three times, indicating that the city itself was under attack. I returned to the hotel roof to see what was happening. The group on the Alliance Française building was still there, still waiting for its sign. Across the river, but not far away, you could see the artillery firing, and the battle lines coming closer. Then two flares went up, one red, one white. Somebody said that the white flare was for surrender. In the restaurant, the waiters sat by the radio. I asked them what was happening. 'The war is finished,' said one.

I looked down into the square. Almost at once, a waiter emerged from the Continental and began to hoist a French tricolour on the flagpole. There were groups of soldiers, apparently front-line troops, sitting down. From the battlefield across the river, the white flares began to go up in great numbers. Big Minh's broadcast had been heard—offering unconditional surrender—and in a matter of minutes the war would be well and truly over.

Under such circumstances, what does one do? For the poor of Saigon, the first reaction was to loot as much as possible. For most of the soldiers, it was to give in as quickly as possible, and make oneself scarce. For the victorious troops, for the students and Vietcong sympathizers within the city, it was a question of taking control as quickly as possible. For the reporter, there was a choice: go out and see what was happening, or write about it. It was a cruel choice, but it was clear that the lines would soon either be jammed or go down altogether. For a stringer, the burden of the choice is even greater, since it is during such moments

that he earns the fat off which he has to live during the lean years. The first two laws of stringing are: the more you file the more you earn; and, the more you file the less you learn. I mention this because, throughout the remainder of the day and in the days that followed, all my reactions were underscored by a worry about getting the thing written up, and not just written up but sent out. Whereas all my instincts were not to write at all. In the end the instincts won, hands down.

I took a lift with Brian Barron of the BBC along with his small crew, who had remained after their American counterparts had already left. We went out towards the Newport Bridge, in a small car driven by a Vietnamese. The Union Jack was flying from the aerial, and the BBC sign was clearly displayed. As we drove along past the lines of anxious faces, it became clear to me that I had come with the wrong crew. The soldiers whom we tried to film thought that the BBC had been on the side of the Vietcong. It had been denounced by Thieu, and now, in the moment of defeat, was no time to be flying the Union Jack. There was a large amount of military activity on the roads: truckloads of soldiers returning from the front. There was one bulldozer racing back from the bridge, with a whole platoon sitting in the scoop. The tanks were waiting by the tank-traps, many of them with their crew still in position. As we stopped to film them, I noticed one soldier fingering a grenade, weighing it thoughtfully in his hand. In the doors of houses, families waited nervously. By Newport Bridge itself, the looting of the American stores was still going on, a desperate last-minute effort which would hold up, in parts of the city, the advance of the victorious troops. The first thing the North Vietnamese and Vietcong saw as they came into Saigon was crowds of looters dragging sacks of rice and cartons of luxury goods. It must have justified their view of the degeneracy of the city.

But they had not yet arrived. Walking up to the top of the bridge, we wondered whether to go on to meet them, or retrace our steps. Then we were called back to the car by the Governor of Gia Dinh.

He looked exceedingly angry and unpleasant—he and one of his officers laden down with pistols and grenades, ready perhaps to make their last stand against the encroaching communists. They were fat men, with twisted faces, gripped no doubt by the bitterness of betrayal.

Where had we been?

To the top of the bridge.

No, they said, we had come from the Vietcong.

We replied that we had been to the bridge because we wanted to film.

'I don't want to hear any more,' said the Governor, 'how much did they pay you? How much did the Vietcong pay you?'

'Look,' said Brian Barron, 'I'm not Vietcong. I'm afraid of the Vietcong. When the Vietcong start shooting, I lie down.'

'Why do you lie to me?' said the Governor of Gia Dinh.

I thought, 'This is it. He's going to kill us.' And apart from the fear of death itself, there seemed to be something particularly bitter and unfair in being killed as a traitor after the defeat. But instead of killing us, the Governor told me to remove the Union Jack from the car, and ordered one of the film crew to take the BBC label off his camera. The Union Jack was stuck to the aerial with Elastoplast and I remember wondering whether my trembling hands would ever get the thing off. The Governor then ordered us to push our car between two tank traps, where it was later found, completely squashed by a tank.

I wanted to get back to the city centre as quickly as possible— we were now going to have to walk—and I couldn't understand why Barron was taking such a long time. He seemed to be looking for something in the car, and later he told me what it was. A few days before, he had been reading Ho Chi Minh's works, and had shoved them under the back seat, out of sight. Now he was afraid that they would suddenly find the book, and shoot us on the spot. He therefore decided to get the thing out and shove it under his shirt. He went back to the car, put his hand under the seat, and discovered that the book was gone.

By now there was chaos on the streets. The trucks which had passed us in one direction as we were coming out of Saigon appeared to have returned. Clearly nobody knew where to go. There was gunfire at the crossroads just ahead, and I think that we all felt, having lost our car, in great danger. We were saved by a taximan who dumped a load of customers and offered to take us back for four thousand *piastres*. I would have paid whatever I had. We got into the car, put our heads down, and sped back to the city centre.

In the Reuters office I was writing an account of what I had just seen when Barron came in again.

'I don't know what's happening,' he said, 'I've just seen a tank with the flag of the National Liberation Front.' I went to the door and looked out to the left, in the direction of Thieu's palace, and saw the tank. Without thinking, I ran after it and flagged it down just as it turned towards the palace gates. The tank slowed down and a North Vietnamese soldier in green jumped off the back and went at me with his gun, as if to hit me. In my confusion, I couldn't remember the NLF salute, or how to explain to the soldier that I wanted a ride. I tried everything—a salute, another salute, a clenched fist, a hitch-hiker's thumb. Finally (after, that is, a few extremely nervous seconds) I held out my hand to shake his. He took my hand abruptly and indicated the back of the tank. I remember worrying, as I climbed on, that I might touch something very hot. Then, as the soldiers told me to keep my head down, I idiotically produced my passport, which they dismissed scornfully. The tank speeded up, and rammed the left side of the palace gate. Wrought iron flew into the air, but the whole structure refused to give. I nearly fell off. The tank backed again, and I observed a man with a nervous smile opening the centre portion of the gate. We drove into the grounds of the palace, and fired a salute.

I had taken a ride on the first tank to reach the palace, but it was not until several weeks later that I realized this was the case: looking up from my crouching position at the back, I saw another vehicle in the grounds (which turned out to be a South Vietnamese tank). Damn, I thought, I was on the second; still, never mind. I wondered whether I was under arrest. I tried to talk to the soldiers, but I did not notice that some of them were captured troops of the South Vietnamese Army who had been co-opted in order to show the way. On the top of the tank was an open carton of Winston cigarettes, which struck me as odd. No doubt it had been thrown up from the looting crowd. I also remember noticing that another tank was passing behind us on the lawn. Its tracks crushed the verge of a flower bed, and I remember thinking: that was unnecessary. Also, I noticed an extraordinary number of dragonflies in the air.

I was very, very excited. The weight of the moment, the privilege of being a witness, impressed itself at once. Over and above my self-consciousness, and the trivial details which were made all the more interesting by the extraordinary nature of the event, there was the historical grandeur of the scene. Events in history are not supposed to look historical: no eye perceived a battlefield at a glance, no dying leader composed his followers around him in the neo-classical manner; many war photographs, even some of the great ones, are said to have been rearranged. The victors write, rewrite, or retouch their history. Indeed in one western account of these events, I noticed that the tank I have just described was meant to have knocked the palace gate to the ground 'like a wooden twig'. The man who opened the gate, a civilian guard, has in this account been subbed out. The guards themselves have fled. Nothing is allowed to interfere with the symmetry of the scene, or interrupt the conquest with wild, flailing arms.

And yet the North Vietnamese do not merely touch-up history. They also enact it in the heroic manner. This was the first time I had seen their genius for imposing their style upon events, for acting in the manner of their propaganda. The spectacle was tremendous and, as one of their officers realized, not to be missed. He ran up to a British cameraman filming the arrival of the tanks, and begged him: 'You take film for us? You take film for us?' The tanks rolled on to the lawn, and formed automatically into a semicircle in front of the palace, firing a salute into the air as they did so. Soon the air became full of the sound of saluting guns. Beside the gate, sitting in a row on the lawn, was a group of soldiers, former members of the palace guard. They waved their hands above their heads in terror. An NLF soldier took his flag and, waving it above his head, ran into the palace. A few moments later, he emerged on the terrace, waving the flag round and round. Later still, there he was on the roof. The red and yellow stripes of the Saigon regime were lowered at last.

I thought, I shall know if I'm under arrest when I jump off the tank. There came suddenly to mind a story of a plane which went through an electric storm: when it touched down, all the passengers were electrocuted on contact with the earth. I jumped off, and noticed that I was still alive and free. The palace grounds filled up with soldiers, and trucks were arriving all the time. The broad avenue towards the cathedral became the centre for the arriving troops. Their vehicles and helmets were covered in leaves, their uniforms were green. A great wave of greenery swept over the city. It blended into the grass and the trees of the avenue. Only the red armbands and the red tags on the guns stood out. Everything had changed in a trice.

For the Westerners present, it was an occasion for overt celebration. I saw Jean-Claude running through the palace gates, his hands over his head, his cameras swinging hectically around his body. Old colleagues greeted each other with delight. We felt bound to congratulate each other, as if we had a right to partake of the victory. For the National Liberation Front troops, on the other hand, such satisfaction as they felt was completely suppressed. They sat down and lit up North Vietnamese cigarettes, like men who had simply done a good day's work—they were justified and did not need praise. Sometimes they shook hands with the foreigners, occasionally they smiled, or waved from the trucks, but never once did I see them lose their self-control.

I walked past the cathedral, and came upon a North Vietnamese soldier in a condition of extreme embarrassment. He was facing a wall, secretly looking at something. I thought he was embarrassed by having to relieve himself in front of a group of interested onlookers, but in fact he was consulting his compass, unsure of where he was supposed to be. The group realized his difficulty, and gave him directions. At this moment the fire brigade drove past, lights blazing, horn blaring, waving their hats in the air, in expressions of wild delight. Further down, along Tu Do street, I met a friend and we walked together to the Ministry of Defence, which was in the process of surrendering. At these ceremonies, a salute was always fired over the building, and so the city must have been full of falling lead, and yet I never heard of anyone being injured from such fall-out. This was one of the many curious features of the day.

The most dramatic change that had taken place was the complete disappearance of the Saigon army. All round the streets one would come across piles of clothes, boots and weapons. Some of the piles were so complete it looked as if their former occupant had simply melted into his boots. And then, in the doorways, one

would see young men in shorts, hanging around with an air of studied indifference, as if to say, 'Don't look at me, I always dress like this—it's the heat, you know.' Where groups of soldiers had been caught and told to surrender, they were made to take off their clothes and sit down. I came across one such group by the town hall.

Slowly the streets were beginning to fill up again. Occasionally the requisitioned jeeps of the former regime came past, full of cheering youths in gear that was intended to look like Vietcong attire. These new revolutionary enthusiasts were immediately distinguished in appearance and behaviour from the real thing. Some of them were disarmed on the spot. Others were to carry on for several days or weeks before being identified, but for the moment they had a great fling, cheering, shouting and riding around. Most people were still indoors, wondering what would happen to them. The first to appear on the streets and talk to the soldiers were the old men, women and young children. They brought out tea to the tired troops, and sat with them, firing questions about what would happen next. The reassurance they received spread visibly throughout the suspicious city, and in a short while the areas where the troops were concentrated (around the palace and the port) took on the air of a massive teach-in.

The sorts of questions being asked were: Would there be revenge? Would those who had left North Vietnam at the time of the division be forced to return? Would the women be forced to cut their hair? Would those with painted nails have them pulled out, *without anaesthetic*? Would the women be forcibly married off to the crippled soldiers of the North? To all such questions, the answer was a gentle no. Another question was, what did the North Vietnamese eat? The fact that such a question could be put shows the ignorance of young Saigon about Hanoi, since the answer of course was rice.

I was getting very hungry and thirsty after the exertions of the day, so I wandered down to my old hotel by the market. The manager was pleased, and rather surprised, to see me. She had obviously assumed that, whatever I said, I would in fact leave with the Americans. I told her what was happening outside. 'We are very pleased to welcome the liberation forces,' she said, through clenched teeth. The night-club dancer, whom I had failed to assist to

leave, was also there. She gave me some very sick looks. She had dressed simply, in black pyjamas, and done up her hair in a bun, in what she imagined would be a manner suitable for receiving the forces of liberation. The landlady and the old doorman produced from the siege rations a meal of bread, olives, walnuts, cheese and beer. It was the first and last time that the landlady ever let me have anything for free.

A phrase ran through my mind, from the time of the arrival of the tanks, and on through the day as I wandered round the streets, meeting people I knew, watching the chatting groups, and seeing how the whole place settled down. The phrase was: 'a permanent and marvellous disgrace'. It seemed to me evident, and bitterly ironical, that all the talk of what the North Vietnamese would do when—*if*—they took Saigon, all of it had been wrong. During the whole of the day I saw only three or four corpses. The North Vietnamese Army were clearly the most disciplined troops in the world. They had done nothing out of order, and it could not be that they were just waiting till the foreigners were out of the way before setting about the rape and pillage which many had prophesied. You could not fake the sort of discipline they had shown, nor could the events of the day be depicted (even by the most bigoted critic) as anything other than a triumph—a triumph that exceeded the expectations of their warmest, most bigoted, admirers. Consequently when the story was told (by now the lines were down), it would disgrace those who had predicted otherwise. It would be a permanent and marvellous disgrace; the CIA and Pentagon boffins, a generation of hawks, would be made to stand forever in the corner, wearing the dunce's cap. I did not think that Saigon had been liberated in the way that would shortly be made out. I did not think that there had been an uprising—I had seen no real evidence for such a thing. But the victorious army had justified itself by its behaviour alone. That I will never forget.

Peace had come, more or less. In the afternoon one desperate group of South Vietnamese soldiers had made a last attempt at a fire-fight right in the centre of town, and sometimes in the distance one would hear explosions, for which I never found the reason. Along the outskirts of the town the looting continued wherever any wealthy establishment had been abandoned, or wherever the troops

had not yet arrived to take control. I went to the Buddhist University, where the students were already organizing the collection of the enormous number of arms that had been abandoned on the streets. Nguyen Huu Thai, the student leader, greeted us and gave us a form of identification which would serve for the next few days. Were we not impressed? he asked. Was it not like the Paris Commune of 1871?

As we drove back, we passed the Taiwanese and Malaysian Embassies, which were being very thoroughly looted. People were stealing everything, including the chandeliers. The young students who had taken it upon themselves to stop the looting tried to do so by firing into the air. When this did not work, one of them adopted a most terrifyingly effective technique. Holding a rifle in his left hand and a pistol in his right, he pointed the pistol at a looter and fired his rifle into the air.

Back at the Caravelle Hotel, I watched the landscape settle down in peace. The flares still went up, on and on into the night. The intense excitement of the past days subsided into an irritable exhaustion. I had a bitter argument with one of my greatest friends, and went to bed in the worst of spirits. As my head sank into the pillow I burst into tears.

After the Fall

May Day 1975 was probably an occasion for world-wide celebration of the liberation of Saigon. I don't know. In Saigon itself, indeed throughout Vietnam, May Day was not celebrated. It had been cancelled by Hanoi, as part of the war effort, and now, the day after the war was over, it was too late to organize. May Day would have to wait.

I went out at dawn on May Day morning. The flares were still going up, and the flags of the National Liberation Front had already appeared on public buildings. NFL washing hung from windows. The soldiers were breakfasting by the parked tanks. They had dug foxholes in the public squares, and slept in Saigon as if in the jungle. The trouserless soldiers of the defeated army wandered around with nothing to do. There were beggars in the doorways, and an old woman asleep and a young girl beside her looking through a work of lurid pornography. There was litter everywhere, military and domestic, and piles of incriminating documents and letters and, in one case, a large stack of seventy-eight gramophone records.

There was a pair of nuns on a motorbike, sporting the NLF flag. Sightseers. Saigon was coming out to see the NLF, and the NLF was being conducted around the city in trucks, gazing up at the buildings. It had been told of the poverty of Saigon. It had never seen such wealth. As yet the spivs, beggars and prostitutes had not come out. But I saw one cripple from the Saigon Army dressed in what he clearly conceived to be the outfit of a guerrilla.

As yet, very few of the guerrillas, the true Vietcong of the South, had appeared. They strolled in in twos and threes, with strangely shaped bombs tied to their belts, and antique weapons. They sometimes had no holsters for their guns, but carried them in their hands or in trouser pockets. Some were barefooted. They wore the same range of cheap man-made fibres in blues and browns. They wore either pith helmets or floppy hats. When I asked them about the difference between these two forms of headgear, they replied that the pith helmets were hard, whereas the floppy hats were—floppy.

I put out my hand to shake that of a Vietcong. He thought I was trying to take the revolver from his hand. Prudently he put the gun behind his back.

Most of the regular troops seemed to come from the north. They arrived in trucks, and all but the officers abandoned their arms. Then they wandered hand in hand through the streets. We rushed down to the port to marvel at the navy in their nineteenth-century suits. At Tan Son Nhuot, the air-force arrived, wearing wings and speaking Russian. Near the still smouldering remains of the DAO compound, these elusive aristocrats of the air could be found drinking Chablis and American beer.

The Saigon bourgeoisie, to meet the occasion, dressed themselves up to the nines and drove round and round the city for days on end, until they were stopped by the price of petrol. Many cars had been destroyed, and lay at the side of the roads. The bourgeoisie then came round and round on Hondas. They were at last admitted to the bar of the Continental Shelf, where they came to be seen. The café crowds came back to their old haunts, and cowboys resumed work, stealing watches and handbags: they thought it good sport to snatch cameras from the necks of NLF soldiers. People were said to have been shot for stealing, but the reports did not deter the criminals.

After a time the beggars returned to their usual patches, and an unusually large number of prostitutes started hanging around the hotels. As Saigon got used to the new soldiers, and realized that their orders were not to intervene, the hope grew that the city might draw these saints into its aged corruption.

It was easy to pick out the stalls of looted goods. Drink was cheap, and since many Embassy wine cellars had been ransacked the quality was high. It was in liberated Saigon that I learned what happens to aged champagne, how it loses its sparkle and turns to a nutty dessert wine. The French residents of Saigon— there were many—descended on the street-markets early and got the best wine home and out of the sun. The journalists—of whom there were not a few—picked off the bottles of genuine spirits: it had been foolish to try to buy whisky in Saigon before; now the real thing was as cheap as the imitation. Over the next three months, the depletion of stocks told you a lot about drinking habits: it was clear, for instance, that since the Americans had left, no one in Saigon could stand tequila, or knew what to do with it. I tried it, and tried to imagine what it would be like with a salted rim. Ten years later the thought still disgusts me.

The chief customers in the market were the NLF. The soldiers had been paid on arrival in Saigon, and with the North Vietnamese *dong* standing at four to five hundred *piastres* (the panic rate) they were richer than they had ever been in their lives. They bought several watches and might wear them all. They bought cigarette lighters with tiny clocks concealed inside them. And the more they acquired, the less they resembled the nineteenth-century army of the early days of liberation. Once they had bought the dark glasses, they had taken on something of the Saigon look.

There were no wounded soldiers. They were not allowed to visit Saigon. The soldiers we met were appalled by what they saw: the beggars, the painted faces of the women, the dishonesty. They spoke of a future in which they would turn Saigon into a beautiful city. They compared it unfavourably with Hanoi.

The soldiers had a mission to perform, but they did not have a missionary's reforming zeal. They knew it was best to take their time, and they had time on their hands. Saigon society slowly returned to abnormal, out of gas and freewheeling downhill. Everyone knew the situation could not last. Nobody knew what would come next.

In those initial days it was possible to travel outside the city, since no formal orders had been given. Indeed it was possible to do most things you fancied. But once the regulations were published restricting us to Saigon, life became very dull indeed. The novelty of the street scenes had worn off, and most journalists left at the first opportunity. I, however, had been asked by the *Washington Post* to maintain its presence in Vietnam until a replacement could be brought in. I allowed the journalists' plane to leave without me, then cabled Washington stating my terms, which were based on the fact that I was the only stringer left working for an American paper. The *Post*, on receipt of my terms, sacked me. I had thought I had an exclusive story. What I learned was: never get yourself into an exclusive *position*. If the *New York Times* had had a man in Saigon, the *Post* would have taken my terms. Because there were no rivals, and precious few Americans, I had what amounted to an exclusive non-story. By now, I was sick of the East, sick of travel, sick of the journalistic life. But I was stuck. I crawled back to the *Post*.

When there was nothing to write about, I described myself, but as this was against house style in an American paper, I had to be thinly disguised: '"It's like a spa at the end of the season," remarked a dejected Englishman, sitting on the empty terrace of the Continental Palace—this abandoned, echoing, colonial hotel. The rains have begun, leaving the air cooler and clearer. Most of the foreigners are preparing to leave.' And I went on to record how the old Assembly building had been turned back into an Opera House, where a brute of a conductor leaped around in tails, and where the mixed evening always included the same programme: a movement of Beethoven's Fifth, some Strauss, and a rendition in Russian of *La*

Donna è Mobile, sung by a Vietnamese tenor with an idea of how to smile like an Italian. The NLF soldiers would listen relaxedly, sticking their bare feet over the gallery. It appears to be an idea common among conquerors that what a fallen city needs is a good injection of culture. After the capture of Berlin, every sector was immediately featuring Russian dancing and lectures by T. S. Eliot. Hanoi sent down pretty well everything it could transport, including massed choirs and an archaeological exhibition of a strongly nationalistic bent.

In early June I went to a reception at the Presidential Palace, to mark the sixth anniversary of the founding of the Provisional Revolutionary Government. Nowadays, I believe, you will find that Vietnam has written the PRG out of history. The process was just beginning then. A particularly frank and cynical guerrilla told me that the talk about the PRG was nonsense. Hanoi called all the shots and it was stupid to believe otherwise. And yet I believe that the members of the southern movement did generally believe in the authority of their own existence. The excitement was, on this occasion, to spot the PRG leaders, such as Huynh Tan Phat, with his face wreathed in smiles, dressed in the kind of khaki suit favoured by foreign correspondents in the tropics, but with the addition of a matching khaki tie.

The person we all wanted to meet was General Tran Van Tra, Saigon's military chief. He was in a terrific mood, and laughed and laughed when we reminded him of some of his previous activities. We would ask: the Americans say you masterminded the Tet Offensive from headquarters in Thu Duc; is this true? And he would reply that he couldn't remember. I'd been reading Lucien Bodard's extraordinary *The Quicksand War*, in which Tran features as having organized a patriotic liquidation campaign against the French. Was that true? He said he wouldn't elaborate. All he would say was that he had been in the environs of Saigon since before 1945.

There was a sense that the life work of such men was coming to fruition, that the plan of years could now be implemented. And the implementation could proceed at its own proper pace. The centre of Saigon was losing its significance. The shops of Tu Do, dealers in luxury goods, were now also soup-stands. But Tu Do itself was deserted. It reminded me of an old French photograph, with a couple of blurred figures in the middle distance, and a cyclo-driver snoozing in the shade.

In the suburbs, by contrast, the mobilization of the youth groups had got under way. They sat around awkwardly singing revolutionary songs, clapping in unison and not wearing jeans. They had turned the task of sweeping the streets into a ceremony. They were tearing down the old police posts, but not all the barbed wire, not all the barbed wire by any means.

The major effort was to get people back from urban squats to their homes in the country. A truck would come through the streets bound for Quang Nam, its destination written in large chalk letters along the side, together with the words 'We drive by night'. That was an astonishing novelty. For over twenty years the golden rule in Indochina was not to be on the roads at night.

Something had to be done about crime. Saigon had lived on crime, all kinds, from the petty to the most highly organized. With the fall of Saigon, prisons were opened, all prisoners released, and judiciary suspended. I spoke to one judge, an opponent of Thieu and yet part of his criminal court. He said that after the liberation he and about a hundred other former judges had presented themselves and asked for pardon. The pardon had been given, after they had informed on their fellow judges. Since that time they had gone to their place of work every day, and waited for the arrival of the new Minister of Justice. Finally he came and looked round the tribunal, delivering himself of one sentence: 'Comrades, continue your work.' So a hundred judges sat around and waited. In the provinces it was said that they received unwelcome visits from men they had sentenced.

Justice took to the open streets, and in one week the official newspaper (the old papers had been closed down) gave two front-page stories showing robbers executed by the liberation forces. Both accounts emphasized the popular support for the executions. In the first case, a Honda-cowboy was killed trying to escape. Support was *ex post facto*. In the second, the photograph showed a former 'puppet soldier' tied to crossed planks in the manner of Spartacus. Public support preceded the action. The man had been caught attempting to steal a watch at gunpoint, had resisted arrest, and, not having repented when finally caught, had committed further 'savage' actions. So: 'In order to protect the tranquil life of the Saigon population and in accordance with the aspirations of the people, the revolutionary law shot the thief Vo Van Ngoc.'

In another case, three thousand people assembled in order to judge three thieves. They climbed up on buildings to witness the popular tribunal, which sentenced one of the culprits to death. He was shot 'before the joy of the people', whom the newspaper showed in a rather blurred photograph waiting for the event.

That a thief had not repented was a serious point to be held against him. In the judicial and moral climate of the day, repentance was of prime importance, and obstinacy was a political category. Re-education, *Hoc Tap*, was under way, and everyone was talking about it. It appeared that the private soldier or NCO could go along for the three-day political education session: if he performed well he would be praised, whereas if he was uncooperative he would be told to emulate those singled out for praise. It sounded an absurdly lenient programme—perhaps merely a way of filling in the time and keeping idle officers off the street. But later on, the same people who had spoken with modest pride of their good performances in *Hoc Tap* came back to say that *Hoc Tap* was not yet over. It was becoming inexorable; it was impossible to extricate oneself from the guilt of being associated with the Thieu army. In South Vietnam, men of military age had had no choice but to join the army: they were conscripts. And yet they seemed to be asked to share the guilt of Thieu.

It was, in fact, over the question of re-education that the new regime showed its true character, and it brought to an end the long period in which the Saigonese were prepared perhaps to give their conquerors the benefit of the doubt. One morning my Vietnamese assistant burst into my room. 'It's sensational, all the officers have to leave home for a month's course. They're going to be re-educated.'

I got back into bed, crossly, and asked why that was so sensational.

'Don't you think it's harsh? They're to be separated from their families for thirty days.'

I replied that in the case of the generals I thought the whole thing pretty lenient.

The details of the announcement were extraordinary. You were told exactly how much money you would need for the course, for the purchase of food, and you were advised to bring three kilos of rice as emergency rations. In addition, you needed a change of clothes, blanket, towel, mosquito net, mat, raincoat, pullover, toothpaste, toothbrush, bowl, cigarettes (if a smoker), paper, pen, health card and medicines. It seemed to indicate a trip to the Central Highlands, and looking at the list I was foolish enough to express the wish that I was going too.

That there was a ten-day course for junior officers seemed to indicate that the duration of the course was seriously meant. The officers put on their raincoats and went off to their departure points, joking that if they tell you to shower and don't provide the soap you are not to go in. They left, and as long as I was there they didn't come back.

The officers had been duped, and you might almost say that the deception was justifiable: there were decades of corruption in an army that was going to be extremely difficult to incorporate into the new society. But the ruse was exacerbated by the way it was reported. In the days of Thieu there had been a press of sorts, and spokesmen of the Provisional Revolutionary Government used to be eloquent in its defence. Then, with the end of the war, they came in and closed the papers down, replacing them with *Giai Phong*.

The new official press hated mentioning disasters of any kind. A friend of mine sent a report abroad concerning a road accident. This was censored, and the rumours began. There was a rumour that two truckloads of former officers had been ambushed, or had hit a minefield, somewhere near Tay Ninh. The rumour grew until I was assured by one woman that two thousand former officers had been killed. The women of Saigon went into shell shock. There were gatherings, real demonstrations in the streets, and slanging matches between the innocent soldiers of the north and the very down-to-earth wives of Saigon. The women wanted to know from General Tran Van Tra what had happened. The soldiers seemed completely unnerved. Worse, there were more officers waiting to leave on similar 'courses', and so there was always a group of tearful women waiting behind the Post Office to learn when their husbands were due to go. I was told that four officers had returned from re-education in coffins.

It was becoming impossible for me to work as a journalist. Up to now my stories had all had the theme of life returning to normal, but when the censorship began it was very difficult to describe normality truthfully. I wrote a story about how a fishnet factory had been ordered to stay open with full employment, even though there was no nylon thread for the nets (the implication being that the employer would soon become impoverished). No one questioned the truth of the story, it was that they wanted me to say simply: the factory has been ordered to stay open *despite all the difficulties*. If they could not admit that there was no thread, how could they allow us to say that no one seemed to have returned from the re-education camps? And if one could not write such a story, how could one justify giving a general impression of normality in other stories? In one I mentioned that a man had committed suicide in the ruins of an old military monument. But the outside world was not allowed to know that there had been a suicide in Saigon.

I began to wonder if there was a code word to explain to my employers on the *Washington Post* that my copy was being censored. The thought, judging from the subjects they asked me to write about, hadn't occurred to them. I had retained from the *Post*'s bureau (before I handed it over to the authorities) a copy of a handbook for the paper's correspondents. I looked up censorship. There was no entry. I looked up Moscow, where the most I learned was that a correspondent should beware of making unflattering personal references to Lenin and to the way Jews were treated in Russia. I decided to solve the censorship problem by stopping writing and applying to leave. It was not a solution, but I could no longer bear Vietnam.

I had a spacious but gloomy old flat in Tu Do street. If I looked out of my window any time during the day, there would be a bum swinging in the window opposite, which belonged to a body-building club. If I looked down at the street to the corner slightly

left, my eye would immediately be caught by a tiny cyclo-driver in a panama hat, who had decided that I was the only generous customer left in the city, and that he might as well specialize. I was under a kind of commercial house arrest, genial enough, but unrelenting. If I told the cyclo-driver I was walking today, I would still have to go past my spastic beggar, the one who was all smiles and whom I was supposed never to let down. But he was generous enough in a way. One day I carefully crossed the street to avoid him on my usual walk. I was studiously pretending not to be anywhere near him when I happened to see he was doubled up in laughter. He knew exactly what pressure he was putting on me every day, and he seemed to think it well within my rights occasionally to refuse.

Early in the morning at, say, 5.30, you would hear the bells ringing in the military billets. Then there was a noise—a great tearing sound—which I thought must belong to some extraordinary contraption for removing the surface from the road. I rose and threw open the mosquito blinds: it was a company of soldiers sprinting along the street in their Ho Chi Minh sandals. The soldiers were relaxed and cheerful at this time of day. They shouted a few slogans, exercised, listened to what sounded like a little pep-talk for about ten minutes and then went off to breakfast.

These soldiers—the *bo doi*, as we all now called them—were members of the best army in the world, disciplined in war and extraordinarily well-behaved in peace. But they had no gift for drill—even their gymnastics were uncoordinated—Saigon rooked them something rotten. The stall-holders persuaded the *bo doi*, when they suspected the dud watches they had been sold, that the only foolproof test was to put a watch in your mouth, block your ears and close your eyes. If you could hear it ticking, it was kosher.

The *bo doi* hated keeping order. They did at one stage execute thieves in the street, but that was at the height of the crime wave in May. Later I saw a robber trying to escape from a pursuing crowd. The *bo doi* were appealed to, but were reluctant to interfere: because the *bo doi* had a great deal of sympathy for the poor of Saigon, and all the people they had put out of work by winning. They believed their own propaganda. They *were* heroes. A story was told in the early days after the fall that a *bo doi* had been driving

104

a truck carelessly and had killed a child. His commanding officer said to him: you have been a good soldier and have sacrificed much for the revolution—the time has come to make the final sacrifice. Whereupon the *bo doi* shot himself. The fact that the Saigonese told these rumours says something for the reputation of the *bo doi*. Even so, they were sometimes stabbed in the back streets, and once or twice one would hear gunfire at night.

If I had been able to talk to the *bo doi*, Saigon would have been the most interesting place in the world. But I mean really talk. They were forbidden to chat to *us*. Once one told me: 'I always liked going into battle because the atmosphere was so good. Everybody knew they were going to die. They had no food, and nothing to drink for days. If a man had something to eat, he would share it with you, and if you had nothing to give in return, you would show him the letter you had just got from your wife. Everybody loved each other, because they all knew they were going to die.' But then he became embarrassed at confessing all this to a foreigner.

Part of our admiration for the *bo doi* derived from what, in contrast, we were now learning of the Khmer Rouge after the fall of Phnom Penh. Large numbers of refugees had been making their way from the evacuated Cambodian capital across the border into Vietnam and, in some cases, to Saigon itself. The stories they told made it clear that the Khmer Rouge had not just instigated a bloodbath, they had no plan for the governing of the country they had won. If you could persuade a Vietnamese officer to talk about the Khmer Rouge, the best he would say, with a shudder, would be that they do not respect the laws of Ho Chi Minh. But it was obvious now that the regime was one of unparalleled savagery, and the Vietnamese were shocked by what they knew of it.

What was happening in Cambodia meant far more to me personally than the events I was witnessing in Vietnam, and I spent some time cultivating contacts with those who had escaped the Khmer Rouge regime. In particular, there were nine officers who had been associates of Son Ngoc Thanh, the former Cambodian prime minister and leader of the Khmer Krom (the ethnic Cambodians from South Vietnam). They had now requested asylum in Vietnam, as they were terrified of repatriation. But

nobody knew precisely what the relationship between the authorities in Saigon and the Khmer Rouge would be.

The officers were living with their families in a Cambodian pagoda not far from the city centre. They were free to go around town. One day, one of them came to see me in the hotel. He asked if he could borrow my spare bed. I asked him why. He explained that over the last few days a particular car had been arriving at the pagoda and taking people away. The pretext was that the officers and the head of the monastery, the Venerable Kim Sang, were to meet with Son Ngoc Thanh himself. Four people went and did not return. Nobody knew if they had been arrested by the Provisional Revolutionary Government, or if Khmer Rouge undercover agents were involved.

I told the officer that he could stay the night, but he would not be able to continue in the hotel for a long time, or he would draw suspicion on both of us. We sat up and talked until late into the night. As it happened I had Sihanouk's memoirs with me, which included a long attack on the CIA and Son Ngoc Thanh for undermining his regime. The officer agreed with much of Sihanouk's account, and admitted to me that he had been involved with the CIA. I asked him a number of times where Son Ngoc Thanh was now. It took a long time before he would say. Finally, he admitted that Son Ngoc Thanh was in Saigon. I said that it seemed very strange, if the man had been an associate of the CIA, that he should have stayed on in Saigon. The officer replied that Ho Chi Minh and Son Ngoc Thanh, both being nationalist leaders, had a respect for each other, and that there was a stipulation in Ho's will that Son Ngoc Thanh must not be harmed in any way. He had nothing to fear from the PRG.

Once his story was out, the officer began to talk about his fears that the Khmer Rouge would catch him. He recounted his escape from Cambodia. He talked about the screams he had heard from the undergrowth, when they had taken away suspected officers. He talked about the beatings. He was still pleading for help and he believed that I had influence. I remember his soft voice from the next bed asking if I could imagine what it was like to be put in a cage and left all day in the sun, 'like a wild animal, like a wild animal.'

That night, every time I fell asleep, there was a loud knocking at the door. I would wake fully, then wait, my heart beating, to see whether the knocking was real. I would doze off again. Then the knocking would resume. The next day the officer left to find a new hiding place.

I was out of my depth entirely, and confided my problem to a colleague who was not only very curious to know who had spent the night in my room and why, but also seemed very well-connected. A few days later he came rushing into my room and said that if I could find my lieutenant-colonel, the one who was supposed to have done stuff for the CIA, he couldn't guarantee anything but he just might be able to help him. But it had to be straight away. I said it was impossible. I couldn't find him. He was in hiding.

Later on, the desperate officer came to see me in my flat. His wife, who was still at the pagoda, had been threatened by the same mysterious men in the car; if her husband did not come with them, they said, she would be beaten up. It was I think on this visit that the officer found something I had not told him I possessed—a copy of the last will and testament of Ho Chi Minh. I had not told him about it because I knew that in the published version at least there was no reference to Son Ngoc Thanh. He flicked through the little pamphlet desperately, and had to agree that unless there was a secret codicil, his hero and mentor was entitled to no special protection from the Vietnamese. And that meant perhaps that his position was even worse than he had thought.

I still do not know what to make of this story. I do not know why Son Ngoc Thanh stayed on in Saigon, or who was causing the disappearance of the Cambodian officers. But the reason I tell the story is this: those who actually set out to see the fall of a city (as opposed to those to whom this calamity merely happens), or those who choose to go to a front line, are obviously asking themselves to what extent they are cowards. But the tests they set themselves— there is a dead body, can you bear to look at it?—are nothing in comparison with the tests that are sprung on them. It is not the obvious tests that matter (do you go to pieces in a mortar attack?) but the unexpected ones (here is a man on the run, seeking your help—can you face him honestly?).

At that time in Saigon there was a craze for a cheap North Vietnamese soup called *bun bo*. All the shops in Tu Do seemed to be serving it in the hope of attracting military customers. Some friends called on me and suggested we should go for lunch in one of these establishments. As we were crossing the road, I bumped into the Cambodian officer, with his pockmarked face and his pleading smile. Something very important has happened, he said, I must talk to you. I told him I was going with some friends for a bowl of *bun bo*. He was welcome to join us. No, he said, this was very urgent; and he added meaningfully that this might be the last time we met. He had hinted at suicide before, and on this occasion my heart hardened. I told him I was going with my friends for a bowl of *bun bo*. The incident was over in the time that it took to cross the road, and I never saw the officer again. But I can remember where I left him standing in the street.

It takes courage to see clearly, and since courage is at issue I know that I am obliged to address myself to the questions raised at the outset of the journey. I went as a supporter of the Vietcong, wanting to see them win. I saw them win. What feeling did that leave me with, and where does it leave me now? I know that by the end of my stay in Saigon I had grown to loathe the *apparatchiks*, who were arriving every day with their cardboard suitcases from Hanoi. I know that I loathed their institutional lies and their mockery of political justice.

But as the banners went up in honour of Lenin, Marx and Stalin, I know too that I had known this was coming. Had we not supported the NLF 'without illusions'? Must I not accept that the disappearances, the gagging of the press, the political distortion of reality was all part of a classical Stalinism which nevertheless 'had its progressive features'? Why, we supported unconditionally 'all genuine movements of national independence'. I must be satisfied. Vietnam was independent and united.

In my last days in Saigon I began to feel that it had all been wrong. But when, on a plane between Vientiane and Bangkok, I learned from a magazine that Solzhenitsyn had been saying precisely that, and condemning the Americans for not fighting more ruthlessly, I was forced to admit that I still believed in the right of

Vietnam to unity and independence. The French had had no right in
Vietnam. The Japanese had had no right in Vietnam. The British
had had no right to use Japanese troops to restore French rule in
Vietnam. Nor had the Americans had any right to interfere in order
to thwart the independence movement which had defeated the
French. Many of my bedrock beliefs were and are such as one could
share with the most innocent *bo doi*. 'Nothing is more precious than
independence and liberty'—the slogan of Ho that had driven me
wild with boredom in the last few months, broadcast over the p.a.
system through the streets, and emblazoned on all those banners—
but it is a fine motto.

But the supporters of the Vietnamese opposition to the United
States had gone further than that, and so had I. We had been
seduced by Ho. My political associates in England were *not* the kind
of people who denied that Stalinism existed. We not only knew
about it, we were very interested in it. We also opposed it. Why then
did we also support it? Or did we?

I was forced to rethink this recently when I read a remark by
Paul Foot: 'No revolutionary socialist apart from James Fenton was
ever under the slightest illusion that Vietnam could produce
anything at all after the war, let alone socialism.' My first thought
was: what about the poor old *bo doi*? Do *they* count as revolutionary
socialists? And my second point may be illustrated by an editorial in
New Left Review ten years ago: 'In achieving the necessary
combination of national liberation and social revolution the
Vietnamese Communists drew on many of the best traditions of the
international workers' movement which produced them.'

The editorial—written by Robin Blackburn, a Trotskyite as
influential as Paul Foot in securing the support of my generation for
the liberation struggle of the Vietnamese—never mentions that the
victory of the Vietnamese was a victory for *Stalinism*, because to do
so would have muddied the issue. The great thing was that the
évents of ten years ago represented a defeat for American
imperialism. The same issue of *New Left Review* quotes Lukács:
'The defeat of the USA in the Vietnamese war is to the 'American
Way of Life' as the Lisbon earthquake was to French
feudalism . . . . Even if decades were to pass between the Lisbon
earthquake and the fall of the Bastille, history can repeat itself.'

Stirring words, and—look—we don't have to support the Lisbon earthquake in order to support the Fall of the Bastille.

Blackburn's editorial ended by saying that the success of a socialist opposition against such odds would have 'a special resonance in those many lands where the hopes aroused by the defeat of fascism in the Second World War were to be subsequently frustrated or repressed: in Madrid and Barcelona, Lisbon and Luanda, Milan and Athens, Manila and Seoul.' An interesting list of places, and a reminder of the variousness of political change. The example of Madrid, for instance, would I think be much more inspiring to anybody in Seoul than the example of Saigon. We seem to have learned that dictatorships can be removed without utter disaster. Is this thanks to the Vietnamese? Maybe in some very complicated and partial way. But Madrid has not yet been 'lost to capitalism' like Indochina.

While I was working in Vietnam and Cambodia I thought that I was probably on the right track if my reports, while giving no comfort to my political enemies, were critical enough to upset my friends. I knew something about the thirties and I absolutely did not believe that one should, as a reporter, invent victories for the comrades. I had the illusion that I was honest, and in many ways I was. What I could not see in myself, but what I realize now is so prevalent on the Left, is the corrupting effect of political opportunism. We saw the tanks arriving and we all wanted to associate ourselves, just a little bit, with victory. And how much more opportunistic can you get than to hitch a ride on the winning tank, just a few yards before the palace gates?

When the boat people later began leaving Vietnam there was an argument on the Left that this tragic exodus was a further example of the pernicious effects of US foreign policy. Yet it is striking that for three decades after the Second World War such a mass departure did not take place. It is only in the decade since unification that people have been trusting themselves to flimsy vessels in the South China Sea. A recent report described a group of North Vietnamese villagers who acquired a boat and were setting out in the dead of night when they were noticed by another village. The second group said, Let us come too. The first group did not have enough space for safety, but they were afraid that if they did not agree the other villagers would raise the alarm. So the boat was impossibly crammed.

The boat people are not merely 'obstinate elements' or Chinese comprador capitalists on their way to new markets. They are simple people with no hope.

For two months after the fall there had been no banking facilities in Saigon. Petrol was expensive and it was not unusual to see students directing the traffic in streets where there was no traffic to be directed. Everything changed when the authorities allowed the withdrawal of small amounts of cash, and when petrol prices were reduced. The rich brought out their cars again. The Hondas reappeared. And the whole bourgeoisie went into the café business.

You borrowed an old parachute from a friend. You got hold of a few small stools, brought your crockery from home and you were in business. Every day I walked the length of Tu Do, looking to see if my name had come up on the departures list at the Information Ministry, and one day I counted seventy of these stalls, excluding the allied trades—cake vendors, cigarette stands, booksellers, manufacturers of Ho Chi Minh sandals, and the best example of Obstinate Enterprise, the man who sat outside the re-education centre making plastic covers for the new certificates.

The parachutes were strung between the trees for shade. With their varying colours and billowing shapes, they made the city utterly beautiful. The tables had flowers. The crockery was of the best and the service—inexperienced. It was all an economic nonsense. There was a group of students who ran a bookstall but spent all their time in the café across the street, watching for custom. During the day they might just make enough money for soft drinks. If more, they moved further up the street to drown their sorrows in a spirit called *Ba Xi De*, 'the old man with the stick'. With this they ate dishes of boiled entrails, and peanuts which came wrapped in fascinating twists of paper—the index of an English verse anthology, or a confidential document from some shady American organization.

In Gia Long Boulevard, by the tribunal where the judges were twiddling their thumbs, proprietors and clients came from the legal profession. The proprietor of 'The Two Tamarind Trees' told me she made about a thousand *piastres* a day. Previously she had made two hundred thousand *piastres* a case (755 *piastres* to a dollar). On the street beneath the Caravelle Hotel, there was the Café Air France, known to us as Chez Solange. Solange came from a rich family. She was beautiful. One day she brought two rattan bars and a set of bar-stools from her house, and set up shop. I was one of her first clients, and she told me over a breakfast of beer and beer what it had been like to become a barmaid.

Her elder brothers had told her she was mad to try it. They dropped her off with her things, but later would have nothing to do with her. Her younger brothers had been more helpful. But: 'This morning when the first customer came for coffee, I was so ashamed that I couldn't serve him. And then when I did serve him, I couldn't decide how much to charge him.' But once the business was established, the elder brothers relented and were to be seen lounging at the bar most of the day, except during the heat.

Solange had come down in the world. There was a thing called *bia om*, meaning beer and a cuddle, a half-way house to prostitution. The client ordered the beer. With it he paid for the company of an attractive girl. The open-air cafés were not great places for a cuddle, but the suggestion was still there. The new slang term was *caphé om*, coffee and a cuddle, reflecting the diminishing spending power of the bourgeoisie.

The morality of the cafés was attacked in the newspapers, particularly on the grounds that the bourgeoisie were procrastinating. What role were they going to play in the future society? I sometimes asked these people, particularly students, why they didn't try going to the countryside as teachers or in some professional capacity. Of course they were horrified. One man told me that he wanted to stay on in the capital in order to read foreign newspapers (there were no foreign newspapers). Another girl said she couldn't teach in the countryside because peasant children didn't go to school (they did go to school).

The *bo doi* occasionally came along with loudhailers, clearing the cafés away. But a few days later the obstinate economy was back in place. And it was still there when I finally got permission to leave.

The majority of the emigrants at this stage belonged to the French community, and it was obvious at the airport that they had spent their last *piastres* very well. We were going out on a plane provided by the United Nations High Commission for Refugees. You should have seen the kind of refugees we were. I had a Leica and two *Washington Post* typewriters. That was my loot. They, the French, had ransacked the market for hi-fi systems of the very highest quality, and they had snapped up the best of the leather jackets and coats in Tu Do, where for some reason you could get very good calf. Their photographic equipment was luxurious, but the thing that held us all up was the censorship of photographs.

Vietnam had become known throughout the world through photos of a kind which emphasized the grain of squalor. The *bo doi* did not like these photographs, and they weren't fools either: if they found a print of an unacceptable image, say a poor woman squatting, they took the print and insisted on a search for the negative. Everyone's attempts to be better than Don McCullin were confiscated, and the process took a long time. There were more mysterious reasons too: I was told that a *bo doi* confiscated a photo of a flower: when asked why, he explained that there was a kind of powder on the flower; if you enlarged the photo enough, you would see a grain of the powder, and if you enlarged that grain enough— you would see a photograph of the whole of Vietnam.

As I waited for the French to clear their loot, a panic seized me which was just like the panic I had had all those months before. I would never escape from Vietnam. The *bo doi* would never get through all those enormous suitcases. And besides the runway was absolutely dancing with rain. We would be sent back to Saigon, and then we would be forced through the whole process again. It had happened to others and it could happen to us. I wished those fucking French would get a move on.

And then at last we were let through. The man in front of me had too much hand-luggage and I offered to help. I took from him the French Embassy's diplomatic bag and we all ran together across the tarmac through the cloudburst. My last memory, as we entered the aircraft, is of the overpowering smell of tropical rain on very expensive new leather.

TEN YEARS ON:
THREE VIEWS

Frank Snepp
Toothpaste

'A day or so before the collapse of Saigon, a Vietnamese friend of mine called me at the Embassy and said, Please, help me to get out of the country. I said, I can't—I was writing up a report for the US Ambassador Graham Martin, hoping to change his mind and induce him to accelerate the American evacuation. I said, Call me back, I'm too busy right now, I can't do anything. When she called back an hour later I was away from the telephone, down in Martin's office trying to sell him my analysis. I never heard from her again. But later I was told—although I've never found out for sure—that my friend killed herself. She killed herself because I couldn't get her out. It's a terrible thing to think back on. Her name was Mai Ly and it's to her that I dedicated my book *Decent Interval*.

That was the problem with the Americans in Vietnam: they always seemed to have their priorities wrong. It took that terrible

Frank Snepp was the CIA's principal analyst of North Vietnamese political affairs, and, on his second tour of duty, was based in Saigon from 1972 until the fall of the city on 30 April 1975. He resigned from the CIA in 1976 to write *Decent Interval*, an account of the last years of the American presence in Vietnam. As Snepp cannot publish writing without its first being scrutinised by the CIA, for reasons explained in the pages that follow, this text was not written by Snepp but is based on an interview conducted by Eric Burns.

thing at the end, that terrible evacuation, to show me how badly my own priorities had become skewed. When I came off the Embassy roof, everything caved in—all the barriers of cynicism the CIA's training had helped erect—it all fell away. For the first time I was no longer insulated against the consequences of my actions and inefficiency. During and immediately after the evacuation I felt like a B-52 pilot who, after flying a bombing-strike at sixty thousand feet, had somehow managed to swoop down and witness at very close range the damage he had done. That's when I suffered my epiphany. That's too elegant a word for it: the complete shock of what had happened set in. I experienced horror and a terrific revulsion at once. A terrible feeling of guilt remains with me to this day. I suffer still from the memory of some Vietnamese who didn't escape. I am still trying to get them out.

Our delusion was profound, our wishful thinking right up to the end monumental. It need not have been that way, and that is the real theme of *Decent Interval*. The whole thrust of the book is that the CIA failed to protect its own: its agents in Vietnam, its documents, and more broadly our allies there. With all our resources in Vietnam, the communists beat the United States in the field of intelligence for one reason: they believed theirs. They accepted their Saigon sources' reports that Thieu's South Vietnamese government was in disarray during those last weeks before the collapse, and that the North could take an advantage—even if they were surprised in the end by how rapidly they achieved their victory. If we had believed our intelligence, we would have known what was going to happen, and taken action accordingly.

I spend a lot of time mulling over what happened in Vietnam and what its impact has been. I'm afraid it's not a very happy experience. Time seems cyclical: we're going back there now. We militarized our foreign policy in Lebanon, just as we had in Vietnam, with disastrous results. When Ambassador Martin was trying to push an aid bill for Vietnam through on Capitol Hill, we would distort the intelligence from Saigon to fit his particular agenda. We're still seeing that happen: in September 1982 Congress criticized the CIA for bending analysis concerning our involvement in Nicaragua to fit administration interests. Every few weeks the Reagan administration doctors photographs to show war materials passing from Nicaragua into El Salvador. Recently two CIA analysts found enough of their conscience to resign over the matter generally.

We really learned *nothing* from Vietnam about approaching intelligence with more integrity. Within a few years of Saigon's collapse we did the same thing in Iran. We embraced the Shah as tightly as we had Thieu, and with the same consequences. Even the evacuation that should have taken place in Iran failed for the same reasons it was so badly handled in Vietnam: it was planned too late, with documents left behind, not to mention most of the Embassy staff. One of the great ironies surrounding the recent libel suit brought by General William Westmoreland, the commander of US forces in Vietnam, against the broadcasting network CBS is that so many CIA officers have only now discovered their consciences. Somewhat late in the day they have testified, in support of the claims made by a CBS documentary on the war, that they should have challenged Westmoreland's cooked figures concerning Communist troop strength years ago. I don't want to sound maudlin, but I think your duty is to tell the truth. That was what I was trying to do when I asked the CIA to let me write an after-action report on those last two years leading up to the evacuation and the fall of Saigon. When they turned me down, I went away and wrote *Decent Interval*.

The Vietnam war was conceived in secrecy, and one of the saddest things to me is that such secrecy has only been increased in its wake. For a while, as a result of Watergate and past CIA excesses, official secrecy fell into disrepute, but the lawsuit against *Decent Interval* was primary in the backlash against the forces of openness.

There were no secrets in my book—the Justice Department itself indicated as much. Admiral Stansfield Turner, head of the CIA at the time the lawsuit was brought, openly stated that I had been very circumspect. I come in fact from a rather conservative background: the last thing I viewed my book as being—as one secret session of the Senate Intelligence Committee claimed—was treason. Unlike so many commentators during the war, I didn't approach the Vietnamese communists as romantic revolutionaries. My book was a protest, but not of the old anti-war type: it was meant to reveal a number of fantasies sustained not just by the American public but the CIA. The CIA then wanted to punish me for unauthorized disclosures—even though none contained classified information. Theirs was the old 'scarecrow' argument: that I had frightened off our allies abroad and Agency collaborators. They claimed, for example, that because of *Decent Interval* British intelligence would stop co-operating with the CIA—complete nonsense, since the British need American intelligence just as we need theirs: it's a marvellously symbiotic relationship that has weathered even Kim Philby's disclosures, which were considerably less benign than mine.

The Supreme Court ruling against me, handed down in 1980, was pretty draconian. It entitled the government to seize all my past, present and future profits from *Decent Interval*—they currently total about $200,000—and imposed on me a life-long gag order, requiring me to clear just about *everything* I write—fiction, non-fiction, screenplays, poetry—with the CIA, even if the material is not related to it. When the Agency gets around to reviewing my writing—and it has thirty days to complete its review—it may under law, or at least its own interpretation of the law, remove material that is both classified and *classifiable*, whatever that means. With the stroke of a pen and a new executive order, each presidential administration can expand the limits of what is considered secret or confidential. I can never be sure exactly what I am finally going to be allowed to print.

My lawsuit marked a real watershed in American law: through a jerry-built ruling the government set up and justified the punishment of anyone who makes non-confidential, benign disclosures. This is exactly what the British Official Secrets Act is supposed to do at its most extreme—but my ruling goes *even* further. In Britain, a newspaper warned under one of the Act's D-

Notices not to go forward with publication still has the choice of doing so—the old Blackstonian doctrine of punishment after the fact. My lawsuit authorized prior restraint. In early 1983 the Reagan administration turned my Supreme Court ruling into a mandate for censorship throughout the government, ordering the heads of major executive agencies to impose written or implicit secrecy strictures on all employees—including a provision for censoring employees' writings, even after they leave the civil service.

'The Reagan administration has now instituted secrecy such as we have never seen before. It recently introduced a measure enabling it to reclassify *what is already public*. Quite obviously, if the material is available to the public it will be available to our enemies: it's like putting toothpaste back into the tube. Such an expedient can only be used to cloak embarrassing information—*not* secrets.

Ironies resonate throughout my career. My three-year bout with the government gave me a real grounding in law, and, although not a lawyer, I now teach the First Amendment law protecting free speech. I also do a lot of public speaking on the question of secrecy in government and what the CIA is doing. But, on the whole, my book has not commended me to any particular interest group—either the Left or the Right. I have found myself alone, and I mean *really* alone. I don't want to sound like a cry-baby, but my appearances before Congress have been anything but sanguine. I'm regarded as a traitor. Moreover, my book is seen more and more as simply unimportant. During the lawsuit against *Decent Interval*, the CIA's Admiral Turner stated that my book was about a piece of history that is not particularly relevant. And, in fact, as memories dim and as various interest groups—the military, the diplomatic community, the government—close ranks around their own, you discover how particularly irrelevant this piece of history can be. Ambassador Martin said after the publication of my book that history would eventually vindicate him. It is a melancholy fact that the revisionists will ensure that it does.'

Norman Podhoretz
Impotence

'*A*s a result of Vietnam, the Pentagon has grown extremely gun-shy. These days it is virtually pacifist: it buys a lot of weapons, but doesn't really like the idea of using them. The Secretary of Defence, Caspar Weinberger, may be regarded as very much a hardliner, but the conditions he spelled out recently governing American use of military force would seem to exclude all grounds short of an outright invasion of the United States.

This is a direct response to the Vietnam war, and to my mind a bad response: a misreading of what happened. It begins from the assumption that the United States went into Vietnam without popular support. In fact, in the early years American intervention was overwhelmingly supported—by the public, Congress and the media alike. Only after the 1968 Tet offensive did that support begin to ebb as people felt the war was being lost, or was simply not winnable. Back in 1954 we had indeed refused to intervene in Vietnam on the side of the French—there *was* little enthusiasm then for American involvement. The memory of Korea was too fresh. More importantly, it would have been backing French colonialism. But the American intervention in 1961 and 1962 represented something different: an attempt to support an indigenously Vietnamese anti-communist government, the victim of an aggressive guerrilla movement ostensibly operating within the country, but in reality directed from the north. The United States was coming to the aid of a country over whose birth it had presided in the Geneva accords of 1954: a country that was trying to build a pro-Western, democratic, anti-communist society. In the early Johnson years there was still overwhelming support for Vietnam: the 1964 Gulf of Tonkin Resolution, extending extraordinary war-making powers to the president, was passed with only two dissenting votes. A glance at the contemporary editorials in the *New*

125

York Times, Washington Post, Time and *Newsweek*, and at TV coverage of the period shows them all backing the prevention of a communist takeover.

There was, it is true, a credibility gap during the early years of Vietnam between the government's and the media's versions of the war. This does not bear on the fundamental premises of the intervention at all, however: it arose because the media took up the position that almost everything in the official version of events must be false, and assumed the responsibility of poking holes in it. It was not that the press or the anti-war movement really lacked knowledge: they had it —the government was providing evidence and white papers. But having for a time been perhaps too credulous towards official statements, as the press *felt* itself to have been in the fifties, it now committed the opposite sin—of assuming that almost anything an American spokesman or indeed any Western leader said about anything was probably untrue.

It would probably be undesirable to try to place any legal restraints on the power of the media, but we need non-systematic means of dealing with its distortions. The libel cases brought by former Israeli defence minister Ariel Sharon against *Time* magazine and General William Westmoreland against CBS Television have arisen from widespread public dissatisfaction with the power of the media: strengthening the libel laws is one way of forcing it to be more scrupulous, especially in sensitive situations. Such lawsuits have what the press always describes as a 'chilling effect' upon journalism, and assumes to be necessarily bad. But the positive side is to force the media to make certain that what they say can be backed up by evidence. After all, newpapers are also private corporations and they can't afford to alienate their customers too much: already they are responding to public unease by trying to compensate for the natural liberal bias shared by a very large number of their reporters.

The irony where Vietnam was concerned is that government briefings were on the whole amazingly truthful and accurate, and have now been vindicated by what we know, including what we know from North Vietnamese sources. The only misleading statements made by the military in Saigon and the government in Washington—those which exaggerated the extent to which the American side was winning—are hardly surprising. Very few nations at war tell the people back home that the war is going badly. Nevertheless, the press gradually exposed those misleading accounts as false. And in the early years even someone like the *New York Times*'s David Halberstam (later a famous opponent of the entire American intervention), while saying that things were not going well, still favoured the government's policy. In a book published as late as 1965, Halberstam argued that Vietnam was one of the United States' two or three most vital interests: his criticisms were directed not at trying to get the US out, but at improving the situation and making a victory more likely.

'*T*he objective of Vietnam was not only morally justified, but noble: to save South Vietnam from the horrors that, as a result of the triumph of communism, have now overtaken it. But achieving a particular objective always presumes the means to do it; there is the possibility, too, that that achievement might actually do more harm than good. The question of whether the United States had the means to fight that kind of war in Vietnam successfully was never satisfactorily addressed, and events demonstrated that it did not: intervention was a reckless, quixotic act.

When formulating political and military policy, one never knows as much about other countries as one ideally should. To imagine oneself capable of fully understanding an alien society and culture is foolish. The lesson to be drawn is that, when you do intervene, relative ignorance limits severely what you can expect to accomplish. Instead of acting, as at the outset, as adviser and helper to a country fighting its own war, the United States made the great mistake of allowing itself to take over the conduct of the war in Vietnam. In clamouring for the replacement of the South Vietnamese President Ngo Din Diem in 1963 the Kennedy administration, the media and the liberal community displayed an arrogance it's hard to imagine anyone falling into today. They thought they knew how to remake South Vietnamese society. It's difficult enough to fight a war successfully. With El Salvador the United States is risking the same major mistake. Except in the most general terms, it doesn't know what to do about El Salvador's social, economic and political problems. That's not saying it can't make an intelligent military assessment—something much easier to do, in fact almost a technical problem. But how a war should be fought in a particular terrain is one thing; the political reconstruction of an alien society quite another.

Nevertheless, within the limits of prudence the United States has an obligation to itself, its values and its own security, indeed a moral imperative, to oppose the spread of communist totalitarian regimes—not only, but especially, when they are allied to and backed by the Soviet Union. During the Angolan civil war, though—a war won by communists with the Soviet Union's help, and using Cuban troops—Congress absurdly forbade the Ford administration even to send aid to the pro-Western forces. Now it is trying to do the same thing with respect to Nicaragua. We have a moral and political obligation to support the Contras in Nicaragua—the freedom fighters, as President Reagan now rightly calls them. Our efforts to dictate their internal policies are probably futile, and also a species of arrogance: we have to allow them to determine their political future within the broad limits they profess. That is, to establish a democratic regime in Nicaragua by overthrowing the Sandinistas, who have stolen and betrayed the democratic revolution against Somoza; who, proclaiming a 'revolution without frontiers', will not peacefully co-exist with the other regimes in the region; and who are trying to establish an anti-democratic, communist totalitarian regime.

Resisting the spread of communist power in Central America now is a necessary precondition for the establishment of democratic institutions in that part of the world. Richard Nixon once described the United States in Vietnam as a 'pitiful, helpless giant'. If it fails in Central America, the United States will convey, once again, the same message to the rest of the world: America is impotent.'

Text based on an interview conducted by Jonathan Levi

Noam Chomsky
Dominoes

*I*n one of his sermons on human rights, President Carter explained that we owe Vietnam no debt, because 'the destruction was mutual'. What is interesting about this statement is the reaction to it among educated Americans: nil.

This should not be surprising. Contrary to much illusion, there was little principled opposition to the Indochina war among the articulate intelligentsia—that is, among writers, historians and members of the media. One detailed study undertaken in 1970, at the peak of the anti-war protest, revealed that the 'American intellectual elite' came to oppose the war for the same 'pragmatic reasons' that had convinced business circles to abandon it: Indochina was a bad investment. Very few opposed the war on the grounds that led all to condemn the Soviet invasion of Czechoslovakia: not that it failed, or was too bloody, but that aggression is wrong. In contrast, as late as 1982 over seventy percent of the general population (but far fewer 'opinion leaders') still regarded the war as not merely 'a mistake' but 'fundamentally wrong and immoral'.

The technical term for this failure to indoctrinate the general population is the 'Vietnam syndrome', a dread disease that spread over most of the United States with such symptoms as a distaste for aggression and massacre—what Norman Podhoretz calls the 'sickly inhibitions against the use of military force', which he hopes were finally overcome with the grand victory in Grenada. The malady, however, persists, and continues to inhibit the US government from actively intervening in Central America and elsewhere. The major US defeat in Indochina was at home: much of the population rejected the hitherto established stance of passivity, apathy and obedience. Great efforts were made in the 1970s to overcome this 'crisis of democracy', but with less success than reliance on articulate opinion would suggest.

Of course, there was debate over the wisdom of the war among educated Americans. The hawks, such as Joseph Alsop, argued that with sufficient violence the United States could succeed in its aims; the doves doubted this conclusion, though emphasizing that 'we all pray that Mr Alsop will be right' and that 'we may all be saluting the wisdom and statesmanship of the American government' [if it succeeds in subjugating Vietnam while leaving it] . . . 'a land of ruin and wreck' (Arthur Schlesinger). Few would deny now that the war began with 'blundering efforts to do good' (Anthony Lewis) in 'an excess of righteousness and disinterested benevolence' (John King Fairbank), that it was 'a failed crusade' undertaken for motives that were 'noble' though 'illusory' and with the 'loftiest intentions' (Stanley Karnow, in his best-selling *Vietnam: A History*). These are the voices of the doves. As noted, much of the general population rejected the hawk-dove consensus of elite circles, a fact of lasting significance.

*I*t is worth recalling a few facts. The United States was deeply committed to the French effort to reconquer their former colony, recognizing throughout, as internal documents reveal, that the enemy was the nationalist movement of Vietnam. The resultant death toll was about half a million. When France withdrew, the United States dedicated itself at once to subverting the 1954 Geneva settlement, installing in the south a terrorrist regime that by 1961 had killed perhaps 70,000 'Vietcong', evoking resistance supported after 1959 from the northern half of the country. In 1961 and 1962 President Kennedy launched a direct attack against rural South Vietnam with large-scale bombing and defoliation, as part of a programme designed to drive millions of people to camps where they would be 'protected' by armed guards and barbed wire from the guerrillas whom, the United States conceded, the rural population was willingly supporting. The United States claimed that it was invited in, but as the *Economist* has accurately proclaimed, 'An invader is an invader unless invited in by a government with a claim to legitimacy.' The United States never regarded the clients it installed as having any such claim, and in fact regularly replaced them when they failed to exhibit sufficient enthusiasm for the American attack. In short, the United States invaded South Vietnam. (The *Economist*, of course, was not referring to Vietnam but to a similar Soviet fraud concerning Afghanistan. With regard to official enemies, Western intellectuals are able to perceive that $2+2=4$.)

From 1961 to 1965 the United States devoted itself to its war against South Vietnam, while fending off the threat of any kind of political settlement with the North—an intolerable prospect since, as Douglas Pike candidly explained, our 'minnow' could not compete with their 'whale'. In 1965, the United States began the direct land-invasion of South Vietnam—which, throughout, bore the brunt of US aggression—along with a systematic bombardment that was *three* times greater than the bombing of the North. By then, some 160,000 South Vietnamese had been killed, many of them 'under the crushing weight of American armor, napalm, jet bombers and, finally, vomiting gases,' in the words of the hawkish military historian Bernard Fall. The United States then escalated the war against the South, as well as extending it to Laos and Cambodia, where perhaps another million were killed. The Vietnamese death toll may have been as high as three million. In 1967, Bernard Fall warned that 'Vietnam as a cultural and historic entity . . . is threatened with extinction.' By that time, though elite groups remained loyal to the cause, popular protest had reached a significant level. After the murderous post-Tet pacification campaigns and other atrocities in Laos and Cambodia, it appeared that US policy would, as I wrote in 1970, 'create a situation in which, indeed, North Vietnam will necessarily dominate Indochina, for no other viable society will remain.' Later, this consequence of US savagery would be exploited as a *post hoc* justification for it, in a propaganda achievement that Goebbels would have admired.

It is revealing to note how history depicts the American attack against South Vietnam, launched by Kennedy and escalated by his successors. History records only a 'defense of freedom' (Charles Krauthammer, *New Republic*), a 'failed crusade' that was, the doves maintain, perhaps unwise. At a comparable level of integrity,

Soviet party hacks extol the 'defense of Afghanistan' against 'bandits' and 'terrorists' organized by the CIA.

The United States did not achieve its maximal goals in Indochina, but it did gain a partial victory. The primary US concern was not Indochina, but rather the 'domino effect', the development that might cause 'the rot to spread' to Thailand and beyond. This threat was averted. The countries of Indochina will be lucky to survive; they will not endanger global order by a social and economic independence that denies the West the freedom to exploit them; they will not infect the regions beyond, as had been feared, by a model of social reform that might be meaningful to impoverished peasants.

Postwar US policy has been designed to ensure that the victory is sustained by maximizing suffering and oppression in Indochina. Since 'the destruction was mutual'—as is readily demonstrated by a stroll through New York, Boston, Vinh, Quang Ngai province and the Plain of Jars—we are entitled to deny reparations, aid, and trade, and to block development funds. The extent of US sadism is noteworthy. When in 1977 India tried to send one hundred buffalos to replenish the herds destroyed by US violence, the United States threatened to cancel 'food for peace' aid, while, as proof of Communist barbarity, the American press featured photographs of peasants pulling ploughs. The Carter administration even denied rice to Laos (despite a cynical pretence to the contrary), whose agricultural system was destroyed by US terror bombing. In 1983 Oxfam America was not permitted to send ten solar pumps to Cambodia for irrigation. Meanwhile, from the first days of the Khmer Rouge takeover, the West was consumed with horror over their atrocities, which caused perhaps another million deaths. Contrast this with the reaction to comparable and simultaneous atrocities in Timor: here the United States bore primary responsibility and could have terminated the atrocities at once, whereas in Cambodia nothing could be done, but the blame could be placed on the enemy. I do not, incidentally, exempt myself from this critique. I condemned the 'barbarity' and 'brutal practice' of the

Khmer Rouge in 1977, long before writing a word on the US-backed atrocities in Timor, which on moral grounds posed a far more serious issue for those in the West. It is difficult for even the most sceptical to extricate themselves from a propaganda system of overwhelming efficiency.*

Now, Western moralists remain silent as their governments provide the means for the Indonesian generals to consummate their massacres. The United States backs the Democratic Kampuchea coalition, largely based on the Khmer Rouge, because of its 'continuity', the State Department explains, with the Pol Pot regime. The prime motive is to 'bleed Vietnam', to ensure that suffering and brutality reach the highest possible level. We can then exult in our benevolence of earlier years, in undertaking our 'noble crusade'.

The elementary truths about these terrible years survive in the memories of those who opposed the US war against South Vietnam, then all of Indochina. There is no doubt, however, that the approved version will sooner or later be established by the custodians of history, perhaps to be exposed by crusading intellectuals a century hence, if 'Western civilization' endures that long.

---

*In December 1975, Indonesia invaded the territory of East Timor, with diplomatic and material support from the United States and its allies. The atrocities, supported throughout by the United States, left a death toll as great as several hundred thousand. Those who survived were reduced to a level of existence comparable to that of the refugee camps along the Thai-Cambodian border. For further details see my book *Towards the Cold War*.

NADINE GORDIMER
THE ESSENTIAL
GESTURE: WRITERS
AND RESPONSIBILITY

When I began to write at the age of nine or ten, I did so in what I have come to believe is the only real innocence: an act without responsibility. I was alone. I did not know how my poem or story came out of myself. It was directed at no one, was read by no one.

Responsibility is what awaits outside the Eden of creativity. I should never have dreamed that this most solitary and deeply marvellous of secrets—the urge *to make* with words—would become a vocation for which the world and that life-time lodger, conscionable self-awareness, would claim the right to call me and all my kind to account. The creative act is not pure. History evidences it. Ideology demands it. Society exacts it. The writer loses Eden, writes to be read, and comes to realize that he is answerable. The writer is *held responsible*, and the verbal phrase is ominously accurate; for the writer not only has laid upon him responsibility for various interpretations of the consequences of his work, he is 'held' before he begins by the claims of different moralities asserted upon him: artistic, linguistic, ideological, national, political and religious. He learns that the creative act was not pure even while being formed in his brain. Already it carried congenital responsibility for what preceded cognition and volition: for the class represented in the genetic, environmental, social and economic terms when he was born of his parents.

In *Writing Degree Zero,* Roland Barthes wrote that language is a 'corpus of prescriptions and habits common to all the writers of a period.'

He also wrote that a writer's 'enterprise'—his work—is his 'essential gesture as a social being'.

Between these two statements I have found my subject, which is their tension and connection: the writer's responsibility. As the transformation of thought into written words, language is not only 'a' corpus but *the* corpus common to all writers. From the corpus of language, within that guild shared with fellow writers, the writer fashions his enterprise—what, in being fashioned, then becomes his 'essential gesture as a social being'. Created in the common lot of language, that essential gesture is individual, but in making it the writer quits the commune of the corpus: he enters the commonalty of society, the world of other beings who are not writers. He and his fellow writers are at once isolated from each other by the varying concepts in each different society of what the essential gesture of the writer as a social being is.

By comparison of what is expected of them, writers often have little or nothing in common. There is no responsibility arising out of the status of the writer as a social being that could call upon Saul Bellow, Kurt Vonnegut, Susan Sontag, Toni Morrison or John Berger to write on a subject that would result in their being silenced under a ban, banished to internal exile or detained in jail. But in the Soviet Union, South Africa, Iran, Vietnam, Taiwan, certain Latin American and other countries, this is the kind of demand that responsibility for the social significance of being a writer exacts: a double demand, the first from the oppressed to act as spokesperson for them; the second, from the state, to take punishment for being that spokesperson. Conversely, it is inconceivable that a Molly Keane or any other writer of the quaint Gothic-domestic cult recently discovered by discerning critics and readers in the United States and Britain would be interpreted or taken seriously in terms of the 'essential gesture as a social being' demanded in countries such as the Soviet Union and South Africa if he or she lived there. Still less likely would he or she then be taken up by discerning critics and readers in the United States and Britain: those who live safe from the midnight arrests and the solitary confinement that is the dark condominium of East and West make their demands upon the writer, too. For them, his essential gesture as a social being is to take risks that these critics and readers do not know that they themselves would take.

This demand results in some strange and unpleasant distortions in the personality of some of these safe people. Any writer from a country of conflict will bear me out. When abroad, you often disappoint interviewers: you are there, and not in jail in your own country. And since you are not—why are you not? Aha. . . does this mean you have not written the book you should have written? Can you imagine this kind of self-righteous inquisition being directed against a John Updike for not having made the trauma of America's Vietnam war the theme of his work?*

There is another tack of suspicion. The *Daily Telegraph* reviewer of *Something Out There*, my recent book of stories, said I must be exaggerating: if my country really was a place where such things happened, how was it I could write about them? And then there is the wish-fulfilment distortion, arising out of the homebody's projection of his dreams upon the exotic writer: the journalist who makes a bogus hero out of the writer who knows that the pen, where he lives, is a weapon not mightier than the sword.

One thing is clear: ours is a period when few can claim the absolute value of a writer without reference to a context of responsibilities. Exile as a mode of genius no longer exists. In place of Joyce we have the fragments of works appearing in *Index on Censorship*. These are the rags of suppressed literatures, translated from a Babel of languages; the broken cries of real exiles, not those who have rejected their homeland but those who have been forced out—of their language, their culture, their society. In place of Joyce we have two of the best contemporary writers in the world, Czeslaw Milosz and Milan Kundera; but both regard themselves as amputated sensibilities, not free of Poland and Czechoslovakia in the sense that Joyce was free of Ireland—whole: out in the world but still in possession of the language and culture of home. In place of Joyce, one might argue, we have Borges; but in his old age, and out of what he sees in his blindness as he did not when he could see, Borges has spoken wistfully for years now of a desire to trace the trails made by ordinary lives instead of the arcane pattern of abstract forces of which those lives are the finger-painting. Despite his rejection of ideologies (earning the world's

---

*American and British societies do not demand this 'orthodoxy' of their writers, because (arguably) their values are not in a crisis of survival concentrated on a single moral issue: which does not authorize self-appointed cultural commissars to decide whether or not writers from other countries are fulfilling their 'essential gesture' in their own societies.

inescapable and maybe accurate shove over to the ranks of the Right) even he senses on those lowered lids the responsibilities that feel out for writers so persistently in our time.

What right has society to impose responsibility upon writers and what right has the writer to resist? I want to examine not what is forbidden us by censorship—I know that story too well—but to what we are bidden. I want to consider what is expected of us by the dynamic of collective conscience and the will to liberty in various circumstances and places; whether we should respond, and if so, how we do.

'It is from the moment when I shall no longer be more than a writer that I shall cease to write.' One of the great of our period, Camus, could say that. As a writer he accepted, in theory at least, the basis of the most extreme and pressing demand of our time. The ivory tower was finally stormed, and it was not with a white flag that the writer came out, but with manifesto unfurled and arms crooked to link with the elbows of the people. And it was not just as their chronicler that the compact was made; the greater value, you will note, was placed on the persona outside of 'writer': to be 'no more than a writer' was to put an end to the justification for the very existence of the persona of 'writer'. Although the aphorism in its characteristically French neatness appears to wrap up all possible meanings of its statement, it does not. Camus's decision is a hidden as well as a revealed one. It is not just that he has weighed within himself his existential value as a writer against the value of other functions as a man among men, and found independently in favour of the man; the scale has been set up by a demand outside himself, by his world situation. He has, in fact, accepted its condition that the greater responsibility is to society and not to art.

Long before it was projected into that of a world war, Camus' natal situation was that of a writer in the conflict of Western world decolonization—the moral question of race and power by which the twentieth century will be characterized along with its discovery of the satanic ultimate in power, the means of human self-annihilation. But the demand made upon him and the moral imperative it set up in himself are those of a writer anywhere who lives among people—

or any sections of them marked out by race or colour or religion—
who are discriminated against and repressed. Whether or not he
himself materially belongs to the oppressed makes his assumption
of extraliterary responsibility less or more 'natural', but does not
alter much the problem of the conflict between integrities.

Loyalty is an emotion; integrity is a conviction adhered to out
of moral values. Therefore I speak here not of loyalties but
integrities, in my recognition that society's right to make
demands on the writer is equal to the writer's commitment to his
artistic vision. The conflict is between what demands society makes
and how they should be met.

In this conflict, the closest any writer comes to reconciliation
seems to me to be achieved in my own country, South Africa,
among some black writers. It certainly cannot be said to have
occurred in two of the most important African writers outside South
Africa, Chinua Achebe and Wole Soyinka. They became 'more
than writers' in answer to their country's—Nigeria's—crisis of civil
war, but in no sense did the demand develop their creativity. On the
contrary, in both, the energy of their creativity was sacrificed for
some years to the demands of activism, which for Soyinka included
imprisonment. The same might be said of Ernesto Cardenal. But it
is out of being 'more than a writer' that many black men and women
in South Africa *begin* to write. All the obstacles and diffidences—
lack of education, a tradition of literary expression, even the chance
to form the everyday habit of reading that germinates a writer's
gift—are overcome by the imperative to give expression to a
majority not silent, but one whose deeds and whose proud and
angry volubility against suffering have not been given the eloquence
of the written word. For these writers, there is no opposition of
inner and outer demands. As they are writing, they are at the same
time political activists in the concrete sense: teaching, proselytizing,
organizing. When they are detained without trial it may be for what
they have written, but when they are tried and convicted on crimes
of conscience it is for what they have done as 'more than a writer'.
'Africa, my beginning . . . Africa my end'—these words from the
epic poem written by Ngoapele Madingoane epitomize this

synthesis of creativity and social responsibility: what moves him, and the way it moves him, are perfectly at one with his society's demands. Without those demands he is not a poet.

In *The Necessity of Art*, the Marxist critic, Ernst Fischer, reaches anterior to my interpretation of this synthesis with his proposition that 'the artist who belonged to a coherent society [here, read preconquest South Africa] and to a class that was not yet an impediment to progress [here, read not yet infected by white bourgeois aspirations] did not feel it any loss of artistic freedom if a certain range of subjects was prescribed to him' since such subjects were imposed 'usually by tendencies and traditions deeply rooted in the people.' Of course, this same proposition may provide, in general, a sinister pretext for a government to invoke certain tendencies and traditions to suit its purpose of *proscribing* writers' themes, but applied to black writers in South Africa, history evidences its likely truth. For more than three hundred years, the tendency and tradition of black writers in South Africa has been to free themselves of white domination.

A rt is on the side of the oppressed. Think before you shudder at the simplistic dictum and its heretical definition of the freedom of art. For if art is freedom of the spirit, how can it exist within the oppressors? And there is some evidence that it ceases to. What writer of any literary worth defends fascism, totalitarianism, racism, in an age when these are still pandemic? Ezra Pound is dead. In Poland, where are the poets who sing the epic of the men who have broken Solidarity? In South Africa, where are the writers who produce brilliant defences of apartheid?

It remains difficult to dissect the tissue between those for whom writing is a revolutionary activity, no different from and to be practised concurrently with running a political trade union or making a false passport for someone on the run, and those who interpret' their society's demand to be 'more than a writer' as something that may yet be fulfilled through the nature of their writing itself. Whether this demand can be fulfilled by the writing itself depends on the society within which the writer functions. Even 'only' to write may be to be 'more than a writer' for one such as Milan Kundera, who goes on writing what he sees and knows from within his situation—his country under repression—until a ban on publishing his books strips him of his 'essential gesture' of being a writer at all. Like one of his own characters, he must clean windows or sell tickets in a cinema booth for a living. That, ironically, is what being 'more than a writer' would be for him, if he had opted to stay on in his country; something I don't think Camus quite visualized.

There are South Africans who have found themselves in the same position—for example, the poet Don Mattera, who for seven years was banned from writing, publishing, and even from reading his work in public. But in a country where the majority is totally repressed, as in South Africa, and where literature is nevertheless only half-suppressed because the greater part of the black majority is kept semi-literate and cannot be affected by books, there is—just—the possibility for a writer to be 'only' a writer, in terms of activity, and yet 'more than a writer' in fulfilling the demands of his society. An honourable category has been found for him. As 'cultural worker' in the race/class struggle he still may be seen to serve, even if he won't march towards the tear gas and bullets. In this context, long before the term 'cultural worker' was taken over from the vocabulary of other revolutions, black writers had to accept the social responsibility white ones didn't have—of being the only historians of events among their people. H. I. E. Dhlomo, Solomon T. Plaatje, and Thomas Mofolo created characters who brought to life and preserved events either unrecorded by white historians or recorded purely from the point of view of white conquest.* From this beginning there has been a logical intensification of the demands of social responsibility, as over decades discrimination and repression set into law and institution, and resistance became a liberation struggle. This process culminated during the black uprising of 1976, calling forth poetry and prose in an impetus of events not yet exhausted or fully explored by writers. The uprising began as a revolt of youth and it brought to writers a new consciousness—bold, incantatory,

---

*See H. I. E Dhlomo's *Valley of a Thousand Hills,* Solomon T. Plaatje's *Mhudi, Native Life in South Africa,* and *Boer War Diary,* and Thomas Mofolo's *Chaka.*

messianically reckless. It also placed new demands upon them in the essential gesture that bound them to a people springing about on the balls of their feet before dawn–streaks of freedom and the threat of death. Private emotions were inevitably outlawed by political activists who had no time for any; black writers were expected to prove their blackness *as a revolutionary condition* by submitting to an unwritten orthodoxy of interpretation and representation in their work. I stress unwritten because there was no Writers' Union to be expelled from. But there was a company of political leaders, intellectuals, and the new category of the alert young, shaming others with their physical and mental bravery, to censure a book of poems or prose if it was to be found irrelevant to the formal creation of an image of a people anonymously, often spontaneously heroic.

Some of my friends among black writers have insisted that this 'imposition' of orthodoxy is a white interpretation; that the impulse came from within to discard the lantern of artistic truth that reveals human worth through human ambiguity, and see by the flames of burning vehicles only the strong, thick lines that draw heroes. To gain his freedom the writer must give up his freedom. Whether the impulse came from within, without, or both, for the black South African writer it became an imperative to attempt that salvation. It remains so; but in the 1980s many black writers of quality have come into conflict with the demand from without—responsibility as orthodoxy—and have begun to negotiate the right to their own, inner interpretation of the essential gesture by which they are part of the black struggle.* The black writer's revolutionary responsibility may be posited by him as the discovery, in his own words, of the revolutionary spirit that rescues for the present —and for the post-revolutionary future—that nobility in ordinary men and women to be found only among their doubts, culpabilities, shortcomings: their courage-in-spite-of.

---

*Among the most recent examples, Njabulo Ndebele's *Fools,* Ahmed Essop's *The Emperor*, and Es'kia Mphahlele's *Africa my Song*.

To whom are South African writers answerable in their essential gesture if they are not in the historical and existential situation of blacks, and if they are alienated from their 'own', the historical and existential situation of whites? Only a section of blacks places any demands upon white writers at all—that grouping within radical blacks which grants integrity to whites who declare themselves for the black freedom struggle. To be one of these writers is firstly to be presented with a political responsibility if not an actual orthodoxy: the white writer's task as 'cultural worker' is to raise the consciousness of white people, who, unlike himself, have not woken up. It is a responsibility at once minor, in comparison with that placed upon the black writer as composer of battle hymns, and yet forbidding, if one compares the honour and welcome from blacks that await the black writer, and the branding as traitor, or, at best, turned backside of indifference that await the white, from the white establishment. With fortunate irony, however, it is a responsibility which the white writer already has taken on, for himself, if the other responsibility—to his creative integrity—keeps him scrupulous in writing about what he knows to be true whether whites like to hear it or not: for the majority of his readers are white. He brings some influence to bear on whites, though not on the white-dominated government; he may influence those individuals who are already coming-to bewilderedly out of the trip of power, and those who gain courage from reading the open expression of their own suppressed rebellion. I doubt whether the white writer, even if giving expression to the same themes as blacks, has much social use in inspiriting blacks, or is needed to. Sharing the life of the black ghettoes is the primary qualification the white writer lacks, so far as populist appreciation is concerned. But black writers do share with white the same kind of influence on those whites who read them, and so the categories that the state would keep apart get mixed through literature—an unforeseen 'essential gesture' of writers in their social responsibility in a divided country.

The white writer who has declared himself answerable to the oppressed people is not expected by them to be 'more than a writer', since his historical position is not seen as allowing him to be central to the black struggle. But a few writers have challenged this definition by taking upon themselves exactly the same revolutionary responsibilities as black writers such as Alex la Guma, Dennis Brutus and Mongane Serote, who make no distinction between the tasks of underground activity and writing a story or poem. Like Brutus, the white writers Breyten Breytenbach and Jeremy Cronin were tried and imprisoned for accepting the necessity they saw for being 'more than a writer'. Their interpretation of a writer's responsibility, in their country and situation, remains a challenge, particularly to those who disagree with their action while sharing with them the politics of opposition to repression. There is no moral authority like that of sacrifice.

In South Africa the ivory tower is bulldozed anew with every black man's home destroyed to make way for a white man's. Yet there are positions between the bulldozed ivory tower and the maximum security prison. The one who sees his responsibility in being 'only a writer' has still to decide whether this means he can fulfil his essential gesture to society only by ready-packaging his creativity to the dimensions of a social realism which *those who will free him of his situation* have the authority to ask of him, or whether he may be able to do so by work the Western liberal George Steiner defines, in his review of E. M. Cioran's *Drawn and Quartered*, as 'scrupulously argued, not declaimed . . . informed, at each node and articulation of proposal, with a just sense of the complex, contradictory nature of historical evidence.' The great mentor of Russian revolutionary writers of the 19th century, Belinsky, advises: 'Do not worry about the incarnation of ideas. If you are a poet, your works will contain them without your knowledge—they will be both moral and national if you follow your inspiration freely.' Octavio Paz, speaking from Mexico for the needs of the Third World, sees a fundamental function as social critic, for the writer who is 'only a writer'. It is a responsibility that goes back to source: the corpus of language from which the writer arises. 'Social criticism begins with grammar and the re-establishment of meanings.'* This was the responsibility taken up in the post-Nazi era by Heinrich Böll and Günter Grass, and is presently being

---

*Vissarion Belinsky, 1810–48. The quote is from my notebook: unable to locate source.

fulfilled by South African writers, black and white, in exposing the real meaning of the South African government's vocabulary of racist euphemisms, such terms as 'separate development', 'resettlement', 'national states', and its grammar of a racist legislature, with segregated chambers for whites, so-called coloureds and Indians, and no representation whatever for the majority of South Africans, those classified as black.

If the writer accepts the social realist demand, from without, will he be distorting, paradoxically, the very ability he has to offer the creation of a new society? If he accepts the other, self-imposed responsibility, how far into the immediate needs of his society will he reach? Will hungry people find revelation in the ideas his work contains 'without his knowledge'? The one certainty, in South Africa as a specific historical situation, is that there is no opting out of the two choices. Outside is a culture in sterile decay, its achievements culminating in the lines of tin toilets set up in the veld for people 'resettled' by force. Whether a writer is black or white, in South Africa the essential gesture by which he enters the brotherhood of man—which is the only definition of society that has any permanent validity—is a revolutionary gesture.

'**H**as God ever expressed an opinion?' . . . I believe that great art is impersonal . . . . I want neither love nor hatred nor pity nor anger. The impartiality of description would then become equal to the majesty of the law.'

—Flaubert

Nearly a century passed before the *nouveau roman* writers attempted this kind of majesty, taking over from another medium the mode of still-life. The work aspired to be the object-in-itself, although made up of elements—words, images—that can never be lifted from the 'partiality' of countless connotations. The writers went as far as is possible to go from any societal demand. They had tried so hard that their vision became fixed on Virginia Woolf's mark on the wall—and as an end, not a beginning. Yet the anti-movement seems to have been, after all, a negative variation on a kind of social responsibility some writers have assumed at least since the beginning of the modern movement: to transform the world by style. This was and is something that could not serve as the writer's essential gesture in countries such as South Africa and Nicaragua, but it has had its possibilities and sometimes proves its validity where complacency, indifference, accidie, and not conflict, threaten the human spirit. To transform the world by style was the iconoclastic essential gesture tried out by the Symbolists and Dadaists, but whatever social transformation (in shaping a new consciousness) they might have served in breaking old forms was horribly superseded by different means: Europe, the Far, Middle and Near East, Asia, Latin America and Africa overturned by wars; millions of human beings wandering without the basic structure of a roof.

The Symbolists' and Dadaists' successors, in what Susan Sontag terms 'the cultural revolution that refuses to be political' have among them their 'spiritual adventurers, social pariahs determined to disestablish themselves . . . not to be morally useful to the community'—the essential gesture withheld by Céline and Kerouac.* Responsibility reaches out into the manifesto, however, and claims the 'seers' of this revolution. Through a transformation by style—the laconic word depersonalized almost to the Word—Samuel Beckett takes on as his essential gesture a responsibility direct to human destiny, and not to any local cell of humanity. This is the assumption of a messenger of the gods rather than a cultural worker. It is a disestablishment from the temporal, yet some kind of final statement exacted by the temporal. Is Beckett the freest writer in the world, or is he the most responsible of all?

Kafka was also a seer, one who sought to transform consciousness by style, and who was making his essential gesture to human destiny rather than the European fragment of it to which he belonged. But he was unconscious of his desperate signal. He believed that the act of writing was one of detachment that moved

*In 'Approaching Artaud', *Under the Sign of Saturn*: 'Authors . . . recognized by their effort to disestablish themselves, by their will not to be morally useful to the community, by their inclination to present themselves not as social critics but as seers, spiritual adventurers and social pariahs.'

writers 'with everything we possess, to the moon.'* He was unaware of the terrifyingly impersonal, apocalyptic, prophetic nature of his vision in that ante-room to his parents' bedroom in Prague. Beckett, on the contrary, has been signalled to and consciously responded. The summons came from his time. His place—not Warsaw, San Salvador, Soweto—has nothing specific to ask of him. And unlike Joyce, he can never be in exile wherever he chooses to live, because he has chosen to be answerable to the twentieth century human condition which has its camp everywhere, or nowhere—whichever way you see Vladimir, Estragon, Pozzo and Lucky.

Writers who accept, as a professional responsibility, the transformation of society are always seeking ways of transforming their societies in ways they could not ever imagine, let alone demand: asking of themselves means that will plunge like a drill to release the great primal spout of creativity, drench the censors, cleanse the statute books of their pornography of racist and sexist laws, hose down religious differences, extinguish napalm bombs and flame-throwers, wash away pollution from land, sea and air, and bring out human beings into the occasional summer fount of naked joy. Each has his own dowsing twig, held over heart and brain. In *Gemini*, Michel Tournier sees writers' responsibilities as the obligation to 'disrupt the establishment in exact proportion to their creativity.' This is a bold global responsibility, though more Orphic and terrestrial than Beckett's; more human, if you like. It also could be taken as admission that this is *all* writers can do; for creativity comes from within: it cannot be produced by will or dictate if it is not there, although it can be crushed by dictate. Tournier's—this apparently fantastical and uncommitted writer's—own creativity is nevertheless so close to the people, that he respects as a marvel—and makes it so for his readers—the daily history of their lives as revealed in city trash dumps. And he is so fundamentally engaged by what alienates human beings that he imagines for everyone the restoration of wholeness (the totality which revolutionary art seeks to create for alienated man) in a form

---

*Letter to Max Brod, quoted in *Kafka*, by Ronald Hayman.

of Being that both sexes experience as one—something closer to a class–less society than to a sexually hermaphroditic curiosity.

The *transformation of experience* remains the writer's basic essential gesture: the lifting out of a limited category something that reveals its full meaning and significance only when the writer's imagination has expanded it. This has never been more evident than in the context of extreme experiences of sustained personal horror that are central to the period of twentieth century writers. John Bayley has written of Anna Akhmatova: 'A violently laconic couplet at the end of the sections of *Requiem* records her husband dead, her son in prison . . . . It is as good an instance as any of the power of great poetry to generalize and speak for the human predicament in extremity, for in fact she had probably never loved Gumilev, from whom she had lived apart for years, and her son had been brought up by his grandmother. But the sentiment (of the poem) was not for herself but for "her people", with whom she was at that time so totally united in suffering.'

Writers in South Africa who are 'only writers' are sometimes reproached by those, black and white, who are in practical revolutionary terms 'more than writers', for writing of events as if they themselves had been at the heart of action, endurance and suffering. So far as black writers are concerned, even though the humiliations and deprivations of daily life under apartheid enjoin them, many of them were no more among the children under fire from the police in the seventies, or are among the students and miners shot, tear-gassed and beaten in the eighties, or are living as freedom fighters in the bush, than Akhmatova was a heart-broken wife or a mother separated from a son she had nurtured. Given these circumstances, their claim to generalize and speak for a human predicament in extremity comes from their *ability to do so*, and the development of that ability is their responsibility towards those with whom they are united by this extrapolation of suffering and resistance. White writers who are 'only writers' are open to related reproach for 'stealing the lives of blacks' as good material. Their claim to this 'material' is the same as the black writers', at an important existential remove nobody would discount. Their essential gesture can be fulfilled only in the integrity Chekhov demanded: 'to describe a situation so truthfully that the reader can no longer evade it.'*

The writer is eternally in search of entelechy in his relation to his society. Everywhere in the world, he needs to be left alone and at the same time to have a vital connection with others; needs artistic freedom and knows it cannot exist without its wider context; feels the two presences within—creative self-absorption and conscionable awareness—and must resolve whether these are locked in death-struggle, or are really foetuses in a twinship of fecundity. Will the world let him, and will he know how to be the ideal of the writer as a social being, Walter Benjamin's story-teller, the one 'who could let the wick of his life be consumed completely by the gentle flame of his story'?

---

*Quoted by Isaiah Berlin in *Russian Thinkers*.

This month another 5,000 new British books will be published.

How will you know which ones to order?

At a time when it is more important than ever to spend your book budget wisely, it is a curious fact that book selection is often a rather hit or miss affair. Simply finding out what is available (and whether or not it is worth ordering) can be a time-consuming business, particularly overseas.

Every month British Book News gives advance information on some 800 forthcoming books, publishes reviews of 200 recent books and periodicals in all subject areas, and includes news features, a regular selection of paperback reprints, and bibliographical surveys of a wide range of subjects from computers to crime fiction, from poetry magazines to political geography.

1985 subscription rates: £25 (UK) £30 (overseas) $55.50 (USA) $61.50 (Canada). Rates for individual subscribers on request.

Requests for sample copies or orders with payment to Journals Department, Basil Blackwell, 108 Cowley Road, Oxford OX4 1JF, England.

Nadine Gordimer
What Were You
Dreaming?

I'm standing here by the road long time, yesterday, day before, today. Not the same road but it's the same—hot, hot like today. When they turn off to where they're going, I must get out again, wait again. Some of them they just pretend there's nobody there, they don't want to see nobody. Even go a bit faster, *ja*. Then they past, and I'm waiting. I combed my hair; I don't want to look like a *skolly*. Don't smile because they think you being too friendly, you think you good as them. They go and they go. Some's got the baby's napkin hanging over the back window to keep out this sun. Some's not going on holiday with their kids but is alone; all alone in a big car. But they'll never stop, the whites, if they alone. Never. Because these *skollies* and that kind've spoilt it all for us, sticking a gun in the driver's neck, stealing his money, beating him up and taking the car. Even killing him. So it's buggered up for us. No white wants some guy sitting behind his head. And the blacks—when they stop for you, they ask for money. They want you must pay, like for a taxi! The blacks!

But then these whites: they're stopping; I'm surprised, because it's only two—empty in the back—and the car it's a beautiful one. The windows are that special glass, you can't see in if you outside, but the woman has hers down and she's calling me over with her finger. She ask me where I'm going and I say the next place because they don't like to have you for too far, so she say get in and lean into the back to move along her stuff that's on the back seat to make room. Then she say, lock the door, just push that button down, we don't want you to fall out, and it's like she's joking with someone she know. The man driving smiles over his shoulder and say something—I can't hear it very well, it's the way he talk English. So anyway I say what's all right to say, yes master, thank you master, I'm going to Warmbad. He ask again, but man, I don't get it— *Ekskuus*? Please? And she chips in—she's a lady with grey hair and he's a young chap—My friend's from England, he's asking if you've been waiting a long time for a lift. So I tell them—A long time? Madam! And because they white, I tell them about the blacks, how when they stop they ask you to pay. This time I understand what the young man's saying, he say, And most whites don't stop? And I'm careful what I say, I tell them about the blacks, how too many people spoil it for us, they robbing and killing, you can't blame white people. Then he ask where I'm from. And she laugh and look round where I'm behind her. I see she know I'm from the Cape, although she ask me. I tell her I'm from the Cape Flats and she say she suppose I'm not born there, though, and she's right, I'm born in Wynberg, right there in Cape Town. So she say, And they moved you out?

Then I catch on what kind of white she is; so I tell her, yes, the government kicked us out from our place, and she say to the young man, You see?

He want to know why I'm not in the place in the Cape Flats, why I'm so far away here. I tell them I'm working in Pietersburg. And he keep on, why? Why? What's my job, everything, and if I don't understand the way he speak, she chips in again all the time and ask me for him. So I tell him, panel beater. And I tell him, the pay is very low in the Cape. And then I begin to tell them lots of things, some things is real and some things I just think of, things that are going to make them like me, maybe they'll take me all the way there to Pietersburg.

I tell them I'm six days on the road. I not going to say I'm sick as well, I been home because I was sick—because *she's* not from overseas, I suss that, she know that old story. I tell them I had to take leave because my mother's got trouble with my brothers and sisters, we seven in the family and no father. And s'true's God, it seem like what I'm saying. When do you ever see him except he's drunk. And my brother is trouble, trouble, he hangs around with bad people and my other brother doesn't help my mother. And that's no lie, neither, how can he help when he's doing time; but they don't need to know that, they only get scared I'm the same kind like him, if I tell about him, assault and intent to do bodily harm. The sisters are in school and my mother's only got the pension. *Ja.* I'm working there in Pietersburg and every week, madam, I swear to you, I send my pay for my mother and sisters. So then he say, Why get off here? Don't you want us to take you to Pietersburg? And she say, of course, they going that way.

And I tell them some more. They listening to me so nice, and I'm talking, talking. I talk about the government, because I hear she keep saying to him, telling about this law and that law. I say how it's not fair we had to leave Wynberg and go to the Flats. I tell her we got sicknesses—she say what kind, is it unhealthy here? And I don't have to think what, I just say it's *bad, bad*, and she say to the man, *As I told you*. I tell about the house we had in Wynberg, but it's not my grannie's old house where we was all living together so long, the house I'm telling them about is more the kind of house they'll know, they wouldn't like to go away from, with a tiled bathroom, electric stove, everything. I tell them we spend three thousand rands fixing up that house—my uncle give us the money, that's how we got it. He give us his savings, three thousand rands. (I don't know why I say three; old Uncle Jimmy never have three or two or one in his life. I just say it.) And then we just kicked out. And panel beaters getting low pay there; it's better in Pietersburg.

He say, but I'm far from my home? And I tell her again, because she's white but she's a woman too, with that grey hair she's got grown-up kids—Madam, I send my pay home every week, s'true's God, so's they can eat, there in the Flats. I'm saying, *six days on the road*. While I'm saying it, I'm thinking; then I say, look at me, I got only these clothes, I sold my things on the way, to have something to eat. *Six days on the road*. He's from overseas and she isn't one of those who say you're a liar, doesn't trust you—right away when I got in the car, I notice she doesn't take her stuff over to the front like they usually do in case you pinch something of theirs. Six days on the road, and am I tired, tired! When I get to Pietersburg I must try borrow me a rand to get a taxi there to where I live. He say, Where do you live? Not in town? And she laugh, because he don't know nothing about this place, where whites live and where we must go—but I know they both thinking and I know what they thinking; I know I'm going to get something when I get out, don't need to worry about that. They feeling bad about me, now. Bad. Anyhow it's God's truth that I'm tired, tired, that's true.

They've put up her window and he's pushed a few buttons, now it's like in a supermarket, cool air blowing, and the windows like sunglasses: that sun can't get me here.

The Englishman glances over his shoulder as he drives.
'Taking a nap.'
'I'm sure it's needed.'

All through the trip he stops for everyone he sees at the roadside. Some are not hitching at all, never expecting to be given a lift anywhere, just walking in the heat outside with an empty plastic can to be filled with water or paraffin or whatever it is they buy in some country store, or standing at some point between departure and destination, small children and bundles linked on either side, baby on back. She hasn't said anything to him. He would only misunderstand if she explained why one doesn't give lifts in this country; and if she pointed out that in spite of this, she doesn't mind him breaking the sensible if unfortunate rule, he might misunderstand that, as well—think she was boasting of her disregard for personal safety weighed in the balance against decent concern for fellow beings.

He persists in making polite conversation with these passengers because he doesn't want to be patronizing; picking them up like so many objects and dropping them off again, silent, smelling of smoke from open cooking fires, sun and sweat, there behind his head. They don't understand his Englishman's English and if he gets an answer at all it's a deaf man's guess at what's called for. Some grin with pleasure, and embarrass him by showing it the way they'vẹ been taught is acceptable, invoking him as *baas* and *master* when they get out and give thanks. But although he doesn't know it, being too much concerned with those names thrust into his hands like whips whose purpose is repugnant to him, has nothing to do with him, she knows each time that there is a moment of annealment in the air-conditioned hired car belonging to nobody—a moment like that on a no-man's-land bridge in which an accord between warring countries is signed—when there is no calling of names, and all belong in each other's presence. He doesn't feel it because he has no wounds, nor has inflicted, nor will inflict any.

This one standing at the roadside with his transistor radio in a plastic bag was actually thumbing a lift like a townee; his expectation marked him out. And when her companion to whom she was showing the country inevitably pulled up, she read the face at the roadside immediately: the lively, cajoling, performer's eyes, the salmon-pinkish cheeks and nostrils, and as he jogged over smiling, the unselfconscious gap of gum between the canines.

A sleeper is always absent; although present, there on the back seat.

'The way he spoke about black people, wasn't it surprising? I mean—he's black himself.'

'Oh no he's not. Couldn't you see the difference? He's a Cape Coloured. From the way he speaks English—couldn't you hear he's not like the Africans you've talked to?'

But of course he hasn't seen, hasn't heard: the fellow is dark enough, to those who don't know the signs by which you're classified, and the melodramatic, long-vowelled English is as difficult to follow if more fluent than the terse, halting responses of blacker people.

'Would he have a white grandmother or even a white father, then?'

She gives him another of the little history lessons she has been supplying along the way. The Malay slaves brought by the Dutch East India Company to their supply station, on the route to India, at the Cape in the seventeenth century; the Hottentots who were the indigenous inhabitants of that part of Africa; add Dutch, French, English, German settlers whose backyard progeniture with these and other blacks began a people who are all the people in the country mingled in one bloodstream. But encounters along the road teach him more than her history lessons, or the political analyses in which they share the same ideological approach although he does not share responsibility for the experience to which the ideology is being applied. She has explained Acts, Proclamations, Amendments. The Group Areas Act, Resettlement Act, Orderly Movement and Settlement of Black Persons Act. She has translated these statute book euphemisms: people as movable goods. People packed onto trucks along with their stoves and beds while front-end loaders scoop away their homes into rubble. People dumped somewhere else. Always somewhere else. People as the figures, decimal points and multiplying zero-zero-zeros into which individual lives—Black Persons Orderly-Moved, -Effluxed, -Grouped—coagulate and compute. Now he has here in the car the intimate weary odour of a young man to whom these things happen.

'Half his family sick . . . it must be pretty unhealthy, where they've been made to go.'

She smiles. 'Well, I'm not too sure about that. I had the feeling, some of what he said . . . they're theatrical by nature. You must take it with a pinch of salt.'

'You mean about the mother and sisters and so on?'

She's still smiling, she doesn't answer.

'But he couldn't have made up about taking a job so far from home—and the business of sending his wages to his mother? That too?'

He glances at her.

Beside him, she's withdrawn as the other one, sleeping behind him. While he turns his attention back to the road, she is looking at him secretly, as if somewhere in his blue eye registering the approaching road but fixed on the black faces he is trying to read, somewhere in the lie of his inflamed hand and arm that on their travels have been plunged in the sun as if in boiling water, there is the place through which the worm he needs to be infected with can find a way into him, so that he may host it and become its survivor, himself surviving through being fed on. Become like her. Complicity is the only understanding.

'Oh it's true, it's all true . . . not in the way he's told about it. Truer than the way he told it. All these things happen to them. And other things. Worse. But why burden us? Why try to explain to us? Things so far from what we know, how will they ever explain? How will we react? Stop our ears? Or cover our faces? Open the door and throw him out? They·don't know. But sick mothers and brothers gone to the bad—these are the staples of misery, mmh? Think of the function of charity in the class struggles in your own country in the nineteenth century; it's all there in your literature. The lord-of-the-manor's compassionate daughter carrying hot soup to the dying cottager on her father's estate. The 'advanced' upper-class woman comforting her cook when the honest drudge's daughter takes to whoring for a living. *Shame,* we say here. Shame. You must've heard it? We think it means, what a pity; we think we are expressing sympathy—for them. *Shame.* I don't know what we're saying about ourselves.' She laughs.

'So you think it would at least be true that his family were kicked out of their home, sent away?'

'Why would anyone of them need to make that up? It's an everyday affair.'

'What kind of place would they get, where they were moved?'

'Depends. A tent, to begin with. And maybe basic materials to build themselves a shack. Perhaps a one-room prefab. Always a tin toilet set down in the veld, if nothing else. Some industrialist must be making a fortune out of government contracts for those toilets. You build your new life round that toilet. His people are Coloured, so it could be they were sent where there were houses of some sort already built for them; Coloureds usually get something a bit better than blacks are given.'

'And the house would be more or less as good as the one they had? People as poor as that—and they'd spent what must seem a fortune to them, fixing it up.'

'I don't know what kind of house they had. We're not talking about slum clearance, my dear; we're talking about destroying communities because they're black, and white people want to build houses or factories for whites where blacks live. I told you. We're talking about loading up trucks and carting black people out of sight of whites.'

'And even where he's come to work—Pietersburg, whatever-it's-called—he doesn't live in the town.'

'Out of sight.' She has lost the thought for a moment, watching to make sure the car takes the correct turning. 'Out of sight. Like those mothers and grannies and brothers and sisters far away on the Cape Flats.'

'I don't think it's possible he actually sends all his pay. I mean how would one eat?'

'Maybe what's left doesn't buy anything he really wants.'

Not a sound, not a sigh in sleep, behind them. They can go on talking about him as he always has been discussed, there and yet not there.

Her companion is alert to the risk of gullibility. He verifies the facts, smiling, just as he converts, mentally, into pounds and pence any sum spent in foreign coinage. 'He didn't sell the radio. When he said he'd sold all his things on the road, he forgot about that.'

'When did he say he'd last eaten?'

'Yesterday. He said.'

She repeats what she has just been told: 'Yesterday.' She is looking through the glass that takes the shine of heat off the landscape passing as yesterday passed, time measured by the ticking second-hand of moving trees, rows of crops, country-store stoeps, filling stations, spiny crook'd fingers of giant euphorbia. Only the figures by the roadside waiting, standing still.

Personal remarks can't offend someone dead-beat in the back. 'How d'you think such a young man comes to be without front teeth?'

She giggles whisperingly and keeps her voice low, anyway. 'Well, you may not believe me if I tell you . . .'

'Seems odd . . . I suppose he can't afford to have them replaced.'

'It's—how shall I say—a sexual preference. Most usually you see it in their young girls, though. They have their front teeth pulled when they're about seventeen.'

She feels his uncertainty, his not wanting to let comprehension lead him to a conclusion embarrassing to an older woman. For her part, she is wondering whether he won't find it distasteful if—at her de-sexed age—she should come out with it: for cock-sucking. 'No-one thinks the gap spoils a girl's looks, apparently. It's simply a sign she knows how to please. Same significance between men, I suppose . . . . A form of beauty. So everyone says. We've always been given to understand that's the reason.'

'Maybe it's just another sexual myth. There are so many.'

She's in agreement. 'Black girls. Chinese girls. Jewish girls.'

'And black men?'

'Oh my goodness, you bet. But we white ladies don't talk about that, we only dream, you know! Or have nightmares.'

They're laughing. When they are quiet, she flexes her shoulders against the seat-back and settles again. The streets of a town are flickering their text across her eyes. 'He might have had a car accident. They might have been knocked out in a fight.'

They have to wake him because they don't know where he wants to be set down. He is staring at her lined white face (turned to him, calling him gently), stunned for a moment at this evidence that he cannot be anywhere he ought to be; and now he blinks and smiles his empty smile caught on either side by a canine tooth, and gulps and gives himself a shake like someone coming out of water. 'Sorry! Sorry! Sorry madam!'

What about, she says, and the young man glances quickly, his blue eyes coming round over his shoulder: 'Had a good snooze?'

'Ooh I was finished, master, finished, God bless you for the rest you give me. And with an empty stummick, you know, you dreaming so real. I was dreaming, dreaming, I didn't know nothing about I'm in the car!'

It comes from the driver's seat with the voice (a real Englishman's, from overseas) of one who is hoping to hear something that will explain everything. 'What were you dreaming?'

But there is only hissing, spluttery laughter between the two white pointed teeth. The words gambol. 'Ag, nothing, master, nothing, all *non*-sunce—'

The sense is that if pressed, he will produce for them a dream he didn't dream, a dream put together from bloated images on billboards, discarded calendars picked up, scraps of newspapers blown about—but they interrupt, they're asking where he'd like to get off.

'No, anywhere. Here it's all right. Fine. Just there by the corner. I must go look for someone who'll praps give me a rand for the taxi, because I can't walk so far, I haven't eaten nothing since yesterday . . . just here, the master can please stop just here—'

The traffic light is red, anyway, and the car is in the lane nearest the kerb. Her thin, speckled white arm with a skilled flexible hand but no muscle with which to carry a load of washing or lift a hoe, feels back to release the lock he is fumbling at. 'Up, up, pull it up.' She has done it for him. 'Can't you take a bus?'

'There's no buses Sunday, madam, this place is ve-ery bad for us for transport, I must tell you, we can't get nowhere Sundays, only work-days.' He is out, the plastic bag with the radio under his arm, his feet in their stained, multi-striped jogging sneakers drawn neatly together like those of a child awaiting dismissal. 'Thank you, madam, thank you master, God bless you for what you done.'

163

The confident dextrous hand is moving quickly down in the straw bag bought from a local market somewhere along the route. She brings up a pale blue note (the Englishman recognizes the two-rand denomination of this currency that he has memorized by colour) and turns to pass it, a surreptitious message, through the open door behind her. *Goodbye master madam.* The note disappears delicately as a titbit finger-fed. He closes the door, he's keeping up the patter, *goodbye master, goodbye madam,* and she instructs—'No, bang it. Harder. That's it.' *Goodbye master, goodbye madam*—but they don't look back at him now, they don't have to see him thinking he must keep waving, keep smiling, in case they should look back.

She is the guide and mentor; she's the one who knows the country. She's the one—she knows that too—who is accountable. She must be the first to speak again. 'At least if he's hungry he'll be able to buy a bun or something. And the bars are closed on Sunday.'

GEORGE STEINER
A CONVERSATION
PIECE

A humming as of bees, distant.

—But the Master, Eleazer son of Eleazer, in his commentary of 1611 said—

—That Akhiba, may his name shine in glory, had been mistaken—

—When he wrote that Abraham was altogether free, a man at liberty, the father of freedoms, when God, blessed be His unspeakable Name, called upon him to take the boy, Isaac, to the place of burnt offering.

—By which Akhiba meant to signify that God's commandments are spoken to the spirit of man when that spirit is in a state of sovereignty over its own truth, that commandments to the enslaved and the maddened are empty.

—To which Eleazer son of Eleazer, he of Cracow, retorted—

—'What freedom has man in the face of the summons of the Almighty?' When He commands, our freedom is obedience. Only the servant of God, the absolute servant, is a free man.

—Not so, said Baruch to me, he of Vilna. Not so. When God bade Abraham, our father, take Isaac, his only son, to Mount Moriah, He paused for an answer. Abraham could have said 'No'. He could have said: 'Almighty God, hallowed be Thy Name. You are tempting me. You are putting in my path the supreme temptation, which is unthinking, blind obedience. Such is the obeisance demanded by the Dragon Baal, by the empty gods with dog-heads in Egypt's temples. You are not Moloch, eater of children. What you now await from me is loving denial.' So Baruch, my teacher.

—The journey to the mountain took three days. During which Abraham did not speak to Isaac—

—Nor to God. Who listened closely. Hoping for the answer 'No'. Whose patience was without end and who was saddened. So Baruch, in our *schul* at Vilna, where the almond tree—

—That's crazy. God's foreknowing is total. What need

had He to listen to Abraham. He knew that His commandment would be obeyed, that it was not for man to question. I knew Baruch, your teacher. He was so subtle that in his hands words turned to sand.

—Yet God, blessed blessed be the hem of His unsayable Name and the fire-garment of His glory, did not wholly trust Abraham.

—Another madman.

—No. Listen to me. God's confidence in Abraham was not total. Let me hammer out my meaning. Do not interrupt. If God had been utterly certain that Abraham would strike down the boy, He would have let the sacrifice come to pass. And brought Isaac back to life. For is it not said that God can waken the dead? By putting the ram in the thicket, by saving the child, He left uncertain the final obedience of Abraham. Did not Gamaliel the Kabbalist instruct us that there are moments, openings in the universe, during which God questions His own foreknowledge, during which the Angel of the Unknown, of the nameless, passes across the light of being?

—Gamaliel the heretic. The witch and alchemist of Toledo—

Many voices now, close-crowded.

—That accounts for the gloss—

—Gloss? What gloss, chatterbox?

—In the Talmud in the *yeshivah*. Written in by hand.

—Which *yeshivah*?

—Ours. At Bialik. Saying that Abraham was angry. That anger choked him all the way home. That he did not speak once from Mount Moriah back to Beersheba.

—*Angry*? Our father, Abraham, to whom God had restored Isaac?

—Because the Almighty had not kept faith in him. Because God had not been absolutely certain that Abraham would fulfill His commandment and strike the knife into the boy. In the night after he had heard God's voice, and during the unendurable march to the mountain, Abraham had died many deaths. His senses had frozen. His brain had become like black dust. The heart had stopped its song. There was no ground under his feet, no dawn under his eye-lids. His steps were like those of a bullock when it has been stunned, when the blood is already out of its throat. Those who looked on Abraham saw death walking. The faith in him had grown so mighty, the sinews of obedience so stretched, that there was no room for life. There was doubt in Moses, sanctified be his great name and remembrance. Mutiny in Jeremiah. But Abraham, he the father of our fathers, had been made faith. All else had been purged. He was faith in bone and nerve. No hair, no hair of a hair on him or in his unkempt beard but had become faith and obedience harder than steel. The knife was softer than his hand. The blade might snap. That was Abraham's last fear. But God did not know this. He did not choose to know it. His trust in Abraham, His servant, fell short. Now the Almighty would never have proof of Abraham's infinite faith. He would never know how tight was the knot of Abraham's obedience. As life came back into the old man, as pain came home to him, so did a towering anger. That, said the gloss, is why the silence on Abraham's return journey was more terrible than the silence on the road to Moriah.

 —Error. A false gloss. For has not Jehoshuah of Prague cleared up the matter of the silence? Has he not instructed us—

 —That Abraham's anger was the very opposite. He could not at first, and may he be forgiven, find it in his heart to praise, to thank God for the saving of Isaac. The terror had been too sharp. The temptation too severe for a man to bear. Unendurable because twofold. The temptation to obey was murderous and beyond human understanding. How could God ask such a thing of Abraham, his most faithful servant? The temptation to disobey. But is there anything worse than to deny God's voice, to close one's ears against His calling?

That the Almighty had saved the child did not take away even an atom, an atom's breath of terror from His commandment and the three days thereafter. And what if God *had* taken Isaac? What if Abraham's knife had struck? What then? How could the boy's resurrection make up for his sacrifice, for Abraham's act of slaughter? On the way back to Beersheba, Abraham could not speak to God. The hurt, the doubts gagged his soul. Had not the ram appeared too late in the thicket? How could Abraham live after that moment on the mountain, how could Abraham draw breath after he had carried inside him the slaying of his son? Hence the grey sweat on him during the return, hence the total silence. So Jehoshuah, whom they stoned in Prague.

For an instant the voices dropped. But then, like a grape bursting—
    —Foolishness. Foolishness. Hair-splitting.
    Almost in chorus.
    —God had promised Abraham' 'I will make of thee a great nation'. He had promised father Abraham that his seed would be as are the stars, numberless, inextinguishable even when scattered. He had renewed with Abraham the covenant of hope. That Israel would endure, that Abraham's seed would be sown across the earth. Indestructible as is the living wind.
    —That it would endure despite
    —The destruction of the temple and the loss of Zion
    —Despite massacre and dispersal
    —That we should not be consumed, not finally, in the fiery furnace, in the teeth of the mob, in the charnel house or the *pogrom*—
    —That we shall endure even after they have torn the almond tree from its roots—
    —Like hot ashes through the night. Alive even in death. Alive.
    —'A nation and a company of nations shall be of thee,'

said God to our fathers, despite—

—But how then could Abraham have believed, even for a minute, that the Almighty, sung be His Name of Names, would have him slay Isaac? For without Isaac there could be no lineage, no children of Israel? Answer me that.

—Was it all a game? Play-acting, as at *Purim*? When Haman roars through his black beard that all Jews, both young and old, little children and women, shall perish in one day, and the spoil shall be taken from them for a prey? O, that black roaring. How it frightens us, how the children in the hall hold their breath and crowd close to their parents. Though we know that Esther is in the wings and that evil Haman will hang high. God and Abraham acting out the play of Isaac. To make our hearts breathless. To teach us by terror and by joy, as children must be taught. And Abraham was silent because he knew that all would be well, that he would, through Isaac, be a father to nations. Silent as was Joseph when he recognized his brethren and looked on Benjamin.

—But where then would be Abraham's merit? Play-acting? When the being of God is, as Maimonides taught, truth. A truth so pure that there is no shadow, no shadow of a shadow where it prevails. Abraham was an old man, a very old man—

—Who might have forgotten then, in the numbness of that terrible calling, the terms of God's promise, so long ago, in the land of Ur—

—Who might have thought, in the dizziness of his fear, that God would bring to Sara another son, a child of late evening after Isaac—

—Who could have believed that the Lord, blessed be His Name, had changed purpose, that some other people, and not Israel, would be sanctified among nations. Because even Abraham, father of our fathers, had known sin, being a man. Or so it is argued in the commentary of the learned Ephraim of Mainz. I remember the passage.

—And for all these reasons, or others we are too blind,

too unlettered to apprehend, Abraham might have taken for the voice of God that of a demon—

—That of Satan himself.

—Abraham in his numbness, in his dizziness, in his knowledge of imperfection, mistaking the whisper of Satan for the voice of God. For was it not said by Soloviel the Kabbalist that these two voices, that of God whom we must not name and that of un-namable evil, are so utterly alike. That the difference between them is only that of the sound of a rain-drop in the sea?

—It *was* the voice of Satan. God is no play-actor. Neither is he a sadistic tempter. How do we best define God, how do we seek to imagine Him? Precisely as one who *cannot* ask of a man that he stick a knife in the throat of his child. There is no surer proof that God is than the incapacity of our souls, of our minds, to conceive of Him as tempting Abraham to murder his son, to conceive of Him as torturing Abraham our father during the journey to the mount. Even a gentile, albeit the wisest among them, understood that the definition, the being of God, is proved by the impossibility of the commandment to Abraham. That it was Satan who confounded Abraham and seduced him to his devilish purpose.

—A gentile? What gentile?

—He bore a name like ours: Immanuel. He lived in Koenigsberg.

—In Koenigsberg? I have a cousin there. Menachem the draper. Do you know him, the shop in the old town square? Do you know what has happened—

—And having observed the confusion of Abraham, the Almighty betook Himself to Mount Moriah, set an angel to guard Isaac and wove the ram into the thorn-bush. Perhaps the selfsame bush that would burn for Moses.

—Why then, *rebbi*, did God not intervene at once? Why did He not drive Satan from Abraham's door and take the old man out of his agony? The journey took three whole days. Three long nights Abraham lay awake with the face of Isaac before him, with that knife in his belt. An eternity. Why?

—Our time is not His. Perhaps that ram was not yet born or the bush thick enough. Perhaps in His infinite mercy, the Almighty, praised be He, sought to give Satan a chance, to see whether the Fallen One would feel remorse seeing the sweat on Abraham, and undo his evil trick.

—Though you are a learned man, you speak like a simpleton. You say that we know the being of God, the meaning of Him, just because He could not order Abraham to sacrifice Isaac the child, the only son. You would have us believe that so crazy, so obscene a commandment could come only from Satan. God's existence tells us that Abraham was mistaken when he took the voice of the devil for that of the Lord. You cite a wise man of the gentiles. Perhaps he was wise. But no true Christian. For is the God of the Christians not He who gives His only son in sacrifice, who let His son die in bestial pain on the Roman cross?

A rush of voices.

—But that is not our God. Not ours. Not—

—Our God is one. He does not beget. All men are His sons. The Nazarite was no Messiah. Only a man. Mad, perhaps.

—Let me speak. I do not say that their God is ours, or that Christ was His child. I can attach no meaning to such words. But consider this: only Almighty God, only He who spoke to Job out of the whirlwind and slew the first-born of Egypt, could command Abraham to sacrifice Isaac. Abraham was not mistaken. His hearing was good. Listening to those terrible words, words which should never cross the lips of the living, Abraham *knew* that God was speaking. God is what He is because He alone can demand of his most faithful servant that he slit his child's throat. And it was this knowledge, this understanding beyond reason, which made father Abraham speechless on the journey to the mountain and mute on the road back to Beersheba. We who are fallen into the hand of the living God—

Was the sound nearing? A sound slithering, like smoke across sand.

Next, a voice lime-green and acid.

—Who speaks for Isaac?

Not yet a man's voice. Choked by the first starched collar and the bite of the collar-stud.

—Who speaks for Isaac? It was a hard march. His father Abraham walking too fast. Saying nothing, but pulling him by the hand. Black, impatient as Isaac had never seen his father before, but silent. Isaac saw the dry wood and the flint. He knew that his father was carrying a knife and a whetstone. But where was the lamb for the burnt offering? And when he asked, his father said that God would provide. But the words sounded strange, like the beads of sweat on Abraham's lips. Do you think Isaac believed him? I don't. He must have guessed. From the way in which they hurried from the house, from the way they camped in the night, hardly washing, all under one stinking tent-cloth. Oh, Isaac must have guessed and smelled the knife. And fouled himself in his fear. Marching three days with his bowels cold and loose, trying to sleep three short nights in the stench of his fear. Can you imagine their climb up the mountain? It may be that Abraham carried the wood, giving to Isaac the flint and shavings for the fire. But Isaac must have noticed the rope around the logs. Too thick, too freshly woven. A rope with which to tie a man's hands behind his back. Why did he not scream for help or run back to the young servants whom Abraham had left at the foot of the trail? Isaac's friends. The serving men with whom he played in the court-yard of the house, who brought him the new grapes from the vine and cut arrows for him? Surely they would hide him and spirit him home. Why did Isaac not seize his father's hands and cry out for his life? Why did he not snatch at the knife and throw it over the side of the hill?

—Because the spirit of God was upon him, because he was blessed in obedience.

—Because Abraham's ass, the brindled she-ass whom

Isaac fed, had whispered to him that he need not fear, that an Angel was beside him. There is a *midrasch* which says that the beast of burden spoke comfort to Isaac.

—Fairy-tales. Lies. I will tell you why Isaac did not scream for help or run away or try to stop his father. It was because he was too frightened. It was because his voice had frozen inside him. It was because he was ashamed of the hot dirt and smell in his pants. The shame being even greater than his fear of death. But when Abraham bound him and laid him out on the altar, on that dry, sharp wood, when he heard the knife come out of his father's belt, he screamed. No one heard that scream. Because Isaac was vomiting, because the vomit was in his mouth, like a gag. But I know that he screamed.

—Nowhere in the Torah, nowhere in the scrolls of truth—

—But I hear the scream, said the boy. All around me. And inside my head. Since we left for the station. It is Isaac's scream, which has never ceased.

Refutation is made. But gently.

—You must be mistaken, boy. There was no scream. And even if there had been, it stopped at once. The Angel called out. And Isaac's heart leaped and sang at the great blessing: 'I will multiply thy seed as the stars of the heaven, and as the sand which is upon the sea shore; and thy seed shall possess the gate of his enemies.' And when they came home to Beersheba, they feasted and rejoiced in the Lord. The ass was put to pasture and Isaac the child was given the ram's horn, circled with gold, to blow on. It is that horn you hear, calling to the hills.

—I don't believe you. (Even shriller.) I don't believe you. I can't. It's like the sweets they cram in your mouth after you've had a tooth pulled. Do you know what those sweets taste like? You don't, do you! Of blood and pus.

—But Isaac loved Abraham. His love never wavered. It was Abraham his father who chose Rebekah for him. And when Abraham died at 165 years of age, his blessing was on

Isaac and Isaac tore his hair in grief.

—Bed-time stories. No man lives that long. Isaac never trusted Abraham again. Not for one instant. How could he? How could he forget the walk to Moriah, the faggots, the rope, the knife? The taste of his father's hand on his eyes and mouth, of Abraham's knee in his back, never left him. That is why Isaac was deceived by *his* sons, by Esau and Jacob. No Jewish father looks on his son without remembering that he may be commanded to take back his life. No Jewish son looks on his father without remembering that he may be sacrificed by his father's hand. How can there be trust or forgiveness between us? Blood and pus. Don't you smell it, you who call yourselves teachers, masters of the word?

The young voice skidded, like a cracked pipe, soon inaudible. In the droning dark.

And what of Sarah?
—
A woman speaking. An angry chorus.
—Silence. Silence. Is it not ordained by the Law that no woman shall come to the Torah? That women, though blessed and honoured is their mystery, shall not comment on holy writ?

—Then why are we here, behind the same closed door? You have never given us a sabbatical from pain. Never a leave of absence from massacre. Though you would have us be silent, we are branded like you. Sarah *knew*. How could she not have known? How can any mother not know when her child is taken from her to be slaughtered? Old Abraham told her to be silent, to stay out of God's unfathomable way. But she saw the wood, the rope, the knife. She smelled the cold fear in the old man's groin and the hot fear in the boy's hair. They stole away before sun-up, like foxes from the hen-house. But she was awake. She heard their lying steps on the threshold and the drowsy coughs of the serving-men. She lay awake, did Sarah, crazed with fear, her guts turning to stone. Six nights and six days, her eyes so hot with horror that she could no longer weep. And when they came back from the mountain, the men and the boy—her child, her only son— they told her to prepare a great feast, to deck the great table with fresh green, to send for flute-players and dancers from Ashod. When all she wanted was to hold the child, so close he would feel the fire in her bones, and cry out her pain. During those six days and nights, Sarah's whole life had passed before her. How Abraham had handed her over to Abimelech, king of Gerar, how he had handed her over for the king to whore with, lying to save his own precious hide, saying 'she is my sister.' How other women had laughed at her, behind their fluttering hands, when she became pregnant with Isaac, how no one believed that the old frozen man was Isaac's father— did Abraham himself believe it? Sarah saw before her the years during which she had had to endure in her house, in her kitchen, in the vegetable garden, Hagar the Egyptian and the dark son she had borne Abraham, how she had had to endure the scent of burnt almonds from Hagar's skin, Abraham's scent. And even as she lay dying, Sarah heard, in Abraham's train, the chirping of women, of the concubines that came with him to Hebron. Do you really think she did not know, in her parched hollowness, that Abraham would, immediately after her death, take to wife Keturah, the girl with the good teeth? But what did it matter, what did anything matter after those days of Mount Moriah, after this boy's footsteps had been taken from the house? What could make up for that? The Holy Books report nothing of Sarah's torture. No learned commentator reports what she felt when she heard the lick of the ass's hoofs on the cobbles but dared not look whether Isaac was among the men coming home. No man, no one who has not borne a child, can imagine that. We women are not called up to read the Torah. A good thing for you. It is between the lines we would be reading, between every two lines. For in that space lies the silence of women. Who have had no say among you. It is the loudest silence in the world. Loud with the cries of labour and with the cries of all the mothers who have seen their children beaten to death in front of their eyes. But now you must hear it, you men. In this meeting-house we no longer sit and pray apart from you. Here we also are called, we daughters of silence.

Another woman's voice, and a third: Dance, Miriam, dance. In this small house—

Too small, really. Not a dancing-floor at all. Not that it terribly mattered. Men and women, oh, impropriety, young and old, were now welded so close that the merest motion, a raw breath out of a single mouth, quivered through the lot.

—A thousand years you men have argued, ravelled, spun words. You have read yourselves blind, crooked your backs, poring over the single letter or the missing vowel. A thousand years you have chanted and swayed as if truth could be caught in your fingers. You have burrowed for meaning like starved mice and pounded the words so fine they have fallen to dust. Living men, their lips caked with dust, as are the buried. You have hissed and croaked at one another, owls at noon-time. We have heard you when we passed the closed shutters of the schools, we have heard you when you lay beside us in the night, expostulators, litigants, cross-examiners, word-peddlers even in your dreams. To what end? Have you found those syllables which make up the secret name of God? What pun, what game of hidden numbers has made us free? Was it all for *this*?

—Thought is the dance of the mind. The spirit dances when it seeks out meaning, and the meaning of that meaning. Perhaps there is in the forty-ninth letter of the forty-ninth verse of the forty-ninth chapter of the Book of Books, which lies hidden in the Torah as the Torah rolls lie cloaked inside their shrine, a truth so mighty that God Himself must pause when He remembers it. The dance-steps of the soul are words, woman. The lords of the dance are we. Are we not dancing now?

Up steps of air.
    Which grew steeper and steeper.
    Mountainous. Higher than Moriah.
    —Dance, Miriam, dance, said the spigot in the ceiling.
    —There is no ram now and the bush is burning.

Dancers, their mouths wide open. So that the hive swarmed into their throats. And hummed to them the slurred slow song of ash.

SALMAN RUSHDIE
ON GÜNTER GRASS

In the summer of 1967, when the West was—perhaps for the last time—in the clutches of the optimism disease, when the microscopic, invisible bacillus of optimism made its young people believe that they would overcome some day, when unemployment was an irrelevance and the future still existed, and when I was twenty years old, I bought from a bookshop in Cambridge a paperback copy of Ralph Manheim's English translation of *The Tin Drum*. In those days everybody had better things to do than read. There was the music and there were the movies and there was also, don't forget, the world to change. Like many of my contemporaries I spent my student years under the spell of Buñuel, Godard, Ray, Wajda, Welles, Bergman, Kurosawa, Jancsó, Antonioni, Dylan, Lennon, Jagger, Laing, Marcuse and, inevitably, the two-headed fellow known to Grass readers as Marxengels. In spite of all these distractions, however, Oskar Matzerath's autobiography had me hooked, and I stayed hooked all the way from grandmother Anna Koljaiczek's wide skirt, past fizz powder and horse's head full of eels, right up to Anna's dark opposite, the wicked Black Witch.

There are books that open doors for their readers, doors in the head, doors whose existence they had not previously suspected. And then there are readers who dream of becoming writers; they are searching for the strangest door of all, scheming up ways to travel through the page, to end up inside and also behind the writing, to lurk between the lines while other readers, in their turn, pick up books and begin to dream. For these Alices, these would-be migrants from the World to the Book, there are (if they are lucky) books which give them permission to travel, so to speak, permission to become the sort of writers they have it in themselves to be. A passport is a kind of book. And my passports, the works that gave me the permits I needed, were *The Film Sense* by Serge Eisenstein, the 'Crow' poems of Ted Hughes, Borges's *Fictions*, Sterne's *Tristram Shandy*, Ionesco's play *Rhinoceros*—and, that summer of 1967, *The Tin Drum*.

This is what Grass's great novel said to me in its drumbeats: Go for broke. Always try and do too much. Dispense with safety nets. Take a deep breath before you begin talking. Aim for the stars. Keep grinning. Be bloody-minded. Argue with the world. And never forget that writing is as close as we get to keeping a hold on the thousand and one things—childhood, certainties, cities, doubts, dreams, instants, phrases, parents, loves—that go on slipping, like sand, through our fingers. I have tried to learn the lessons of the midget drummer. And one more, which I got from that other, immense work, *Dog Years*: When you've done it once, start all over again and do it better.

Günter Grass, Danzig's most famous son (Lech Walesa, the only other contender for the title, inhabits—it's important to insist—not Danzig but Gdańsk), who now lives partly in Berlin—a city which itself seems to have migrated to a new and starker location—and partly in a north German landscape which reminds him of the wide, diked vistas of his writing and his youth, is a figure of central importance in the literature of migration, and the migrant is, perhaps, the central or defining figure of the twentieth century. And like many migrants, like many people who have lost a city, he has found it in his luggage, packed in an old tin box. Kundera's Prague, Joyce's Dublin, Grass's Danzig: exiles, refugees, migrants have carried many cities in their bedrolls in this century of wandering. And let nobody underestimate the obstinacy of such writers; they will not tolerate the Gdansking of their past. In Grass's transported city Labesweg is still Labesweg, and the shipyard which saw the birth of Solidarity is not called Lenin, but Schichau. (Here, once again, I feel a small affinity. I grew up on Warden Road, Bombay; now it's Bhulabhai Desai Road. I went to school near Flora Fountain; now the school is near Hutatma Chowk. Of course the new, decolonized names tell of a confident, assertive spirit in the independent state; but the loss of past attachments remains a loss. What to do? Shrug. And pickle the past in books.)

In one sense, Grass is less than a complete migrant. A full migrant suffers, traditionally, a triple disruption: he loses his place, he enters into an alien language, and he finds himself surrounded by beings whose social behaviour and code is very unlike, and sometimes even offensive to, his own. And this is what makes migrants such important figures: because roots, language and social norms have been three of the most important parts of the definition of what it is to be a human being. The migrant, denied all three, is obliged to find new ways of describing himself, new ways of being human.

Well, Grass certainly lost his place (and, as I suggested, found that he'd brought it along with him). It's possible to argue that he lost a part of his language, the Kashubian dialects of his youth which he attempted to preserve in his literature; but here I'm on thin ice, as my knowledge of German is probably about as great as Grass's knowledge of Urdu . . . . At any rate, apart from the dialects, it seems difficult to suggest that Grass is a writer out of language, and certainly he has remained within a society whose social mores are known to him. Indeed, as his essays show, his dedication to the idea of a German civilisation which embraces both West and East Germany and which finds its true expression in the German language, is complete. One may therefore legitimately ask how useful this notion of a half-migrant Grass, a maybe-only-one-third-migrant Grass, really is.

I think it is useful, because there are other senses in which Grass seems to me very much more than merely a fragment or percentage of a migrant writer. Migration across national frontiers is by no means the only form of the phenomenon. In many ways, given the international and increasingly homogeneous nature of metropolitan culture, the journey from, for example, the Scottish Highlands to London is a more extreme act of migration than a move from, say, Bombay. But I want to go further than such literalistic discussion: because migration also offers us one of the richest metaphors of our age. The very word *metaphor*, with its roots in the Greek words for *bearing across*, describes a sort of migration, the migration of ideas into images. Migrants—borne-across humans—are metaphorical beings in their very essence; and migration, seen as a metaphor, is everywhere around us. We all cross frontiers; in that sense, we are all migrant peoples.

Günter Grass is a migrant from his past, and now I am no longer talking about Danzig. He grew up, as he has said, in a house and a milieu in which the Nazi view of the world was treated quite simply as objective reality. Only when the Americans came at the war's end and the young Grass began to hear how things had really been in Germany did he understand that the lies and distortions of the Nazis were not the plain truth. What an experience: to discover that one's entire picture of the world is false, and not only false, but based upon a monstrosity. What a task for any individual: the reconstruction of reality from rubble.

I am suggesting that we can see this process as an act of migration, from an old self into a new one. That the end of World War II was for Grass, as it was for Germany, as tough and disrupting a frontier to cross as any one can imagine. And if we call Grass a migrant of this type, we quickly discover that the triple dislocation classically suffered by migrants has indeed been in operation in the case of Migrant Grass, the man who migrated across history. The first dislocation, remember, is the loss of roots. Grass lost not only Danzig: he lost—he must have lost—the sense of home as a safe, 'good' place. How could it retain that feeling in the light of what he learned about it at the war's end? The second dislocation is linguistic. We know—and Grass has written often and eloquently— of the effect of the Nazi period on the German language, of the need for the language to be rebuilt, pebble by pebble, from the wreckage; because a language in which evil finds so expressive a voice is a dangerous tongue. The practitioners of 'rubble literature'—Grass himself being one of the most prominent—took upon themselves the Herculean task of re-inventing the German language, of tearing it apart, ripping out the poisoned parts, and putting it back together.

And the third disruption is social. Once again we can argue that the transformation in German society, or, rather, in the Germany that the growing Grass knew and experienced, was of the same order as the change in social codes that a migrant from one country to another experiences: that Nazi Germany was, in some ways, another country. Grass had to unlearn that country, that way of thinking about society, and learn a new one.

I see Grass, then, as a double migrant: a traveller across borders in the self, and in Time. The vision underlying his writing, both fiction and non-fiction, is in many ways, I believe, a migrant's vision.

This is what the triple disruption of reality teaches migrants: that reality is an artefact, that it does not exist until it is made, and that, like any other artefact, it can be made well or badly, and that it can also, of course, be unmade. What Grass learned on his journey across the frontiers of history was Doubt. Now he distrusts all those who claim to possess absolute forms of knowledge; he suspects all total explanations, all systems of thought which purport to be complete. Among the world's great writers, he is quintessentially the artist of uncertainty, whose symbol might easily have been the question mark if it were not the Snail. To experience any form of migration is to get a lesson in the importance of tolerating others' points of view. One might almost say that migration ought to be essential training for all would-be democrats.

About that Snail. This social-democratic mollusc, under whose spiralling shell are housed the ideas of hurrying slowly, caution, circumspection, and gradualism, has served Grass well, and also earned him his share of brickbats from those who advocate more rapid rates of advance. I don't want to enter that dispute here, noting only that there are times—for instance during his advocacy of nuclear disarmament—when Grass himself appears far from Snailesque. But I should like to use the Snail as evidence that Grass lives more comfortably in images, in ideas, than in places. This, too, is a characteristic of migrants. He is, after all, a metaphorical being.

The migrant intellect roots itself in itself, in its own capacity for imagining and re-imagining the world. This can lead to difficulties: is it because the United States is a migrants' culture that its citizens can, at times (election campaigns, for instance), appear to prefer image to substance? But the love of images also contains great potential. When the world is seen through ideas, through metaphors, it becomes a richer place. When Grass looks at Czechoslovakia through the writing of Kafka, or contemporary Japanese urban sprawl through the images of Alfred Döblin, he helps us see more, and more clearly.

A writer who understands the artificial nature of reality is more or less obliged to enter the process of making it. This is perhaps why Grass has so determinedly sought a public rôle, why he has used his great fame as a novelist as a platform from which to speak on the many issues—the bomb, the invasion of our privacy by data banks, the relationship between the nations of the rich North and the poor South—which concern him. And since to argue about reality is to be at once creative and political, it is not surprising that when Grass writes about literature he finds himself writing about politics, and when he discusses political issues, the quirky perspectives of literature have a habit of creeping in.

In his essay 'The Destruction of Mankind Has Begun' Grass makes the telling point that, for the first time in the history of the species, writers can no longer assume the existence of posterity. He says that, as a result, 'the book I am planning to write . . . will have to include a farewell to the damaged world, to wounded creatures, to us and our minds, which have thought of everything and the end as well.' The composition of elegies is indeed one of the proper responses for a writer to make when night is drawing in. But outside his fiction, in his political activities and writings, Grass is making a second, and equally proper response. What this work says is: we aren't dead yet. We may be in deep trouble but we aren't done for. And while there is life, there must be analysis, struggle, persuasion, argument, polemic, re-thinking, and all the other longish words that add up to one very short word: hope.

GÜNTER GRASS
THE TIN DRUM
IN RETROSPECT

In the spring and summer of 1952 I hitch-hiked back and forth across France. I lived on nothing. I sketched on wrapping paper and, infected with logorrhea, wrote and wrote. Along with a number of exceedingly derivative cantos about the pilot Palinurus who fell asleep at the helm, I turned out an endlessly proliferating poem in which Oskar Matzerath, before assuming that name, made his appearance as a stylite saint.

A young man, an existentialist in accordance with the fashion of the day. A mason by trade. He lived in our times. A savage, rather haphazardly well read, not afraid of quotation. Even before prosperity erupted, he was disgusted by prosperity and in love with his disgust. Right in the middle of his small town (which remained nameless), he therefore built himself a pillar and chained himself to the top. His vituperative mother handed up his meals in a dinner pail fixed to a pole. Her attempts to lure him down to earth were supported by a chorus of young girls with mythological hair-dos. The small town's traffic circled round his pillar, friends and enemies gathered, and in the end a whole community was looking up at him. He, the stylite, high above them all, looked down, nonchalantly alternating fixed leg and free-moving leg; he had found his perspective and expressed it through a volley of metaphors.

This long poem was a flop. I left it somewhere, and I remember only fragments, which show, if anything, how much I was influenced by Trakl, Apollinaire, Ringelnatz, Rilke, and the wretched German translations of Lorca, all at once. Its only interesting feature was my quest for a perspective. But the stylite's elevated situation was too static: it would take a diminutive three-year-old Oskar Matzerath to provide both distance and nobility. You might call Oskar Matzerath a converted stylite.

In the late summer of that same year, while crossing Switzerland on my way from southern France to Düsseldorf, I not only met my future wife Anna for the first time, but also saw something that brought my saint down from his pillar. One afternoon I saw among a group of adults drinking coffee a three-year-old boy with a tin drum. I was struck by the three-year-old's self-absorbed concentration on his instrument, his disregard of the world around him (grown-ups chatting over their afternoon coffee), and the image has stayed with me.

189

For at least three years my find remained buried. I moved from Düsseldorf to Berlin, changed sculpture teachers, met Anna again, married her a year later, dragged my sister (who had got herself into a mess) out of a convent, sketched and modelled bird-like figures, grasshoppers and filigree chickens, and botched my first attempt at a prose piece—that was called *The Barrier*, patterned on Kafka, and derived its plethora of metaphors from the early Expressionists. Only then, being more relaxed, did I succeed in writing my first occasional poems, casual offerings accompanied by drawings, that were detached and independent enough from their author to be publishable. *The Advantages of Windhens* was the title, my first book.

With the baggage of stored-up material, vague plans and precise ambitions—I wanted to write my novel and Anna was looking for more rigorous ballet training—we left Berlin early in 1956 and, penniless but undaunted, went to Paris. Not far from the Place Pigalle, Anna found an exacting Russian ballet teacher in the person of Madame Nora. And I, while still putting the finishing touches to my play *The Wicked Cooks*, set to work on the first draft of my novel, whose title changed from *Oskar the Drummer* to *The Drummer* to *The Tin Drum*.

At that precise point my memory cuts off. I remember drawing up a number of outlines mapping out my epic material, and filling them with catchwords, but the outlines cancelled one another out and were dropped as the work progressed. The manuscripts of the first, second and finally third drafts fed the furnace which was located in my work room.

'Granted: I am an inmate of a mental hospital . . .'—with that first sentence my block was gone. Words pressed in on me; memory, imagination, playfulness and an obsession with detail gave themselves free rein: chapter engendered chapter. When a gap emerged, breaking the flow of my story, I hopped over it. History came to my aid with local offerings—as if little jars were sprung open, releasing smells. I took on a wildly proliferating family. I argued with Oskar Matzerath and his clan about tram lines, about simultaneous events and the absurd pressure of chronology, about Oskar's right to tell his story in the first or third person, about his desire to beget a child, about his real transgressions and his feigned feelings of guilt.

My attempt to give Oskar the loner a vicious little sister was thwarted by Oskar's objection; it seems quite possible that the excluded sister later insisted on her right to literary existence under the name of Tulla Pokriefke in *Cat and Mouse* and *Dog Years*.

Far more distinctly than the process of writing I remember my work-room: a damp hole on the ground floor. It was also my art studio, but once I started putting *The Tin Drum* on paper, my sculpture casts crumbled away. My work-room was also the furnace room for the tiny two-room apartment upstairs. My activities as fireman and writer were closely meshed. Whenever the writing met with a snag, I'd go and get two buckets of coke out of the cellar. My work-room smelled of mould and the cozy aroma of gas. Dripping walls kept my imagination flowing. The dampness of the room may have encouraged the dryness of Oskar Matzerath's wit.

Because my wife is Swiss I was allowed once a year to write for a few weeks during the summer in the fresh air of the Ticino. I would sit at a stone table in an arbour of grape-vines, gaze at the shimmering subtropical stage set and, sweating, write about the frozen Baltic.

Sometimes for a change of air I'd scribble outlines of chapters in Paris bistros straight out of old movies: surrounded by tragically enlaced lovers, old women hidden in their coats, wall mirrors and Art Nouveau decorations, I'd write something about elective affinities: Goethe and Rasputin.

And yet during all that time I must still have lived energetically, cooked usefully, and, owing to the pleasure I took in Anna's dancing legs, danced whenever opportunity offered. Because in September 1957—I was in the midst of the second draft—our twin sons Franz and Raoul were born. The problem wasn't literary, only financial. We lived on the carefully apportioned 300 marks a month that I earned more or less in passing. Sometimes I think that what saved me—much as it distressed my father and mother—was the mere fact of not graduating from secondary school. With a degree I'd have become a night programme television director and kept my manuscript in the drawer and, prevented from writing, I'd have developed an increasing grudge against all those free-ranging scribblers whom the heavenly father feedeth all the same.

191

In the spring of 1958 my work on the final draft of the chapter about the defence of the Polish Post Office in Danzig necessitated a trip to Poland. Höllerer arranged it; Andrzey Wirth wrote out an invitation, and I went to Gdańsk via Warsaw. Looking for Danzig in Gdańsk, and on the assumption that some of the defenders of the Polish Post Office would still be alive, I inquired at the Polish Ministry of the Interior, which maintained a bureau devoted to documenting German war crimes in Poland. There I was given the addresses of three former Polish postal clerks (the most recent address dating from 1949), but I was also informed that these alleged survivors had not been recognized by the Polish Postal Workers' Union, or any other official body: because in the autumn of 1939 both German and Polish official sources had reported that these men had all been court-martialed and shot; that their names had accordingly been inscribed on a memorial tablet; and that people incised in stone are dead.

Eventually, I found two of the former Polish postal clerks. They'd since gone to work in the shipyard, where they were earning more than they had at the post office. All in all, they were content with their lack of recognition, but their sons wanted to regard their fathers as heroes and had tried without success to get them acknowledged as resistance fighters. From the two Post Office employees (one had delivered money orders) I obtained detailed accounts of what happened in the Post Office during its defence. Their escape routes were something I could not have made up.

In Gdańsk I retraced the routines of a Danzig schoolboy, spoke in graveyards with tombstones that made me nostalgic, sat as I had as a boy in the reading room of the municipal library, leafing through piles of the *Danziger Vorposten*. I smelled the Mottlau and the Radaune. In Gdańsk I was a stranger, but in fragments I rediscovered everything: bathing establishments, walks in the woods, brick Gothic, and the apartment house on Labesweg between Max-Halbe-Platz and Neuer Markt; and revisited, on Oskar's advice, the Church of the Sacred Heart: still the same old Catholic fug.

Then I stood in the kitchen-cum-living-room of my Kashubian grand-aunt Anna. She didn't believe who I was until I showed her my passport: 'My goodness, Günter child, you've got so big.' I stayed a while and listened: when the defenders of the Polish Post Office surrendered, her son Franz had indeed been shot. I found his name incised in stone on the memorial tablet: officially recognized.

In the spring of 1959, when I'd finished work on my manuscript, corrected the galleys and dispatched the page proofs, I was given a four-month travel grant. Once again Höllerer had pulled strings. The idea was for me to go to the United States and answer students' questions now and then. I never went. To get a visa in those days you had to submit to an exacting medical examination. I submitted and was told that tuberculomas—bone-like nodules—had been found here and there in my lungs; when tuberculomas break open, cavities form.

For that reason, and also because after one night in the custody of the Paris police (by that time de Gaulle had come to power) I was overcome by a positive longing for the West German police, we left Paris soon after *The Tin Drum* was published (and soon after it left me), and moved back to Berlin. There I had to take afternoon naps, do without alcohol, be examined at regular intervals, drink cream, and three times a day swallow little white pills called Neoteben—all of which cured me and made me fat.

While still in Paris, however, I had done some preparatory work on my novel *Dog Years*. Originally it was called 'Potato Peelings', a short-winded project that got off to a bad start. It took my novella *Cat and Mouse* to make me drop it. By then I was already famous, though, and no longer had to stoke the furnace while I wrote. Since then I've found it harder to write.

Translated from the German by Ralph Manheim

Nº 4 – Printemps 1985

LETTRE

INTERNATIONALE

Directeurs A.J. LIEHM, PAUL NOIROT

MILAN KUNDERA
ENCORE SUR LE ROMAN

**LES RICHES
LES PAUVRES
LES AUTRES**

R. DAHRENDORF
J.K. GALBRAITH
H. SCHMIDT E. NOSOV

**DU
MODERNISME
DE L'ART
DE L'ARGENT**

R. BARILLI
R. SHATTUCK
A. SAURA
R. HUGHES

PETER WEISS
LES VAINCUS

W. CROMWELL F. ETKIND J.M. SIMMEL

MAX
FRISCH
L'EXIL

J. BERGER
H. NEF
K. MICHAŁ
G. KUNERT

Le numéro 30 F. Abonnement 100 F, étranger 140 F.
14-16, rue des Petits-Hôtels, 75010 Paris Tél. (1) 523-48-40 – FRANCE

JOHN BERGER
GO ASK THE TIME

Once there was a young man who said to himself: this story about everybody having to die, that's not for me. I'm going to find a place where nobody ever dies. And so he says goodbye to his parents and his family, and he sets off on a journey. And after several months, he meets an old man, with a beard down to his chest, trundling rocks in a wheelbarrow off a mountainside. And he says to the old man: Do you know that place where nobody ever dies?

The old man says: Stay with me, and you won't die until I have carted away in my wheelbarrow all this mountain.

How long will that take?

Oh, at least a hundred years.

No, said the young man, I'm going to find that place where nobody ever dies.

He travels on, and he meets a second old man with a beard down to his waist. This old man is on the edge of a forest that seems to go on for ever and ever. And he's cutting branches off a tree. The young man says: I'm looking for that place where nobody ever dies.

Stay with me, says the old man, and you won't die until I've cut off the branches of every tree in this forest.

How long will that take?

At least two hundred years.

No. I'm going to find that place where nobody ever dies.

He meets a third old man with a beard down to his knees, and this old man is watching a duck drinking sea water from the ocean. Do you know that place where nobody ever dies?

And the old man answers: Stay with me and you won't die until this duck has drunk the whole ocean.

How long will that take?

Oh, at least three hundred years, and who wants to live longer than that?

The young man went on. And he came to a castle. The door opened and there was an old man, with a beard reaching down to his toes. I'm looking for that place where nobody ever dies.

You've found it, replies the old man.

Can I come in?

Yes, I would be glad, very glad, of company . . . .

Time passes. And one day the young man says: You know, I'd like to go back—just for a moment, I won't stay. I just want to go back to say hello to my parents and to see where I was born.

The old man says: Centuries have gone by, they're all dead.

I'd still like to go back if only—if only to see the street where I was born.

So the old man says: All right, follow my instructions carefully. You go to the stable, you take my white horse, a horse as fast as the wind, and never get off him. If you get off that horse, you'll die.

The young man mounts the horse and rides away. After a while he comes to the beach where the duck was drinking the sea. The sea bed is now as dry as a prairie. The horse stops at a little heap of white bones—all that is left of the old man with a beard down to his knees. How right I was not to stop here, says the young man to himself. And he goes on, and he comes to where he saw the forest. The forest is now pasture land—not a single tree is left. The young man goes on and comes to where the mountain was. The mountain is as flat as a plain. For the third time he says to himself: How right I was not to stop here!

Finally he arrives at the town where he was born. He recognizes—nothing. Everything has changed. He feels so lost, he decides to go back to the castle. One day on his return journey, towards nightfall, he sees a cart drawn by an ox. The cart is piled high with old, worn-out boots and shoes. As he passes, the carter cries out: Stop, stop! Please get down. Look, a wheel of my cart is stuck in the mud. I'm alone. Please help me.

The young man answers back: I'm in a hurry, I won't stop and I can't get off my horse.

The carter pleads: It will be dark in a moment, it'll freeze tonight, I'm old and you're young, please help me. So, out of pity, the young man gets off his horse. Before his second foot is out of the stirrup, the carter grasps him by the arm and says: Do you know who I am? I am Death. Look in the cart at all those boots and shoes I wore out chasing you! Now I have found you. Nobody ever escapes me . . . .

The two Italian stories narrated in this essay were occasioned by Italo Calvino's collection *Italian Folk Tales*.

This story, first told centuries ago near Verona in Italy, can still speak to us. The inexorability of time, the inevitability of death, the desire for immortality—none of this has changed. Yet something has changed. The original listeners to the story would, I think, have attributed the young man's vain and useless attempts to escape death to a lack of wisdom. They would have found in him a blindness to what was important, to what lay beyond the temporal. They would have seen him as a kind of opportunist. Today we would simply say the young man lacked realism. We see him not as an opportunist, but as a kind of dreamer.

The difference between the two understandings of the story is related, in part, to the decline of religious faith, but it is also related to a change in the way we approach the enigma of time. For the original listeners in Verona there lay, beyond the centuries which the young man cunningly acquired for himself, the domain of the timeless, of that which is outside or beyond time. For us the timeless does not exist; there is no place for it. Or at least no rational place.

Here is another story; it happened a little while ago in the next village. Jean, who works in the sawmill, lived with a woman whom he called Mother. She was about ten years older.

This woman had run away from her husband and children in the northern coal-fields, and had come to work as a servant in the local hotel. There, one morning, Jean noticed her because she was crying while picking beans in the vegetable garden behind the hotel kitchen. She said she couldn't bear the thought of returning to the north—her husband beat her—could she stay with him in the village? She would cook for him.

She wore short dresses and had pretty legs. She cried and laughed unselfconsciously. Although fifty-years old, she seemed, a little, as if she had just left school. He told her she could stay with him.

They lived together for four years and then she fell ill. She lost her memory. She could no longer pick beans or untie knots. If she went to the village, she couldn't find her way home. She accused Jean of being unfaithful. She forgot to dress properly, and now it was Jean who cooked for her.

Eventually the doctors named her illness 'premature senility'. To Jean it seemed that she was returning to childhood. Then they told him her blood pressure was too low, so she must be sent to hospital. He accompanied her.

Just slip away, the doctor at the hospital said to Jean, don't let her know you are leaving.

When two days later he went back to the hospital to visit her, she was tear-stained and cowed like a prisoner. The specialist in his white coat behind an oak desk told Jean that her illness was incurable. There was nothing to be done. She would get worse and worse and the illness would kill her.

Jean pondered the matter for a long while. He thought about it when he was sawing wood, when he was sleeping in the bed they used to share. One day he announced: I'm going to fetch Mother on Saturday afternoon.

The young doctor on duty at the hospital refused to give his permission.

Who are you anyway? he asked Jean.

I'm the only person she has in the world.

You are not even a relative, and you're not her husband.

I'm taking her away.

It's I who give orders here! the doctor shouted.

No. About Mother you have no right. And you can listen to me. I'm taking her home.

Get out of my sight—both of you!

This is how the doctor admitted his defeat. Mother was the first to understand what this admission meant, and her whole face became radiant.

Jean took her back to the ward and dressed her. He put on her black stockings—although it was the month of June—because she said she wanted to look smart, now that she was free.

Are you hungry Maman? he asked her in the car.

It was like a prison inside there.

Don't think about it.

They locked me in my room.

Don't think about it.

They treated me so badly.

I'm taking you home, said Jean, and I've cooked us tripe for lunch.

I didn't eat for a week.

We'll eat some tripe and then you can sleep, Maman.

By the door of their house, the dog jumped up to lick her face. When she was in the armchair, one of the cats settled on her lap. Jean came into the kitchen with four tiny kittens, two in each hand. She took his hands and she rubbed the kittens against her cheek.

Jean! How happy we are!

Ah! Maman! Now we are all happy, he said, we are all happy! In this story Jean and his Mother live one Saturday afternoon as if the future did not exist. As if a Saturday were exempt from time. For all their difference of style, the two stories have something in common.

Aneed for what transcends time, or is mysteriously spared by time, is built into the very nature of the human mind and imagination.

Time is created by events. In an eventless universe there would be no time. Different events create different times. There is the galactic time of the stars; there is the geological time of mountains; there is the lifetime of a butterfly. There is no way of comparing these different times except by using a mathematical abstraction. It was man who invented this abstraction. He invented a regular 'outside' time into which everything more or less fitted. After that, he could, for example, organize a race between a tortoise and a hare and measure their performances using an abstract unit of time (minutes).

'Time is not an empirical conception. For neither co-existence nor succession would be perceived by us, if the representation of time did not exist as a foundation *a priori* . . . . Time is nothing else but the form of the internal sense, that is, of the intuitions of self and of our internal state.' Kant, *Critique of Pure Reason*.

A problem remains, however. Man himself constitutes two events. There is the event of his biological organism, and in this he is like either the tortoise or the hare. And there is the event of his consciousness. The time of his life-cycle and the time of his mind. The first time understands itself, which is why animals have no philosophical problems. The second time has been understood in different ways in different periods. It is the first task of any culture to propose an understanding of the *time of consciousness*: of the relation between past, present and future, realized as such.

The explanation offered by European culture of the nineteenth century—which for nearly two hundred years has marginalized most other explanations—is one which constructs a uniform, abstract, unilinear law of time which applies to everything that exists, including consciousness. Thus, the explanation whose task is to 'explain' the time of consciousness, treats that consciousness as if it were comparable to a grain of rice or an extinct sun. If European man has become a victim of his own positivism, the story starts here.

The truth is that man is always between two times. Hence the distinction made in all cultures, except our own, between body and soul. The soul is first, and above all, the locus of another time, distinct from that of the body.

'I see,' wrote Blake, 'the past, present and future existing all at once before me.'

The great Lebanese poet Adonis writes:

Do you remember the house
ours alone
among the olive trees and the figs
with the source sleeping tight
against the orphans of the eye

Do you remember why the woods
beat their wings like butterflies
the earth's first night . . . .

The night . . . .

Drill wells in your breast
be labyrinth and take me in

Everyone knows that stories are simplifications. To tell a story is to select. Only in this way can a story be given a form and so be preserved. If you tell a story about somebody you love, a curious thing happens. The story-teller is like a dress-maker cutting a pattern out of cloth. You cut from the cloth as fully and intelligently as possible. Inevitably there are narrow strips and awkward triangles which cannot be used—which have no place in the form of the story. Suddenly you realize it is those strips, those useless remnants, which you love most. Because the heart wants to retain all.

> A dog barking shows
> how threadbare is
> the fabric of time.
> Through the frayed repetition at dusk—
> dogs were barking here
> since the river was bridged
> and the first dwellings built—
> you can see
> the centuries approaching
> in single file.

Rembrandt painted Hendrickje Stoeffels, who was the great love of his life, many times. One of his most modest paintings of her is, for me, one of the most mysterious. She is in bed. I reckon the picture was painted a little before the birth of Cornelia, Hendrickje's daughter by Rembrandt. She and Rembrandt had lived together, as man and woman, for twenty years. In about two years time Rembrandt would be declared bankrupt. Ten years earlier, Hendrickje had come to work in his house as a nurse for his two-year-old son from his previous marriage. Hendrickje will die, although younger than Rembrandt, six years before him.

It is late at night; she has been waiting for him to come to bed. He has just entered the room. She lifts up the curtain of the bed with the back of her hand. The face of its palm is already making a gesture, preparatory to the act of touching his head or his shoulder, when he bends over her. In this portrait of Hendrickje she is entirely concentrated on Rembrandt's sudden appearance. In her eyes we can read her portrait of him. The curtain she is holding up divides two kinds of time: the daytime of the daily struggle for survival, and the night-time of their bed.

Rembrandt must have painted the picture partly from memory, recalling the times he had come to bed late and Hendrickje had been waiting for him. To this degree it is a remembered image. Yet what it shows is a moment of anticipation—hers, and his by implication. They are about to leave the world of debts and monthly payments for the instantaneity of desire, or sleep or dreams.

The picture was painted three hundred years ago. We are looking at it today. There is such a tangle of times within this image that it is impossible to *place* the moment it represents. It resists the mechanism of clocks or calendars. I do not believe it is therefore less real.

The image of Hendrickje in bed was preserved thanks to Rembrandt's art. Yet the need to preserve an image is felt by us all at certain moments.

There is a photograph by the great Hungarian photographer, André Kertesz, in which we see a mother with her child looking very intently at a soldier. We do not, I think, require the caption in order to know that the soldier is about to leave. The great-coat hung over his shoulder, his hat, the rifle, are evidence enough. And the fact that the woman has just walked out of a kitchen and will shortly return to it is indicated by her lack of outdoor clothes. Some of the drama of the moment is already there in the difference between the clothes the two are wearing. His for travelling, for sleeping out, for fighting; hers for staying at home.

The caption reads: *A Red Hussar leaving, June 1919, Budapest.* How much that caption means depends upon what one knows of Hungarian history. The Hapsburg monarchy had fallen the previous summer. The winter had been one of extreme shortages (especially of fuel in Budapest) and economic disintegration. Two months before, in March, the Socialist Republic of Councils had been declared, under Bela Kun. The western allies in Paris, afraid that the Russian and, now, the Hungarian example of revolution should spread throughout Eastern Europe and the Balkans, were planning to dismantle the new republic.

A blockade was already imposed. General Foch himself was planning the military invasion being carried out by Rumanian and Czech troops. On 13 June 1919, Clemenceau sent an ultimatum by telegram to Bela Kun, demanding a Hungarian military withdrawal, which would have left the Rumanians occupying the eastern third of their country. For another six weeks the Hungarian Red Army fought on but was finally overwhelmed. By August, Budapest was occupied. The first European fascist regime, under Horthy, had been established.

If we are looking at an image from the past and we want to relate it to ourselves, we need to know something of the history of that past. And so the above information is relevant to the reading of Kertesz's photograph.

Everything in it is historical: the uniforms, the rifles, the corner by the Budapest railway station, the identity and biographies of all the people who are (or were) recognizable—even the size of the trees on the other side of the fence. Yet it also concerns a resistance to history: an opposition.

This opposition is not the consequence of the photographer having said, 'Stop!' It is not because the resultant static image is like a fixed post in a flowing river. We know that in a moment the soldier will turn his back and leave; we presume that he is the father of the child in the woman's arms. The significance of the instant photographed is already claiming minutes, weeks, years. The opposition exists in the parting *look* between the man and the woman.

Their look, which crosses before our eyes, is holding in place what *is*: not specifically what is there around them outside the station, but what *is* their life, what *are* their lives. The woman and the soldier are looking at each other so that the image of what *is* shall remain for them. In this look their being is opposed to their history, even if we assume that this history is one that they accept or have chosen.

How close a parting is to a meeting!

Everywhere in the world people have invented stories about the Beginning, about how the universe was created. All mythologies are a way of coming to terms with the fact that man lives between two times. He is born and he dies like every other animal, yet he can imagine the origin and the end of everything. And as a result of this imagining, he lives with the eternal, with that which preceded time and will follow it, with that which is continually there behind time. The Red Hussar and his wife, like two people feeling their way round the furniture in a pitch-dark room, are looking for a door which opens on to what is behind time.

The Adams and Eves
continually expelled
and with what tenacity
returning at night!

Before,
when the two of them
did not count
and there were no months
no births and no music
their fingers were unnumbered.

Before,
when the two of them did not count
did they feel
a prickling behind the eyes
a thirst in the throat
for something other than
the perfume of infinite flowers
and the breath of immortal animals?
In their untrembling sleep
did the tips of their tongues
seek the bud of another taste
which was mortal and sweating?

Did they envy the longing
of those to come after the Fall?

Women and men still return
to live through the night
all that uncounted time.

And with the punctuality
of the first firing squad
the expulsion is at dawn.

Twenty years ago I saw a photo by Lucien Clergue, one of a series of photographs of a woman in the sea. For millennia, the look of a woman's body in water has changed no more than the look of the waves. What we see in the photo must have been seen in the Egypt of the Pharaohs, in ancient China. Yet this changelessness represents only an instant when placed in the context of another 'time-scale'.

Scientists now estimate that life first appeared on this planet four thousand million years ago. The story began with the coming into being of single organic molecules. These were produced, mysteriously, by the action of ultra-violet light on certain mineral elements. Then, after many many trials—and it's difficult to avoid the notion of a will—the first single organic cells produced something capable of reproduction.

Thus it can be said that it took four thousand million years to produce the form and surface of the human body. Clergue's camera recorded this image in less than one hundredth of a second. Do these incomprehensible figures touch the mystery of the sight of the figure in the sea? In a sense they do. What they cannot touch is the *urgency* of the image. What impresses or moves us always has an urgency about it.

In this case, the sense of urgency might be explained by the nature of human sexuality and by cultural conditioning. It can be put into its place within the history of our biological and social evolution. Yet such an explanation remains unsatisfactory because, once again, it ignores the fact that consciousness cannot be reduced to the laws of unilinear time. It is always, at any given moment, trying to come to terms with a whole.

From the idea of the whole come all the variants of the notion—ranging from astrology to the Koran—that everything that happens has already been conceived, has already been told.

There's another Italian story, this time from the Piedmont. One day a farmer was on his way to the town of Biella. The weather was foul and the going was difficult. The farmer had important business, and so he went on, despite the driving rain.

He met an old man and the old man said to him: Good day to you. Where are you going in such a hurry?

To Biella, answered the farmer, without slowing down.

You might at least say: 'God willing'.

The farmer stopped, looked the old man in the eye and snapped: God willing, I'm on my way to Biella. If God isn't willing, I've still got to go there all the same.

The old man happened to be God. In that case, said the old man, you'll go to Biella in seven years. In the meantime, you'll jump into that pond and stay there for seven years!

Abruptly the farmer changed into a frog and jumped into the pond. Seven years went by. The farmer came out of the pond, slapped his hat back on his head, and continued on his way to Biella. After a short distance he met the old man again.

Where are you going to in such a hurry? asked the old man.

To Biella, replied the farmer.

You might at least say: 'God willing'.

If God wills it, fine, answered the farmer, if not, I know what is going to happen, and I'll jump into the pond of my own free will!

What I find wise in this story is the space it offers for the co-existence of free-will and a form of determinism. The 'God willing' offers a promise of a whole. The 'God willing' also, of course, poses insuperable problems. But to close this contradiction is more inhuman than to leave it open. Free-will and determinism are only mutually exclusive when the timeless has been banished, and Blake's 'Eternity in love with the productions of time' has been dismissed as nonsense.

It seems to me that throughout the course of a life the relation between space and time sometimes changes in a way that is revealing.

To be born is to be projected—or pulled—into time/space. Yet we experience duration before we experience extension. The infant lives minutes—without being able to measure them—before he lives metres. The infant counts the temporary absence of his mother by an unknowable time unit, not by an unknowable unit of distance. The cycles of time—hunger, feeding, waking, sleeping—become familiar before any means of transport. Most children face the experience of being lost in time before the experience of being lost in space. The first vertigo—and the rage it produces—is temporal. Likewise time brings arrivals and rewards to the infant before space does.

This is all the more striking if one compares a baby with a newborn animal. Many animals—especially those which graze—begin, within minutes of being born, a spatial quest which will continue all their lives. The comparative immaturity of the human baby, which obliges a long period of physical dependence, but which also permits a much longer and freer learning potential, encourages the primacy of time over space. Space is to animals what time is to sedentary man.

This human predisposition is linked with the early development of the human will. The will develops slowly—along with the ability to stand up, to walk, to talk, to name what one wants. But the will exists from birth onwards. (It is born from that expulsion.) In infancy the will selects very few objects from the full display of the existent. These few isolated objects, invested with desire or fear, then provoke *anticipation* and are thus delivered to the realm of time.

With age some people become more contemplative. Yet what is contemplation if it is not the acknowledgement, the celebration, of the spatial and the forgetting of the temporal? (For which the precondition is the abandonment of the personal will.)

Within the act of contemplation the spatial does not exclude time but it emphasizes simultaneity instead of sequence, presence instead of cause and effect, ubiquity instead of identity.

Curiously, when I write those words I do not think of a passive hermit, but of a dead friend who died because of his active politics.

His name was Orlando Letelier, a Chilean. He liked music. He was witty and debonair. And he had extraordinary courage.

He had been a minister in Allende's government. When Allende was murdered and Pinochet seized power, Orlando and many others were arrested, held in prison, and tortured. Eventually Orlando was released on the condition that he left Chile. He travelled around the world, talking about the fate of his country. He encouraged other exiles. He persuaded certain governments to reduce or to stop their trade with Chile. He was eloquent and effective. Pinochet decided that Letelier had to be got rid of. His secret police arranged for a bomb to be planted in his car in Washington. One morning, when Orlando was driving to his office, with an American girl who was acting as his secretary, his car blew up. The girl was killed immediately, and Orlando, after he had lost both legs, died.

A day after I heard the news of his assassination, I heard the following:

> Once I will visit you
> he said
> in your mountains
> today
> assassinated
> blown to pieces
> he has come to stay
> he lived in many places
> and he died everywhere
> in this room
> he has come between the pages
> of open books
> there's not a single apple
> on the trees
> loaded with fruit this year
> which he has not counted
> apples the colour of gifts
> he faces death no more
> there's not a precipice
> over which his corpse
> has not been hurled
> the silence of his voice
> tidy and sweet as the leaf of a beech
> will be safe in the forest
> I never heard him speak
> in his mother tongue
> except when he named the names
> of patriots
> the clouds race over the grass

faster than sheep
never lost
he consulted the compass of his heart
always accurate
took bearings from the needle of Chile
and the eye of Santiago
through which he has now passed.

Before the fortress of injustice
he brought many together
with the delicacy of reason
and spoke there
of what must be done
amongst the rocks
not by giants
but by women and men
they blew him to pieces
because he was too coherent
they made the bomb
because he was too fastidious
what his assassins whisper to themselves
his voice could never have said
afraid of his belief
in history
they chose the day
of his murder.

He has come
as the season turns
at the moment of the blood red rowanberry
he endured the time without seasons
which belongs to the torturers
he will be here too
in the spring
every spring
until the seasons returning
explode
in Santiago.

To the questions I ask of time, I have no answers. I only know that such questions are of the human essence and that any system of habits or of reasoning which dismisses them does violence to our nature. Since I first started writing I have been labelled a Marxist. A convenient category for others, sometimes a shelter for me. I believe in the class struggle and the historical dialectic; I am convinced by Marx's understanding of the role and mechanisms of capitalism. Within the world historical arena, the fighting is mostly as he foresaw. The questions I ask now are addressed to what surrounds the arena.

I began with a story, I will end with story-telling.

Imagine a character in a story trying to conceive of his origin, trying to see beyond what he knows of his destiny, before the end of the story. His inquiries would lead him to hypotheses— infinity, chance, indeterminacy, free-will, fate, curved space and time—not dissimilar to those at which we arrive when interrogating the universe.

The notion that life—as lived—is a story being told, has been a recurring one, expressed in multiple forms of religion, popular proverbs, poetry, myth, and philosophical speculation. Nineteenth century pragmatism rejected this notion and proposed that the laws of nature were ineluctably mechanical. Recent scientific research tends to support the assumption that the universe and its working processes resemble those of a brain rather than a machine.

What separates the story-teller from his protagonists is not knowledge, either objective or subjective, but *their* experience of time in the story he is telling. (If he is telling his own story the same thing separates him as story-teller from himself as the subject.) This separation allows the story-teller to hold the whole together; but it also means that he is obliged to follow his protagonists, follow them powerlessly *through* and *across* the time which they are living and he is not. The time, and therefore the story, belongs to them. Its meaning belongs to the story-teller. Yet the only way he can reveal this meaning is by telling the story to others.

A story is seen by its listener or reader through a lens. This lens is the secret of narration. In every story the lens is ground anew, ground between the temporal and the timeless.

Ryszard Kapuściński
A Warsaw Diary

During a period of crisis I experience more acutely the contradiction between subjective and objective time: between the time I experience, personally and privately, and the time witnessed by generations, epochs and history. The more ruthless we perceive history to be in realizing its grand, long-range goals, the less chance we have of fulfilling our own individual lives in it. The more space history usurps for itself, the less there is for us. We feel redundant, having always to justify our existence (the very fact of which, the fact that I *am*, is, in any event, sufficient reason for me to be accused and persecuted). Your plans, your ambitions, your dreams? All appear trivial, a stage-set shredded by a bomb. Without meaning, a *raison d'être*, a purpose, to whom does one turn? What can one say?

In an epoch of lawlessness, the ordinances and decrees are so thick on the ground that, often without realizing, you step into a trap every day. Every day you end up infringing some law. You are meant to live with a constant sense of guilt, and you grow weaker and weaker. To confront authority—or even the thought of the authorities themselves—inspires fear, terror and humility. And in you—deformed, humiliated—the half-formed thought occurs that perhaps you really are guilty, and that perhaps the authorities may, to an extent, actually be in the right. Among them, we tolerate lawlessness far more than we ever would among private individuals. Imagine: a man, completely innocent, is arrested. We know he is innocent, but at least once, even if only momentarily, we reflect: perhaps he really has done something wrong, broken some law. Official lawlessness feeds on the moments of our imbalance and confusion.

But then there is what the authorities think of you. And there are the rules of the game that have to be followed. They know that you break the law daily, that you, therefore, are a criminal. They wait, perfidious and self-assured. They watch, studying your movements, listening to your words. Do not be misled by the fact that you are at liberty and relatively free; that for the moment you are not under lock and key: you have simply been granted a reprieve. But take care! You will continue to be at liberty provided you don't take a step that the authorities will question and judge as hostile. Then comes the blow, and you realize that your whole life has been a series of unpardonable errors and serious, punishable crimes.

Poland's contorted fate: every few years we create a new stage; every few years a new scene, a new order. There is no continuity. The future does not develop from the past. What was important yesterday is today attacked, or, having lost its significance, no longer matters. Nothing adds up, nothing can be gathered together, nothing can be given shape. You need to start, again, from the beginning—with the first brick and the first furrow. Whatever you have built will be abandoned and what has grown will wither. Everything, then, is constructed without conviction; everything built is make-believe. Only the irrational endures—myths, beliefs, illusions—only this is firmly rooted.

There are two kinds of impoverishment: material impoverishment and an impoverishment of needs. Both are convenient to the authorities: the first because poverty weakens and oppresses the individual, renders him submissive, deepens his sense of inferiority; the second, because an individual, whose needs are small, isn't even aware that there are things he could demand and fight for.

In Poland we read every text as allusive; every situation described—even the most remote in time and space—is immediately applied to Poland. Every text is a double text. Between the lines we look for the message written in an invisible ink, and the hidden message we find is treated as the only true one. This results, in part, from the difficulty of speaking openly; it also results from having suffered every possible experience, and still being exposed to so many varied and different trials that each Pole naturally sees in other, alien histories allusions to his own.

Degrees of barbarism. This is how: first you destroy those who create values. Then you destroy those who know what the values are, and who also know that those destroyed before were in fact the creators of values. But real barbarism begins when no one can any longer judge or know that what he does is barbaric.

A's mistake: he assumes, as a matter of course, that the authorities' intentions are basically good. Does he really think that men seek power for the good of others? Men in authority do good only when it serves their basic aim—to maintain power. And if there is a relationship between power and public good, it depends not on individuals but on the system in which they work.

When is a crisis reached? When questions arise that can't be answered.

While talking with a man from Switzerland I suddenly feel tempted to say: Dear friend, what do you know about life? You live like a lord, you have everything, you fear no one.... In a moment like this, my friend has made me jealous. But at other moments I believe that we compensate for this jealousy in the strange satisfaction that we—*not* they—have reached the truth about life, by having had to taste its bitter essence and penetrate its mystery. This belief presupposes that life is ultimately an inferno, and that calm, comfort and contentment are, by nature, rare, accidental and fragile. It presupposes that life is truly known only to those who suffer, lose, endure adversity and stumble from defeat to defeat.

He is dead.

He was bestial and base. But now that he lies under the earth, we forgive him everything. He can no longer arouse our powerful feelings—neither terror nor hate nor condemnation. Truly, sincerely, unconditionally, we allow him to rest in peace. Amen.

I used to admire his poetry—until learning that no one could trust him. His poetry lost its lustre, and I all desire to read it. I couldn't separate literature from life.

Here everything is based on a certain principle of asymmetrical verification: the system promises to prove itself *later* (announcing a general happiness that exists only in the future), but it demands that you prove yourself now, *today*, by demonstrating your loyalty, consent and diligence. You commit yourself to everything; the system to nothing.

In a society of little economic development, universal inactivity accompanies universal poverty. You survive not by struggling against nature, or by increasing production, or by relentless labour; instead you survive by expending as little energy as possible, by striving constantly to achieve a state of immobility. And fatalism is your philosophy. Man is not the lord of nature, but its slave, humbly accepting commands, reacting to the world around him. He is a dumb servant of a fate from which he can't escape. Fate is the deity. To oppose it is to commit sacrilege and condemn oneself to hell.

Arms, idiocy and fear: there is no worse combination, and, with it, there is nothing worse to expect.

Be careful: they have arms, and no alternatives.

An open confrontation with the authorities is the only real and unforgivable crime. *All* other abuses may be seen as crimes, but not necessarily.

Our salvation is in striving to achieve what we know we'll never achieve.

This disorientation—this feeling of always being lost—derives in part from a distorted sense of time, finding it difficult to grasp. The past—all of it—is unclear: constantly recalled and dismissed, praised or condemned. There is no enduring support or guidance—no positive inspiration. The present too is deprived of certainty and of a spirit of encouragement: we feel we are its guests or even its victims, not its creators or rulers. And the future appears more like an ambush and a mystery than a crystal palace in which servants are about to switch on the lights and prepare for us a feast.

Terror creates nothing; it is barren. And so is our concern with terror. Its mechanism is that of a malignant cancer. A terrible and monotonous world, frightening and empty, a grey earth, hollow men, squeals and cries, vast areas of silence and a relentless prison walk: circling in numbness and pain.

The so-called 'masses' (or, the simple folk) take life as it comes: literally, tolerantly and fatalistically. They regard the whims of history in the same way they understand the whims of nature (droughts and floods): as the natural mutations of fate to which these simple folk must try to adjust. Hence the rare gestures of revolt: the sources of revolutionary strength are not in the misery of poverty—which quenches, not inflames protest—but in a living, independent consciousness and in a conviction of being in the right.

Unhappiness is a self-seeding growth: one unhappy man makes those around him unhappy. He is a poison and his unhappiness is a pain that spreads.

When man meets an obstacle he can't destroy, he destroys himself. This terrible union is the cause of breakdowns and depression, the source of alcoholism and drug dependence.

A man of compromise, an elastic man: the kind of man we don't like; we say he is ambiguous. In Poland a man must be one thing: white or black, here or there, with us or against us—clearly, openly, without hesitations. Our vision is Manichaean: we see from the front. We are anxious when the picture of contrasts is upset. We lack the liberal, democratic tradition rich in all its gradations. We have instead the tradition of struggle: the extreme situation, the final gesture.

For a civilization to turn from democracy to totalitarianism is always to have regressed.

Z, who has suffered much, offers me the following advice: at the end of the day you should say, 'Things will never be as good as they were today!'

The ease with which the human mind can be manipulated arises from man's very nature. He *receives*; he doesn't *seek*. Indolent, passive, unimaginative, he is satisfied by whatever information or opinion comes his way—the more simplified, embellished or nonsensical, the better. Nonsense has features characteristic of the fairy-tale and often of kitsch: it appeals easily to the popular imagination.

Some believe that by withdrawing from areas of public activity—by simply diminishing their presence—they will increase the extent of the liberty they can privately enjoy. So they strive to shrink, to impoverish themselves, and turn into dust. They expect the authorities to lose interest: for them, only those who are visible exist or those with something that can be taken away.

We follow the mystics. They know where they are going. They, too, go astray, but when they go astray they do so in a way that is mystical, dark, and mysterious. This attracts us.

In times of calamity or tragedy, the colours and variations of the natural world seem to disappear. We perceive only humankind and its drama, and, self-absorbed, do not see the trees or the sky. What was autumn like in 1348 when the Black Death descended on Europe? What did Johann Wolfgang von Goethe see through the window as he lay dying on that day in March 1832? A pale, barely spring-like sun? Rain falling since dawn?

Man and war: it shapes his psychology, his outlook and his patterns of thought. Once experienced, war never ends: he will always think in its images, imposing them on each new reality—a reality from which he is always partly estranged. Reality is time-present, but he is possessed by time-past, constantly returning to what he has lived through and how he survived it. His thinking is obsessively repeating, obsessively retrospective.

What does it mean to think in images of war? It means to see the world in its greatest tension, in terror and cruelty. The reality of war is the world reduced to its Manichaean extremes: a merciless elimination of colour that confines everything to a sharp aggressive counterpoint of black and white and the most primitive struggle of good and evil. There is no one else on the battlefield: only the good—we—and evil, what opposes us.

It is a world of force constantly manifest: that is the image of war—overflowing, ceaselessly, ostentatiously, brutally, every time a boot strikes the pavement or a rifle-butt the skull. Force is the sole criterion of value: the blind cult of force, arrogant and imperial, disdaining nuance, reflection, half-tone or subtle colour. Conflict is resolved not by compromise but by destroying the adversary within the acceptable means: within, that is, the law of immediate effectiveness.

War is, finally, a world in which all is magnified—emotion, exultation, fury and obduracy—and in which we are constantly deafened, enervated, and, above all, threatened. It is full of hatred, and gestures, and voices, and fear.

A system is anachronistic when it offers old answers to new questions.

The basic principle: nothing can be good, or at least no good can last for long. It must be destroyed. Doing good is always suspect; it invites punishment. The self-defence of a system, malfunctioning and under-productive, is to destroy whatever is effective and creative. The system exists in slow motion; to accelerate results in a strain and a tension that threaten complete collapse. The system defends itself instinctively against any acceleration, fearing that any excess—of energy, of will, of creativity—will overload and destroy the system itself. To do good, then, to multiply and perfect, is to be in opposition, threatening the existing order by unmasking its weaknesses.

The relationship between idea and structure. In the beginning there is an idea (the word) and the idea calls to life a structure (it becomes flesh). They exist in tension and conflict: the more the structure annexes and subsumes the idea, the more it formalizes and destroys it. The more the idea penetrates and occupies the structure, the more rigid the structure becomes. It is removed from life, ready for its downfall.

To subjugate a society is to reduce it to its most elementary level of subsistence. The decline in living standards, the limiting of comforts, the increased sense of threat—these are not inexplicable or absurd. They are a consequence not of wrong choices but of a policy—the policy of those wishing to consolidate their rule. A population weakened and exhausted by battling against so many obstacles—whose needs are never satisfied and desires never fulfilled—is vulnerable to manipulation and regimentation. The struggle for survival is, above all, an exercise that is hugely time-consuming, absorbing and debilitating. If you create these 'anti-conditions', your rule is guaranteed for a hundred years.

Professor Henryk Wereszycki points out how much you absorb from people you fight.

Evil acts swiftly, violently, and with a sudden crushing force. The good works more slowly, requiring time to reveal itself and bear witness. The good often arrives late. We are always on the look-out, always waiting for it.

The unceasing eruptions and tensions in the world result largely from three historically unprecedented phenomena that appeared simultaneously in the second half of the twentieth century.

1. The conflict between armed ideologies with huge destructive power, each drawing the whole of humanity into its fight for world domination.
2. The emergence of over a hundred new states, each with its own philosophy or religion, and its own mystique, decalogues and priesthood, but each unable to satisfy the ever-growing requirements of existence because the earth lacks the adequate producers, the material means, and the political conditions.
3. Migrations unprecedented in scale from the country to the city, to a mirage of a better life, better job prospects and greater opportunities of social advancement, that have resulted in a disillusionment so severe as to be the source of continual and widespread frustration and revolt.

Uncertainty and bewilderment: from the fact that words have been deprived of their natural primitive meanings; that language has ceased to be an instrument of navigation and orientation, a compass; that language misleads and confuses.

The phrase 'cultural revolution': it should suggest progress, blossoming and light in the darkness; but it means destruction, bullying, the triumph of hysteria and ignorance, awakening revulsion and fear. The struggle for the future of the world—and man's consciousness in it—will take place more and more in the realm of language. Language battles, battles with words are a part of the whole of human history, but, with the advent of the mass media, they have become more intense. Propaganda has become one of every contemporary government's main tools of action. Someone used the word 'aggression' to define propaganda—accurately, to the extent that propaganda engages in the ceaseless attack and conquest of human consciousness.

How little, in the end, do we determine what we are and how we act. To be a human being requires humane conditions, but it is not the human being—the individual—who determines them. In a democratic country, it is easy to live by a code of ethics; under totalitarian rule, it is not. Does this lead to greater mutual tolerance among those living in a totalitarian world? On the contrary! Those in a democracy are more mutually tolerant than those condemned to autocratic power—where we live amid unending ex-communications, condemnations and hatreds. These are two inseparable pairs: democracy and tolerance, and dictatorship and mutual aggression.

The main objective of authoritarian systems: to arrest time, because time brings about change.

If from among many truths you select one and follow it blindly, it will turn into a falsehood and you into a fanatic.

Fanaticism releases more energy in people than gentleness and goodness: it is easy for a fanatic to impose his will and establish his rule.

As he advanced and was promoted he grew distant and cold. When he lost his position, he was again accessible and, in his own way, tolerable.

The relationship between culture and compromise: the more developed the culture, the greater the possibility of resolving conflicts through compromise.

The mass media's enormous influence derives from the fact that they control what we think about, restricting us to the information and opinion that the decision-makers themselves choose and define. Without even realizing it, we think what the decision-makers want us to think. To be independent of the subjects transmitted by the media it is not enough to be critical of them: independent thought is private reflection on observations and experiences independently derived, bypassing whatever the mass media wish to impose.

One may distinguish systems in the following way:
1. Those in which the chief means of advancement are based on merit.
2. Those in which the chief means are based on loyalty.
The first system is dynamic, the second static. Dynamism is constant energy, and a dynamic society demands this energy from its people. In a static system, the object is different: it is to maintain an internal balance, to conserve the structures of permanence. A static system does not want entrepreneurs or independent individuals; it needs loyal, watchful guardians of the existing order.

Can you shape a face—its expression, features, gaze—to fit a hat? Put on the hat of a policeman or of a field-marshall in the army: in time, the wearer's face will change.

In relations between people: the extent of one man's guilt may be defined by how much of it is experienced by the party he injured.

Translated from the Polish by Adam Czerniawski
This is part one of a two-part article

William Humphrey
HOSTAGES TO FORTUNE

Justin Wintle
MORTADELLA

Secker & Warburg

THE · BEST · OF
Spring
FICTION

GRAHAM GREENE
The Tenth Man
£6.95

LYNN GUEST
Yedo
£8.95

BRYAN MacMAHON
The Sound of Hooves and other stories
£8.95   (May)

JON THURLEY
The Burning Lake
£8.95   (May)

PAUL GEDDES
A State of Corruption
£8.95   (May)

RONALD FRAME
Watching Mrs Gordon and other stories
£8.95   (June)

from
THE BODLEY HEAD

MARILYNNE ROBINSON
THE WASTE LAND

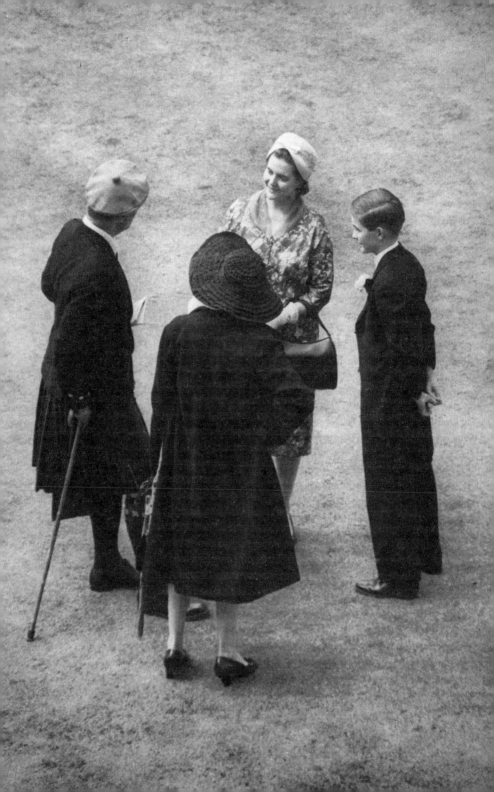

On the coast of Cumbria, in the Lake District, there is a nuclear reprocessing plant called Sellafield, formerly Windscale, that daily pumps up to a million gallons of radioactive waste down a mile and a half of pipeline, into the Irish Sea. It has done this for thirty-five years. The waste contains caesium and ruthenium and strontium, and uranium, and plutonium. Estimates published in *The Times* and in the *Observer* are that a quarter of a ton of plutonium has passed into the sea through this pipeline—enough, in theory, according to *The Times*, to kill 250 million people; much more than enough, in theory, according to the *Observer*, to destroy the population of the world. The plant was designed on the assumption that radioactive waste would lie harmlessly on the sea floor. That assumption proved false, but the plant has continued to operate in the hope that radioactive contamination may not be so very harmful, after all. If this hope is misguided, too, then Britain, in a time of peace, has silently, needlessly, passionlessly, visited upon us all a calamity equal to the worst we fear.

Everything factual that I will relate in this article I learned from reading the British press or watching British television. But it would not be accurate to say that I know, more or less, what a reasonably informed Briton knows about these things, because there is a passivity and a credulousness in informed British opinion that neutralizes the power of facts to astonish.

To understand what I will tell you, you must imagine a country where, though the carcinogenic properties of radioactivity in general and of plutonium in particular are gravely conceded, it is considered reasonable, in the best sense, to permit the release of both of these into the environment until the precise nature of their effect is understood. This notion of reasonableness is, I think, extremely local, but the consequences of such thinking are felt in many places. The Danes object to plutonium on their beaches, as do the Dutch. And of course the Irish, a volatile people at the best of times, are now very much exercised by elevated rates of childhood cancer and Down's syndrome along their eastern coast. They have leaped to the very conclusion the British find too hasty—that the contamination of the environment by known carcinogens is detrimental to the public health. No one disputes that the

229

contamination of these coasts is surely and exclusively owing to British reasonableness, since the Irish have not developed nuclear energy—nor have the Danes, who consider it unsafe—and since the only other fuel reprocessing plant known to release waste into the sea, at Cap de la Hague in France, releases only one percent of the radioactivity that enters the sea from Sellafield.

When I realized what I was reading, I began to clip out articles every day and save them, and I brought them back to America, knowing that my uncorroborated word could not be credited. Travellers to unknown regions must bring back proof of the marvels they have seen. Perhaps the most incredible part of this story is that it has fallen to me to tell it. American scholars and scientists go to Britain in platoons. Many live there. Probably all of them look at the *Guardian* now and then, or *The Times*. Perhaps most of them are more competent to understand what they read there than I am, better schooled in such matters as the particular virulence of plutonium, or the special fragility of the sea. No one had ever hinted to me that for thirty-five years Britain has knowingly befouled itself and its neighbours with radiation, and nothing I had heard or read had prepared me to discover a historical and political context for which the one vivid instance of Sellafield could well serve as an emblem. Yet Sellafield does not depart from, but in fact epitomizes, British environmental practice. This is only to say, read on. This is a tale of wonders.

In November 1983 a family was walking along the beach near Sellafield—it is a major tourist and recreational area—when a scientist who worked at the plant stopped to tell them that they should not let their children play there. They were shocked, of course, and raised questions, and sent a letter to their MP. The scientist was fired, amid official mutterings about his having committed an impropriety in disclosing this information. No doubt he had violated the Official Secrets Act, though so far as I know the matter was not couched in those terms. British workers in significant nationalized industries—for example, British Aerospace, the postal system, and the nuclear industry—are obliged to sign the act, which imposes on them fines and imprisonment if they reveal without authorization information acquired in the course of their work. Only death can release them from this contract. Employees of private industries are in the same position, to all intents and purposes, since the unauthorized use of privately held information is prosecuted as theft. In the democratic kingdom, the exercise of judgement and conscience is the exclusive prerogative of the great.

But I digress. Though the renegade employee was dismissed, the issue of the safety of the beaches was called to public attention, with a number of consequences. A woman who lived in a village near Sellafield sent a bag of dust from her vacuum cleaner to a professor in Pittsburgh, who found that it contained plutonium. Divers from British Greenpeace tried to close the pipeline but were unable to do so because the shape of its mouth had been altered. They discovered an oily scum on the water that sent the needles of their Geiger counters off the scales. The divers and their boat had to be decontaminated. The radioactive slick was said to be the consequence of an error at the plant that had disgorged a radioactive solvent into the sea—an accident that, unlike the normal functioning of the plant, raised questions of competence and culpability. That is to say, this matter was put into the hands of the Director of Public Prosecutions, and quite appropriately. However, it is a curious feature of British law and practice that silence descends around any issue that is about to become the subject of legal action. A judge may remove this restriction in particular cases; murder trials, for example, are reported in lascivious detail. But a newspaper that publishes anything relating to matters prohibited as *sub judice* is subject to catastrophic fines. The manufacturers of thalidomide, the sedative that caused many British children to be born without limbs, kept the question of their liability before the courts for seventeen years, and therefore unresolved and out of public awareness, until the *Sunday Times* defied the law and broke the story. The newspaper took its case to the European Court of Human Rights, and won, but this has had no effect on British law or practice. British justice, which is cousin to British reasonableness, grows squeamish at the thought that the legal process should be adulterated by publicity.

As a third consequence of the attention drawn to Sellafield, Yorkshire Television sent a team there to look into worker safety. The team discovered that children in the villages surrounding the plant suffered leukaemia at a rate ten times the national average. This revelation fuelled public anxiety to such an extent that the government was obliged to appoint a commission to investigate. It recently published its conclusions in the so-called Black Report, named after Sir Douglas Black, president of the British Medical Association and the commission's head and spokesman. Dr Black startled some by assuring a television interviewer that people fear radioactivity now just as they feared electricity one hundred years ago.

The report offers 'a qualified reassurance' to those concerned about a possible health hazard in the area. The *Guardian* said: 'Recognising that radiation is the only established environmental cause of leukaemia in children, "within the limits of present knowledge," the Black team calls for new studies to provide additional potential insights.' Again according to the *Guardian*, 'Despite the high rates of cancer close to Sellafield, the report stresses: "An observed association between two factors does not prove a causal relationship."' This is certainly true. And this is the darling verity of the British government. Souls less doughty than these might feel that exposure to radiation around Sellafield, together with an elevated cancer rate, testifies to a causal relationship between these two factors, but we're not dealing with a bunch of patsies here. In environmental issues, a standard of proof is demanded that makes the claims of the Flat Earth Society look easy.

What do we have here? The better college sophomore has learned that this world does not yield what we call 'proof' of anything. That so weighty an edifice as public policy should be reared upon an epistemological abyss is truly among the world's marvels. Are these decision makers, known to wags as the Good and the Great, cynical connivers, imposing upon what can only be a frighteningly naive and credulous public? Or are they themselves also frighteningly naive? I cannot think of a third possibility. Whatever the cause of their behaviour, its effect, like the effect of the Official Secrets Act and the contempt laws, is to shield government and public and private industries from suspicions of error or wrongdoing, and to blur, fudge, and frustrate questions of responsibility and liability.

You will note that the laws and practices and attitudes I describe here have existed over decades, and have persisted while governments rose and fell. For example, in 1974 the government passed the Control of Pollution Act. To have a proper understanding of 'pollution' in this context it is essential to realize that in Britain, no legal control is exerted over agricultural chemicals or sprays. DDT is still in general use, as are Aldrin and Lindane. I know of no reason to imagine that policies towards industrial pollutants are any less indulgent in effect. Inspectors politely inform manufacturers of their intention to visit, so control of effluents can hardly be stringent. And we are not speaking here of soapsuds. In any case, part two of this Control of Pollution Act is now to be implemented, reports the *Guardian*. The article goes on to say, 'The new measures are expected to have a big impact on the problems of Britain's dirty beaches.' This seems to me a remarkably cheerful thought, considering that, to quote again, 'the measures only apply to new sewage or trade effluent discharges, however. Existing discharges will continue, but "consents" already granted will be subject to public scrutiny.' Well, this looks to me like an act designed to confer legality on the very sources of pollution that already dirty Britain's beaches. However, the act must have a fang, if only a small one, because for ten years it was not implemented. Why? The article offers an explanation from William Waldegrave, Under-Secretary of State for the Environment, who said that 'one of the factors that had held back successive governments was the fear of increasing costs to industry.'

How is one to understand the degradation of the sea and earth and air of the British homeland by people who use the word *British* the way others of us use the words *good*, and *just*, and *proud*, and *precious*, and *lovely*, and *clement*, and *humane*? No matter that these associations reflect and reinforce the complacency that allows the spoliation to go unchecked; still, surely they bespeak self-love, which should be some small corrective. I think ignorance must be a great part of the explanation—though ignorance so obdurate could be preserved only through an act of will.

Marilynne Robinson

The issue of Sellafield is complicated by the great skill the government has shown in turning accidents to good account. You will remember that the Greenpeace divers surfaced through highly radioactive slime. If they had not had Geiger counters with them, no one would have known that an accident had taken place. *Ergo*, one cannot know that *other* accidents have *not* taken place. From which it follows that these accidents, and not the normal functioning of the plant, might be responsible for the cancers and other difficulties and embarrassments. As the *Guardian* said, in its sober and respectful paraphrase of this startling document, the Black Report, 'The possibility of unplanned and undetected discharges having delivered significant doses of radiations to humans via an unsuspected route could not be entirely excluded.' The implication of all this is that the plant can be repaired, improved, and monitored, and then the hazards will go away. Number eight on the list of ten recommendations by the Black inquiry team suggests that 'attention [be] paid to upper authorized limits of radioactive discharges over short periods of time; to removal of solvent from discharges and adequacy of filter systems'—in other words, if occasional splurges are avoided, the level of radioactivity will remain safe and constant. That might well be true, if the substances put in the sea decayed. But as the *Observer* has noted, plutonium remains toxic for at least 100,000 years.

Another accident that has had great effect on the way this affair has been managed is the fact that Yorkshire Television focused its attention on leukaemia among local children. This is understandable, since the deaths of children are particularly vivid and painful to consider. But the limiting of the discussion to childhood cancer in the Black Report is clearly arbitrary and possibly opportunistic. Seascale, the village nearest the plant, where seven children have died of leukaemia in a period of ten years, has a population of 2,000. Children living there are said to have one chance in sixty of developing leukaemia, but the sample is considered too small to be reliable—coincidence might account for the high incidence of the disease.

But why are we talking only about leukaemia? I noted with interest, and added to my collection, a brief report about an inquest into the death of a Sellafield worker from bone cancer. An environmental group (not named) had pointed out that Dr Geoffrey Schofield, the plant's chief medical officer, 'did not mention the three most recent deaths from bone cancer at Sellafield.' The article continues, 'Dr Schofield, quoting a 1981 report on mortality rates among British Nuclear Fuels workers at Sellafield, referred to four cases of myeloma, a bone cancer. These figures over the period 1948 to 1980 were comparable with national figures. Since that report three more workers have died from myeloma and a fourth appears to have contracted the disease.' How do these cancer deaths relate to the cancer deaths among children in the area? Doesn't the concentration on the young actually focus attention on that portion of the population least likely to have developed cancer?

But officially preferred hypotheses are invoked to preclude lines of inquiry that might produce data that would discredit them. What harm could there be in checking for lung cancer deaths in areas downwind of Windscale?* These would certainly be equally relevant to the question of public safety, the real issue here.

---

*A striking feature in all this is the seeming difficulty of obtaining and interpreting information. One would think that a country with a national health service would enjoy centralized and continuous monitoring of health data. One would expect it to encourage preventive practices at both public and individual level, if only on grounds of economy. But the British government has actually suppressed reports on alcoholism and on the relation of cardiovascular disease to diet—the second of these was leaked to the *Lancet*; the first, though joked about in the press, has been dubbed an Official Secret, and its findings may not be published. The British government saves money in the most direct way: by refusing to spend it. In the European Community only Greece spends a smaller share of its wealth on health care. Yet the British are proud of their health system. Margaret Thatcher is fond of saying they get 'good value for money,' and one often sees statements to the effect that indicators of general health show the British system outperforming the big spenders. If this is true—if, with poverty and unemployment and all the problems that attend them; if, with rampant abuse of alcohol and heroin, a polluted

The conclusion reached by James Cutler, the Yorkshire Television producer who first made public the high incidence of leukaemia in Seascale, and the great fear of the chairman of British Nuclear Fuels, who really is named Con Allday, is that anxiety among the public signals a defeat for proponents of nuclear power. Now, I think nuclear power has proved to be a terrible idea, but I do not think the practices associated with Sellafield should ever be spoken of as if they were characteristic and inevitable aspects of its development. To do so would be to obscure the special questions of competence, of morality—of sanity, one might say—that Sellafield so vividly poses. But as I said earlier, I do not wish to imply that what has been done at Sellafield departs radically from the *British* nuclear establishment's behaviour. Ninety percent of the nuclear material that has been dumped in the sea world-wide has been dumped by the British. They have deposited it off the coasts of Spain and France and, of course, Ireland, and elsewhere—in containers, supposedly, though their methods of disposal at Sellafield do not encourage me to imagine that their methods elsewhere should be assumed to be particularly cautious.

I suppose the British make lots of money cleaning spent fuel rods from all over the world, and from their own facilities. To be a source of a substance so prized as plutonium must bring wealth, and influence too. It is certain that they do not do it for their health. Exactly contrary to the universally held view, Britain is an island of unevolved *laissez-faire* plutocracy characterized by unregulated (my translation of the British 'self-regulated') commerce and industry. So far from being lumbered with the costs of runaway socialist largesse, Britain ranks near the bottom in Europe not only in health spending but also in spending for education. In workers' wages and benefits, it has never approached the levels achieved by

---

environment, and immunization policies so casual that Britain still has rubella epidemics; if, with a slow rate of decline in cigarette smoking and rates of breast and lung cancer at or near top of the charts—if Britain still does better than countries that devote more generous portions of larger resources to populations whose conditions of life are distinctly more consistent with well-being, then the National Health Service beggars any praise.

West Germany, Sweden, or the Netherlands. The British seem rather fond of their poverty, which I think is a social and economic strategy rather than the mysterious, intractable affliction it is presented as being. It effectively excuses the state from responsibility for the conditions of life of the poor, and for the quality of life of ordinary people. While lowering public expectations, this 'poverty' justifies the astonishing recklessness of British industries, public and private, and makes it entirely acceptable for government and industry to be in cahoots to a degree that boggles the American mind.

Avoiding costs to industry is treated as an unquestioned good—Britain being so poor, after all. That very little trickles down from these coddled industries is a fact blamed squarely on the British worker, of all people, who, if he is lucky, toils for bad pay in a decaying factory and hopes that his children's lives will not be worse. Only consider: Britain is the world's fourth-largest arms dealer, a major exporter of petroleum, a major exporter of drugs and chemicals, a major centre of banking and insurance, a major centre of tourism. And it has access to the vast literatures of research and technology produced in the United States, the application of which in other countries is slowed and complicated by the problems of translation. This seems to me to be the basis for a presentable economy. But no, Britain is 'poor'—because its workers are sullen and Luddite, or because its governing classes are too haplessly genteel and fair-minded to cope in the hurly-burly of the market-place, or because the national character has grown idle in the embrace of the Welfare State, or because the great forces of entropy and decline have at last overtaken this noble civilization. Or because neither law nor custom encourages the sharing of wealth. Consider: university students are almost entirely subsidized. But only five to seven percent of secondary-school students are admitted to universities. Since nothing is done to compensate for the advantages children of privileged backgrounds bring to examinations and interviews—such education is expensive, and Britain, after all, is poor—the subsidies go to the children of the prosperous. The cost per student of the university system to the state justifies its being kept very small—and this magnifies the value and the prestige that attach to university degrees. That is British socialism.

My point is simply that all the talk of decline, along with the continuous experience of austerity, creates an atmosphere in which the granting of enormous latitude to corporations, whether private or public, seems urgently necessary, and the encumbering of them with codes and restrictions a luxury embattled Britain can scarcely afford. Economic considerations have an importance and a pervasiveness that startle. The *Sunday Times*, reporting on a critical study of the British diet that had been suppressed, laid the blame on a government fear of a negative impact on the food industry, and also on an awareness on the part of the government that old people are expensive: 'Civil servants representing the social services . . . point out that healthy and long-lived citizens will increase the number of old-age pensions.' Britain, you must always remember, is poor.

What a thoroughly miserable business. What arrogance to save a few quid by allowing Sellafield to spew and haemorrhage, again and again, on and on. According to the *Sunday Times*, a spokesman for British Nuclear Fuels agreed that it was 'in everybody's interests to get discharges down as low as possible' but argued that the cost was 'prohibitive.' He said, 'We would have to pass the cost on to our customers, which would mean higher electricity prices. We are already spending £500 million on reducing our discharges. We have reduced them considerably over the past ten years.' Reduced them from what, *to* what? Note how 'everybody's interests' are put in the scales against cost, and with what result. Why should expenses at a fuel reprocessing plant raise the price of electricity, rather than of plutonium? And why should the cost of recycling spent fuel for Japan—to pick a name out of the air—be subsidized by consumers in Britain? The idea is preposterous. We are hearing the same old song: *Shackle us with restrictions and you will pay dearly for it*.

Con Allday, chairman of BNF and, as one may glimpse him through the dark glass of British newspaper journalism, a man of views as emphatic as they are liable to be consequential, and who was quoted in the *Guardian* as saying that 'There is little point in spending additional money simply to be safer than safe,' is well deserving of some attention, while we are on the subject of thrift. This gentleman, according to the *Guardian*, 'announced a new feasibility study into how the company can reduce radioactive discharges into the Irish Sea to "as near zero as possible."' I am quoting this so that you can share my admiration of the language. 'He said: "Public acceptability of nuclear power is so important and the time-scale needed for a swing-round of public opinion is so long that we must be realistic and accept that our discharges must be reduced to very much lower levels than hitherto planned." This was "even though there is no rational, cost-effective basis for doing so on risk assessment grounds."' Weighing cost against risk again. That really is an interesting exercise—quite theological, I think. Considering that the expense involved in running a nuclear plant safely is truly vast, is it possible to say that the value of a given number of lives is exceeded in cash terms by the expenditure that would be required to prevent their loss? Clearly for these purposes the answer is yes, a fact all the more disturbing since the question is gravely distorted by the association of this slovenly enterprise with 'nuclear power' and by the insistence—based on what?—that anyone, least of all an island of coal in a sea of oil, needs nuclear power in any case. Note Allday's impatience with the idea that discharge levels lower than Sellafield's should be achieved. Does this give us insight into the environmental standards maintained at other facilities?

Even Dr Black, whose report found that the connection between radiation and leukaemia at Sellafield was 'by no means proven,' was quoted by the *Guardian* as having said that 'the risks of living near Sellafield were no greater than many of the risks everyone faced in their daily lives.' He compared the increased risk to that of someone who used a private car rather than public transport. This unctuous little simile translates into an admission that there is some measurable risk involved in living near Sellafield. (Risk of what? Leukaemia, surely, among other things. Then is not the presence of leukaemia this very risk actualized? By no means proven!)

How has this happened? I can only speculate that within a tiny community of specialists, where esteem, advancement, and influence travel through a very narrow channel, and where over the life of a new discipline such as nuclear technology the views of a very few people are reflected in policies of great magnitude and consequence, dissent would have little practical or emotional reward. Choices have been made, by scientists, industrialists, and politicians, that have reflected their willingness to accept human deaths at a certain rate, to put a part of the earth at risk, and the sea, contaminating them irreversibly. They have presumed so far on the basis of notions about the hazards involved that they admit to be conjectural. This is an appalling presumption, truly unpardonable if their notions prove wrong. It ought to be expected, therefore, that their standards of proof would be exceptionally rigorous.

Certainly the development of these policies has been very much affected by the dangers, political and diplomatic, of the issues involved. The British would know the effects of radioactivity if they had monitored the Australians who lived in the path of fallout from the huge, misbegotten hydrogen-bomb test at Monte Bello; or the aborigines who drifted across Maralinga, in South Australia, where radioactive detritus was left behind after British weapons testing; or the populations affected by the fire and the radioactive cloud that drifted south-east and west from Sellafield in 1957. They have given themselves many opportunities to look into this question and availed themselves of none of them, no doubt because to do so would undermine their claims that nothing serious has really happened.

There is, as I have said, the continuing threat of economic erosion to keep the public mind focused on the short-term and the local; and there is the image of the government battling to recoup Britain's losses and restore her scanted dignity; and there is the educational system, which trains very few people and these very narrowly, greatly enhancing the authority of specialists while diminishing the content and forcefulness of public debate and the numbers involved in it. And there is the secretiveness that permeates British life, which allows the Foreign Office to impound the records having to do with Argentina's claims to the Falklands;

which prohibits journalists from reporting what they see in prisons; which conceals the identity of those on the committees that choose Britain's magistrates (the magistrates have no legal training—they simply suit some anonymous notion of worthiness); which leads the governing bodies of cities and counties to conduct their business behind closed doors. The Official Secrets Act is simply the most conspicuous manifestation of all this. Granting that it is used as the basis of prosecutions, and assuming that the *Guardian* is accurate in its accounts of mail-openings, phone-tappings, and break-ins practised by MI5, the British secret police, against groups such as Greenpeace, the Friends of the Earth, and the National Union of Mineworkers—nevertheless, it seems to be that the English, at least, have the government they deserve, that they prefer not to know, and that they have very little capacity for exerting power and influence. I think they feel—deeply feel—that their moral rectitude is preserved intact by this means. The Greenham Common women will never encircle Sellafield, though Britain could desist unilaterally from its war against the sea, which is not a terrifying threat, but a terrifying fact.

Then there is the absence of American reaction to consider—especially puzzling since both Greenpeace and the Friends of the Earth have been involved with Sellafield. British Greenpeace was given a heavy fine—paid by public donations—for tampering with the pipeline, and was induced to intervene to prevent Danish and Dutch Greenpeace ships from sending divers down by the threat that all its resources would be sequestered by the court if they did. Why Greenpeace has chosen not to galvanize public opinion outside the range of such restrictions, I cannot imagine. Perhaps regional patriotism has stood in the way of global matriotism. Or perhaps British environmentalists, like many Europeans of advanced views, believe that American public opinion is too brutish to be enlisted in any good cause. It is a treasured faith among Europeans of the Right and the Left that America is a nation of B-movie villains laying waste to the continent and to one another by any means that come to hand, in a sort of frenzy of capitalist rapacity.

Europeans on the Left enjoy the opinion that they are very advanced thinkers. In fact they are simply intellectual cargo-cultists, to whom accident now and then delivers an elaborated policy, a sophisticated idea, or half of one. That crude, capitalist America should enforce higher standards of public conduct than humane, socialist Europe is not to be imagined. So our example in environmental matters is almost never consulted, and our research and experience are almost never invoked.

We in America are greatly at fault in this. There is a streak of pure yokel that reaches straight to the top of American intellectual life, widening as it goes, and it is deference towards all things 'English'. We cannot believe that the English could be stupid or corrupt. We think of them as our better selves, and the source of our most precious institutions—a slander on the dark and the ethnic and a disparagement of the noisy public dramas of advocates and adversaries that provide us with the legal and ethical capacity for discrimination and judgement. We are capable of outrage and we are capable of shame, like a living soul. If we are fortunate in one thing it is in the knowledge that we *can* do evil, and we *can* do injury. A country incapable of scandal is like a mind incapable of guilt or a body incapable of pain.

On 24 July 1984, the *Guardian* concluded its editorial on the Black report, titled 'Lingering Particles of Unease,' with a call for 'one group of inter-disciplinary experts who do nothing else but shadow it round the clock.' In the editorialist's affable view, 'life with [Sellafield] is a tumultuous and ongoing affair.' On 30 July, the *Guardian* wrote that Charles Haughey, the former Irish prime minister, had called the report a whitewash. He said: 'If there is a high incidence of leukaemia in an area where a nuclear plant is situated, surely to God the obvious interpretation is that the plant was responsible for it. These figures alone would in my view justify closing down the plant immediately for further investigation, and certainly putting a lot of people in gaol who have clearly been telling us lies over the past four or five years about this matter.' The words we have longed to hear. But from the wrong side of the Irish Sea.

MICHAEL CRICK
REPORTING THE STRIKE

Grimethorpe, March 1984. My news desk tells me to go to Yorkshire. The Coal Board had just announced that Cortonwood colliery will close in five weeks, followed by twenty other pits, and that 20,000 jobs are to be lost. A national miners' strike looks a strong possibility.

We pick Grimethorpe by selecting a mining village in the heart of Yorkshire: we have heard something about a brass band, but above all the name sounds just right. And it's what we expect: a pit wheel towering above terraced houses, kids and dogs running around in the street—the southerner's idea of a mining community . . . . Since the coal strikes of 1972 and 1974 the miners here have a much higher standard of living than before: around half own their own homes and the high wage-earners—committed to heavy mortgage payments—are into DIY, videos and foreign holidays. There's even a sauna in the village. The miners can't afford to strike. At least, that's our thesis . . . .

In Grimethorpe I first encounter the Yorkshire miners' hostility to the media: 'You're only interested in us when there's a pit disaster or a strike. Bugger off!' When you approach people with a camera and microphone you don't expect everyone to talk, but usually you get enough to put something together. In the miners' clubs things get nasty, and we're told to turn the cameras off. We decide to leave.

Nottingham, April. The National Coal Board's propaganda insists that 'all Notts pits are working normally.' When the Press Association—for many office-bound sub-editors, the primary, even only, source of information on domestic events—constantly pumps out the NCB's figures it's too easy for London news desks to use them uncritically.

My own tour reveals Notts miners on the picket lines, so how can their pits be working normally? At some, half the work-force is on strike. The strike here is badly misrepresented, but where is a version of events from the National Union of Mineworkers?

Television can film the unusual so often that it seems commonplace. Before I went to Beirut in 1982, I had the impression that few buildings would still be standing: every night television showed the city reduced to rubble. I was surprised to find it largely intact. It's the same with pit violence and the number of pickets meant to be outside Nottinghamshire pits. Touring the coalfield in the early morning you find mass pickets at one or two collieries— which can get violent—but at others there is often only a handful of men; at some none at all. Statistically only a quarter of our picket-line coverage has shown scenes of violence. But it's these scenes that stick.

Orgreave, May. Suddenly everyone is interested in this coking plant outside Sheffield that supplies British Steel. For Scargill, it's another Saltley, the coke depot he closed down in 1972 with a mass picket. He has appeared several times, and on each occasion he gets the kind of reception you expect of a pop star. On arrival, he immediately rallies and organizes his troops. When he isn't here, we see some of the dispute's worst violence.

The miners' hositility to the media has increased: we now get continuous verbal abuse, and sometimes we're physically attacked. At an NUM rally in Mansfield an ITN technician is forced to the ground and urinated on by eight drunken miners. A BBC sound recordist, hit in the back by a brick, is off work for several months. Crews have had equipment and vehicles vandalized. Some TV companies, though not ITN, have decided not to publicize these incidents, fearing that they'll be imitated.

While I interview Scargill BBC cameraman Bernard Hesketh has the video lead ripped from his camera. He waves it in front of Scargill, who only mutters that it is what the BBC should expect after its coverage. I ought to back Hesketh, but that might endanger the interview and worsen relations with Scargill. And dozens of pickets are standing round. I say nothing.

Striking miners accuse television of not showing police violence. We show any we manage to film—at Orgreave several horrific incidents of police beating pickets over the head with truncheons. Nevertheless, more is taking place than we can film— much allegedly in police vans or at police stations. But the police are careful: 'Look out, lads, cameras everywhere,' shouts one police sergeant as his colleagues carry away pickets. The police attempt to prevent us filming miners being arrested, or try to move us on for inflaming the situation.

Television crews do film picket lines nearly always from the police side—tending only to show pickets attacking police—but only because crews on the pickets' side are jostled, spat at and often filming is prevented. The intense hostility makes getting a fair picture difficult, and each time we fail, the pickets get more and more hostile. A TV crew tries to film a policeman attacking a miner but is then set upon by pickets. Even the NUM's own video team has been attacked.

Barnsley, June. Arthur Scargill and Ian MacGregor are to prepare their own films for Channel Four News. I'm helping Scargill, and we're filming his piece to camera outside a derelict pit: Scargill does it in one take—something I never manage. He's a natural. He then interviews the colliery's former branch secretary.'It's nothing new to me,' he tells me outside the miners' meals centre, 'I've been doing local and national TV for twenty years.' Scargill understands not just how little one can say in a few minutes on television, but its logistical problems. About ninety percent of television reporting is spent setting up filming opportunities, travelling to locations, arranging camera crews, editing pictures and getting them back to London. The information-gathering and writing of traditional journalism take up very little time.

In the early seventies Yorkshire Television and BBC Leeds indentified Scargill as the articulate spokesman for the left-wing of the union then emerging in the Yorkshire NUM. He was soon known throughout the county and consequently rose higher and higher in the union through a series of election victories. But his attitude to the media is ambivalent: no left-wing figure has been more critical of it. When speaking at rallies, he now begins—it's virtually a ritual—with an attack on the media, directed at the camera crews present. And when interviewed Scargill often evades difficult questions by suddenly accusing the interviewer of 'bias'. But his accusations are not always logical: the only picket-line violence *he* knows about is police violence; on the other hand television never shows police violence. If we are always showing violence, but it is never police violence—whose is it?

Cardiff, July. Wales offers a contrast: the miners are friendly, full of suggestions for things to film—more than we can take up—and their criticisms are constructive and considered. My reports are better than anything produced in Yorkshire because I can get to the heart of the mining communities. The Welsh miners have always been militant and left-wing—their politics are historical, traditional, part of their education—whereas Yorkshire militancy seems to be less deeply rooted, and derives from the power realized in recent picketing successes. And in Yorkshire it is Scargill who has taught the miners to hate the media.

Among the media television teams suffer the most from this hatred, even more than the newspaper journalists, whose papers often vehemently oppose the miners' cause. A *Sun* reporter can hide among the crowd; we can hardly disguise our cameras. Even some sympathetic members of the television union ACTT have lost patience: when one cameraman popped two pounds into a miners' collecting bucket and was then set upon by other miners, he took his money back.

August. The press is obsessed with 'the drift back to work'. Every day men are returning, but in numbers as low as a dozen. But with Parliament away and people on holiday these few miners are made lead stories. I calculate that at this rate the strike will be over by 1994.

Silver Birch, an 'anonymous Notts miner' helping men to return to work, is revealed in the *Mail on Sunday* as Chris Butcher, a blacksmith at Bevercotes. In their eagerness to link him with 'the drift back' few journalists ask who exactly Silver Birch is, or what interests he represents, or the extent of his 'following': is he in fact just a one-man-band playing largely to the media?

Brighton, September. The TUC Congress is dominated by the prospect of yet more coal talks. Even Robert Maxwell is here claiming to have set up new negotiations. Talks are on, then off, and television is always on hand to film each side responding to or insulting the other: it's good viewing, but does little to further a settlement.

When talks do start, the negotiating teams are hunted by the media entourage from one secret location to another. In a rare moment of unity, Scargill and MacGregor emerge together to condemn media harrassment.

October. Two studies show that Scargill has had two to three times more air-time than MacGregor, but Michael Tracey of the Broadcasting Research Unit believes that Scargill's questioning has been more hostile. Certainly Scargill's combative approach encourages an interview to become an argument, and his reluctance to answer in a straightforward way further courts antagonism. Nevertheless, some exchanges with the press are more like interrogations than interviews; on *Panorama* he was asked: 'You're a disaster, aren't you?'

November. The National Coal Board's skilful propaganda claims that men are returning daily in hundreds, even thousands, and detailed figures are supplied first thing to news desks every day. Some journalists don't bother to attribute the figures to the Board (ITN is one of the exceptions), and most have generally adopted the Board's phrase 'the drift back' despite its suggestion of a continuous and inevitable process. In contrast, the Government won't issue full figures for the cost of the dispute—and with independent estimates varying wildly it's impossible to illustrate the rising costs on the news as we can the 'drift back to work.' It's certainly several billion pounds.

December. I'm determined to cover the National Working Miners' Committee—the group largely responsible for the legal actions against the NUM—and particularly its links with the mysterious David Hart, who also advises MacGregor and Mrs Thatcher. I know all the details—it's a good story—but I can't put it together for television. The Chairman won't talk to me—another Channel Four programme, he feels, has misrepresented him—and the committee therefore won't let us film its meetings. David Hart won't do an interview until after the strike, and the former secretary, with plenty of information on the committee's connections with Hart, won't be filmed either. A newspaper could write a report easily, but I'm stuck without decent pictures. The story falls by the wayside.

January 1985. The strike receives almost as much coverage as when it began: the miners generate new television ideas where any other strike would have long since exhausted its visual images. Nevertheless it's too easy to illustrate the strike with violent picket lines and men going back to work: how do you show a pit closing? And too often TV's images have been stereotyped: a colliery must still be a set of winding wheels, although many modern pits don't have traditional winding gear, and mining villages have to be old terraced streets, although many are modern estates. But one of the ironies of our stereotyped images—the *How Green Was My Valley* shots—is that they unintentionally reinforce the miners' case that long-established communities are being destroyed.

Striking miners follow television coverage very closely and frequently discuss with me news items I've done before: in doing a piece now I bear in mind their possible criticisms. They devour information; in the welfare and strike centres they watch *all* the TV news bulletins. Less active miners, at home all day, must watch even more.

Working for 'Channel Four News' I've been more fortunate than most reporters. It was soon the most popular news programme with strikers, partly because the channel had presented several independent companies' sympathetic documentaries on the dispute, but also because at fifty minutes long Channel Four News could allow miners to put their views at length. Some mining communities now know it as 'The Pickets' News'.

February. The NUM could have done far more to publicize its case. The Coal Board has seventy full-time people dealing with press and public relations; the union has one: Nell Myers, Arthur Scargill's personal assistant (a sign of how he regards the media), who is badly overworked and difficult to find. Somehow she manages to live in London and work in Sheffield. I spend hours on the phone to NUM headquarters trying to get some kind of comment from them on the Board's latest back-to-work figures. I usually get nowhere.

'May I speak to Arthur Scargill or Nell Myers?'
'Who's calling?'
'Michael Crick of "Channel Four News"'

'I'm sorry, they're both out at the moment.' Whether they are in seems to depend on who I am. The Coal Board's case wins by default.

Provisional Sinn Fein, the Militant tendency and other left-wing organizations keep in constant touch with the media, and indeed NUM branch officials always give interviews and assist with filming. But not, it seems, the senior people. I have suggested to Scargill that he employ more people on press work: it would make my reporting much easier. But Scargill didn't think much of this: dealing with the press is only a minor part of NUM operations. During a major strike, when public opinion is vitally important? And then why does he appear on television so much?

I suspect Scargill fears losing personal control. He works closely with Nell Myers: every press statement he personally approves; many he writes. Sometimes he will ring up a journalist to complain about some particular point or to offer a piece of information. I once spent twenty minutes going through figures of men on strike with him. It's good that he should do this—I can't imagine Ian MacGregor doing so—but surely it could be left to other NUM people, who might also contact us more regularly?

Cortonwood, March. To the pit where the strike began. I arrive soon after the news from London that the strike is over. As our car draws up the pickets are swigging beer in apparent celebration. Just as soon as we've got the camera gear out the beer cans have disappeared. The pickets don't want to be *seen* to be glad it's over.

PETER GREIG
REVELATIONS

The great era for exposing government lying and 'dirty tricks' was in the United States more than a decade ago. But long after Richard Nixon disappeared, protesting, from the world's televisions, the name 'Watergate' has stuck as a synonym for the shenanigans by which he is probably best remembered. And clearly it stuck in the minds of British government ministers faced with the aftermath of the Belgrano affair in March 1984.

Two years earlier, as the rest of the world looked on, half-amused, half-impressed by this anachronistic twitch of the imperial lion's tail, a large British naval armada sailed south to recover the Falkland Islands by force of arms.

The British government, headed by the famously resolute Mrs Thatcher, said in public that their plans were to use 'minimum force' coupled with diplomatic negotiation, and thus to oust the invading Argentine *junta* from these remote and largely worthless islands, which were only occupied by a handful of British, or near-British, families. In the event, the affair rapidly turned into a full-scale shooting war. With considerable loss of life, the Falklands were re-invaded, the Argentines forced to surrender bag and baggage, and Mrs Thatcher reaped considerable short-term political benefits from a jingoistic public. The long-term consequences, however, left many political commentators aghast; they included not only a long-term garrisoning of 'Fortress Falklands', but also the enormous cost of doing so: so far, more than two billion pounds, plus another half billion every year, indefinitely.

For these reasons, the whole Falklands controversy crystallized very early on around the sinking of the Argentine cruiser *General Belgrano* on 2 May 1982. The cruiser was torpedoed by a British nuclear-powered submarine and sank, killing 368 sailors on board. It was the first serious military clash of the affair, and it came at the moment when the question 'Peace or War?' was most seriously being considered. After the sinking of the *Belgrano*, there was no going back, either for Britain or Argentina.

The question of why the *Belgrano* was sunk at that particular moment was therefore seen—both at the time and subsequently—as of first-class political importance. All the more significant, then, that it has turned out that the British government's initial version of the events surrounding the sinking was, in many parts, incorrect and misleading.

This was the secret discovered in March 1984 by an Assistant Secretary in the Ministry of Defence, Clive Ponting. His political boss, the Defence Secretary Michael Heseltine, was faced with persistent questioning about the affair: he had not been one of the five members of the War Cabinet who had taken the decision at the time, and his predecessor, John Nott, had rather mysteriously retired not only from the job, but from political life altogether.

Heseltine is reported to have made a significant remark: 'I want to make sure there isn't a Watergate in this somewhere.' He ordered Ponting to prepare a secret report, with full access to the most security-sensitive recesses of ministry archives, which would contain the truth about the *Belgrano*'s sinking. Heseltine adopted an even more significant nickname for Ponting's report. He called it the 'Crown Jewels'.

This nickname would have stirred echoes in those who remembered the Watergate years. Part of the unsavouriness of that time was the discovery that the CIA had been engaged in a series of unscrupulous 'dirty tricks'. Faced with the probing of the congressional committee headed by Frank Church, CIA operations director James Schlesinger ordered one of his trusted officials to prepare a similar report. It was to detail all the unconstitutional attempts made over the years by the CIA to assassinate foreign leaders. This compilation of schemes to foist exploding cigars and the like on Castro and other leaders was locked in the safe. It too had a nickname: the 'Family Jewels'.

The contents of the 'Family Jewels' eventually came out. Similarly it is probably now time that the contents of the 'Crown Jewels' emerged.

The basic document is in the form of a chronological log of the events of those few days. It has eighty-six numbered 'serials'. Number one is the declaration of an 'Exclusion Zone' by Britain around the Falklands, and number eighty-six is the text of a warning to all Argentine ships, finally issued by Britain some days *after* she had sunk the *Belgrano*. Attached to the report are the decrypted texts of a number of coded Argentine navy signals obtained by Britain's surveillance chain run from General

253

Communications Headquarters, the GCHQ, at Cheltenham. This chronological log represents the fundamental source of intelligence that at the time lay behind the decision to sink the Belgrano, and it turns out to tell an interesting story.

The 'Crown Jewels' had a very high security classification, presumably stamped on it by Ponting himself. This was: 'TOP SECRET—CODEWORD'. The basic security classification system of British officialdom has four levels: 'RESTRICTED'; 'CONFIDENTIAL'; 'SECRET'; 'TOP SECRET'.

The Crown Jewels went one step higher. The 'CODEWORD' to which it refers requires the most elaborate safety precautions, and restricts, to the greatest extent possible, the number of individuals allowed to see the material. It covers nuclear, intelligence and sensitive diplomatic matters. In the case of the Crown Jewels, the relevant codeword was 'UMBRA'. This meant that they contained extracts from Signals Intelligence, run by GCHQ with the help of the United States.

On 7 April, 1982, Britain announced the imposition of a maritime 'Exclusion Zone' extending 200 miles around the occupied Falklands. This was five days after the Argentine invasion, and the British naval armada was beginning to steam on its long journey 8,000 miles south. Argentina was given 'fair warning': the Zone would not come into effect for another five days, until 12 April. In threatening Argentina in this way, Britain was not declaring war, a course which would have forced the United States into formal neutrality. She was acting with strict legality under Article Fifty-one of the United Nations Charter, giving victims of aggression the specific, but limited right of self-defence. If Argentine ships penetrated the zone, Britain would sink them. The means by which she intended to do so, was the advance guard of a small flotilla of British nuclear-powered submarines, which had been sent ahead.

A fortnight later, on 23 April, the British and Argentine forces were a good deal closer. Peace negotiations mediated by US Secretary of State Alexander Haig were failing to oust the Argentinians. Mrs Thatcher's 'War Cabinet' were attempting, with eventual success, to direct a military assault on the remote and outlying island of South Georgia. The Argentine fleet had put to sea, but was showing no disposition to penetrate the 'Exclusion Zone', or to move on the British armada now well into the South Atlantic.

One British submarine, *Splendid*, was taken off surveillance of Argentina's main naval threat, the aircraft carrier *Veinticinco de Mayo*, but the move was coupled with a public warning. 'Any approach by Argentine warships or military aircraft which could amount to a threat to the task force will be dealt with appropriately.' This threat too was clearly within a legalistic framework of self-defence, but the hawks and doves within the War Cabinet were beginning to surface. Admiral Lewin, Chief of the Defence Staff, says he had washed his hands of diplomacy by now, and indeed navy signals were sent to the fleet promising the virtual certainty of full-scale military action in the Falklands. John Nott, on the other hand, then the Defence Secretary, claims he still had hopes of peace. And, of course, the public posture of the War Cabinet was still that it members wished to see a negotiated settlement, through the good offices of Alexander Haig.

Three days later, the British intelligence machine picked up its first information about the World War II heavy cruiser, the *General Belgrano*. The signals were intercepted, fed back to Cheltenham, decoded, and telexed to two British locations: 10 Downing St and the naval battle headquarters at Northwood. They disclosed that the orders of the *Belgrano* and her destroyer escorts that made up the southern group of Argentina's naval task force were to patrol in a straight line out from the Argentine coast, keeping south of the Falklands and the Exclusion Zone, until they reached a set point beyond the islands. There, they were to turn round and patrol back again. Within twenty-four hours of the GCHQ intercept, another British submarine, *Conqueror*, was taken off tasks in South Georgia (the garrison there had by now surrendered) and ordered towards the Argentine coast to intercept and monitor this new and possibly dangerous group.

3 0 April was the day events came to a military climax. It is hard to avoid the conclusion that this was the day on which Britain decided to go to war. When the War Cabinet met, its members had just been informed that the United States proposed to 'tilt' diplomatically on the side of Britain. Argentina would not submit to British terms. Any military action Britain now took would be with US logistic and intelligence support—in practical terms, this meant fuel supplies would be shipped to the staging-post of Ascension Island, and US satellites would be available both for communications and intelligence. With the approach of carrier-borne British planes and missiles, Argentina had been given another 'fair warning': from the 30 April, the Exclusion Zone would become total, including the invaders' planes as well as its ships.

The War Cabinet met and agreed that diplomacy was, for the time being at least, finished. Instead, a military logic would take over, and Argentine forces would be attacked on and around the Falklands. The idea was partly to frighten Argentina, and partly, in the words of Admiral Woodward, commander of the British fleet: 'to lay on a major demonstration of force . . . to make the Argentines believe that landings were due to take place, and thus provoke a reaction that would enable me to conduct a major attrition exercise.' The 'demonstration of force' consisted of bombing raids, both long-distance from Ascension, and by Harriers from the British task force off the islands. At the same time, British destroyers closed in to Port Stanley, and shelled it.

The War Cabinet took another decision on 30 April. As well as authorizing these attacks, it agreed to put Argentina's most formidable naval unit, the aircraft carrier *Veinticinco de Mayo*, out of action. It was perhaps understandable that, although intending to provoke an Argentine 'reaction', the War Cabinet should not want it to be too formidable: the carrier's Skyhawks had a 500-mile range and the task force was short of air cover. But there was a legal problem—perhaps even, although there is no evidence the War Cabinet considered it in these terms—a moral problem. The aircraft carrier was not attacking the British. Nor was it inside the 'Total Exclusion Zone'. On what basis could the British order it to be torpedoed, no doubt with great loss of life, at a time when not a single British soldier had been killed during the Falklands affair? It might, the War Cabinet agreed, look bad in the eyes of the world.

The doves on this issue included Francis Pym, the Foreign Secretary. The hawks naturally included the military, who said they would only feel secure if the *Vienticinco de Mayo* stayed at least 700 miles away from the Falklands, and close inshore to the Argentine coast, where it could not sally out to intercept the strung-out ships of the British fleet, many still plugging south with men and equipment. The best way of ensuring this, in their view, was to sink the ship. The War Cabinet of Mrs Thatcher agreed not merely to warn off the carrier but to commit what the world might well see as a murderous act. The only moral justification available was that a captured submarine's order in South Georgia had revealed that the Argentine navy had its own instructions to sink British ships, should a suitable opportunity arise.

That night, the orders for the whole major British assault went out. But Pym was deeply disturbed. The next morning, 1 May, he talked to Sir Michael Havers, the government's legal specialist. Before catching a plane for Washington, where a fresh attempt was supposedly to be made to start peace talks with the mediation of Peru, he signed a letter to Mrs Thatcher. A copy was sent to John Nott, the Defence Secretary, and another to Sir Michael Havers. A copy also went to the War Cabinet's other major member, William Whitelaw, and one to Sir Robert Armstrong, the Cabinet Secretary and head of the civil service.

Pym wrote:

Attack on Argentine aircraft carrier

1. Following our decision . . . yesterday to authorise an attack without warning on the Argentine aircraft carrier outside our exclusion zone, I have been giving a further thought to the line we should take in public after the event.

2. After discussion with the Attorney General about the way in which our action would have to be publicly justified and its legality defended, I believe our position would be immeasurably strengthened if we had given a warning to the Argentine government, requiring the aircraft carrier to stay within the narrow zone we discussed yesterday, or within territorial waters south of about 41 degrees South.

3. I attach a draft of a possible warning message which we could ask the Swiss to convey urgently to the Argentine government. This in no way alters the substance of the decision we took yesterday. But I believe it would greatly strengthen our hand in dealing with criticism at home and abroad once an attack on the carrier had been carried out.

Pym attached a draft warning entitled 'NOTIFICATION TO THE ARGENTINE GOVERNMENT'. It said that in the light of Argentina's statement of 30 April—that all British vessels within 200 miles of the mainland, the Falklands, and its dependencies would be considered hostile—the British Government had decided that the *Veinticinco de Mayo* was not to enter what was, in effect, a much larger exclusion zone than the one previously announced. Specifically, the *Veinticinco de Mayo* was not to move east of forty-five degrees longitude or south of thirty-eight degrees latitude or outside a limit of twelve miles from the coast of the mainland or north of forty-one degrees latitude. If it did, the *Veinticinco de Mayo* would be considered hostile and dealt with accordingly. Pym went on to say that 'if any attack anywhere in the South Atlantic is made upon British naval or air forces by an Argentine unit, all other Argentine naval units operating on the high seas, including the carrier THE 25TH OF MAY,' will be considered, regardless of their location, 'hostile and are liable to be dealt with accordingly.'

No such warning was sent.

These rather incriminating documents were listed as 'Serial 24' in the Crown Jewels. But the planned destruction of the *Veinticinco de Mayo* never occurred, in Britian's biggest military error of the affair to that date. When the submarine *Splendid* was ordered to resume contact and go in for the kill, the aircraft carrier could no longer be found.

This made 1 May a rather nerve-wracking day for the British military. The planned bombing and strafing of the Falklands went ahead as planned. What would be the Argentine reaction that this assault was designed to provoke?

An answer came soon enough from the intelligence-gathering machinery of GCHQ. That evening, GCHQ picked up and decrypted Argentine fleet orders. Argentina believed in the British feint, and that it was a full-scale reinvasion attempt. In a do-or-die gesture, two groups of the Argentine fleet, the northern group headed by the *Veinticinco de Mayo*, and a central group of corvettes, were ordered out to engage the British fleet.

In fact, on receipt of the GCHQ decrypts, an intelligence analyst at Northwood wrote an assessment saying that Argentina's *third* naval group, the *Belgrano* and escorts, had also been ordered on to the attack as well. The submarine *Conqueror*, which had previously found and trailed the *Belgrano* as instructed, would have been signalled with this intelligence prediction. Once the *Belgrano* turned north, into the Exclusion Zone, she could, of course, be attacked. The crew of the submarine waited tensely—and, as it turned out, futilely—for the *Belgrano* to become a legitimate target.

The interception of this Argentine navy signal at 19.55 GMT had even wider consequences. It was on the basis of the intelligence summary prepared as a result, that the War Cabinet persuaded themselves they were now entitled to declare all-out war—in effect—on the Argentine navy. They had been triggered into attacking Britain. Britain therefore was entitled, without further warning, to attack all Argentine vessels wherever found on the high seas.

In fact, just as Britain failed to find the Argentine carrier earlier in the day, so the Argentine carrier failed to find the task force as it withdrew eastwards. At around midnight, London time, GCHQ intercepted a second Argentine signal rescinding the previous order. The attack was off.

What was made of the intercepted signal? We can only speculate. Perhaps the Northwood analysts, erring on the side of prudence, interpreted the signal as being of uncertain meaning: perhaps the attack was only temporarily suspended; perhaps, indeed, Argentina knew its codes were being broken, and was sending deliberately misleading signals . . . .

By dawn on 2 May, a further unmistakeable Argentine signal was intercepted. Despatched at 5.19 GMT from Rear-Admiral Lombardo on the mainland to Vice-Admiral Allara at sea on his flagship, it confirmed the previous recall order, stressed the threat the British posed to Argentine ships, and concluded that the British assault on the Falklands had terminated. All elements of the Argentine fleet were retreating from the bloody confrontation which—by accident and good luck—had not occurred.

This signal, once decoded, would have deprived the British navy of any excuse to start shooting on the high seas, at any rate without the previous 'fair warnings' so punctiliously given. Although Labour MP Tam Dalyell claims that this signal, like others, *was* decoded and passed on to the War Cabinet, inquiries conducted last year revealed no trace of the decyphered text. Is it possible to conclude that, among the many messages GCHQ so professionally intercepted and broke, this one was not decoded at the time?

At 9.15 a.m. Lord Lewin, chief of the defence staff, arrived at Northwood Navy Headquarters. He studied the early morning intelligence summary, with its incorrect predictions that Argentina might still be on the attack and that the *Belgrano* was expected to turn north and join in. He was told that Admiral Woodward, in the South Atlantic, had been in touch that very morning, asking anxiously that the rules of engagement be changed so that the *Belgrano* be sunk regardless of its remaining outside the Exclusion Zone.

The true position was in fact that, at virtually the split second Lewin was poring over the intelligence summary, the *Belgrano* was turning round. She had reached the designated limit of her patrol, and following her original and unaltered orders, was reversing course back to Argentina. She was dogged, as she had been for two days now, by the submarine *Conqueror* and its somewhat puzzled and frustrated crew.

Lewin, with his out-of-date, incomplete, and inaccurate intelligence summary, drove down to Chequers, where the War Cabinet was due to meet over lunch. The 'Crown Jewels' do not contain any minute of what occurred at their meeting, so history is likely to remain silent.

What is fact is that Lewin emerged with authority to abandon all the previously restrictive 'Rules of Engagement' which had governed encounters between British and Argentine ships. Without warning, all-out naval war was secretly declared. A signal was immediately sent to the *Conqueror*, authorizing her to sink the *Belgrano* wherever and whenever she liked, and any other ships *Conqueror* could find.

The commander of the *Conqueror* did not respond to the first order he received. He may have been puzzled, because it bore no relation to his previous orders on the subject. And the *Belgrano* was, as he could see, ploughing homewards, attacking no one. He recorded the signal on his log as 'garbled'. Two hours later, he took another sighting of the *Belgrano*, confirming its steady reversal of course. As an automatic repeat of the 'sinking' order came through, the commander transmitted in the opposite direction his up-to-date figures on the *Belgrano*'s course. This information, which appeared significant enough to the *Conqueror*, was ignored at Northwood. Ministers later said that no one told them at the time, but they supposed it was 'irrelevant'.

Only on the third transmission of his orders, six hours after the War Cabinet decision, did the commander signal that he had understood and would comply.

He torpedoed the ship. It was the first major British naval engagement since World War II. The Belgrano went down, and 368 sailors, mainly conscripts, were killed. No British soldier had died, although many were to in succeeding days. Only three hours later, according to the 'Crown Jewels', Foreign Office telegrams arrived telling of what seemed to be promising new peace negotiations via Peru. They were now pointless. Lord Lewin later said, in a phrase which does not appear in the dry recitals of the 'Crown Jewels': 'The sinking was what any reasonably red-blooded Englishman would have done.' From then on, a good deal of blood flowed and it was, as Lord Lewin had said, reasonably red.

QUARTET ENCOUNTER

Quartet Encounter is a vivid and exciting new publishing concept: major European literature, with introductions by distinguished contemporary writers, available in paperback for the first time.

Aharon Appelfeld · *The Retreat*   £3.95
'A small masterpiece . . . the vision of a remarkable poet'
New York Times Book Review

Grazia Deledda · *After the Divorce*   £4.95
'What [Deledda] does is create the passionate complex
of a primitive populace' D.H. Lawrence

Carlo Emilio Gadda · *That Awful Mess on
Via Merulana*   £7.95
'One of the greatest and most original Italian novels of
our time' Alberto Moravia

Gustav Janouch · *Conversations with Kafka*   £5.95
'I read it and was stunned by the wealth of new material
. . . which plainly and unmistakably bore the stamp of
Kafka's genius' Max Brod

Henry de Montherlant · *The Bachelors*   £4.95
'One of those carefully framed, precise and acid studies
on a small canvas in which French writers again and
again excel' V.S. Pritchett

Stanislaw Ignacy Witkiewicz · *Insatiability*   £7.50
'A study of decay: mad, dissonant music; erotic
perversion; . . . and complex psychopathic personalities'
Czeslaw Milosz

Quartet Books Limited
A member of the Namara Group
27/29 Goodge Street, London W1P 1FD

GRANTA

NOTES FROM ABROAD

Ted Solotaroff
Writing in the Cold

During the decade of editing *New American Review*, I was often struck by how many gifted young writers there were in America. They would arrive every month, three or four of them, accomplished or close to it, full of wit and panache or a steady power or a fine, quiet complexity. We tried to devote twenty-five percent of each issue to these new voices and seldom failed to meet the quota. Where were they all coming from? They seemed to come from everywhere: Dixon, New Mexico, and Seal Rock, Oregon, as well as· Chicago and San Francisco, from English departments in community colleges as well as the big creative writing centres. They also came amid the 1,200 or so manuscripts we received each month. Eugenics alone would seem to dictate that half of one percent of the writing population would be brilliant.

What has happened to all of that bright promise? When I look through the cumulative index of the *New American Review*, I see that perhaps one-quarter of our discoveries have gone on to have reasonably successful careers; about the same number still have marginal ones, part of the alternative literary community of the little magazines and small presses. And about half have disappeared. It's as though some sinister force were at work, a kind of literary population control mechanism that kills off the surplus talent we have been developing or causes it to wither slowly away.

Literary careers are difficult to speculate about. They are so individual, so subject to personal circumstances that are often hidden to the writer himself. What is not hidden is likely to be held so secretly that even the editor who works closely with a writer knows little more about his or her sources of fertility and potency than anyone else, and the writers who fail are even more inclined to draw a cover of silence over the reasons. Still, it's worth considering why some gifted writers have careers and others don't. It doesn't appear to be a matter of the talent itself—some of the most natural writers, the ones who seemed to shake their prose or poetry out of their sleeves, are among the disappeared. As far as I can tell, the decisive factor is durability. For the gifted writer, durability seems to be directly connected to how one deals with uncertainty, rejection, and disappointment, from within as well as from without, and how effectively one incorporates them into the creative process itself, particularly in the prolonged first stage of a career. In what follows, I'll be writing about fiction writers, the group I know best. But I don't imagine that poets, playwrights, and essayists will find much that is different.

T hirty years ago when I came out of college and went off to become a writer I expected to remain unknown and unrewarded for ten years or so. So did my few associates in this precarious enterprise. Indeed, our low expectations were, we felt, a measure of our high seriousness. We were hardly going to give ourselves less time and difficulty than our heroes— Joyce and Flaubert, say—gave themselves. It was a dubious career, and none of our families understood, much less supported, us. Nor were there any universities—except for Iowa and Stanford—that wanted us around once we'd got a degree, except as prospective scholars. Not that we knew how to cope with the prolonged isolation and likely poverty that faced us—who does until he has been through them?—but at least we expected them and even understood something of their necessity.

I don't find that our counterparts in the present generation are as aware of the struggle to come. As the products of American postwar affluence and an undemanding literary education, most of them have very little experience with struggle of any kind. Their expectations of a writer's life have been formed by the mass-marketing and subsidization of culture and by the creative writing industry, and their career models are not, say, William Faulkner or Henry Miller but John Irving or Ann Beattie. Instead of the jazz musicians and painters of thirty years ago somehow making do, the other arts provide them with the model life-styles of rock stars and the young princes of New York's Soho. There is not a Guggenheim or Yaddo writers' residency far up the road, but a whole array of public and private grants, colonies and fellowships that seem just around the corner. Most of all, there is the prospect—not immediate but still only a few significant publications away—of teaching, with its comfortable life and free time. As the poet William Matthews recently remarked, 'What our students seem mainly to want to do is to become us, though they have no idea of what we've gone through.'

I don't think one can understand the literary situation today without dealing with the one genuine revolutionary development in American letters during the second half of the century: the rise of the creative writing programs. At virtually one stroke we have solved the age-old problem of how literary men and women are to support themselves: today they teach writing. They place themselves in an environment, mild and relatively static, whose main population is always growing a year younger and whose beliefs and attitudes become the writer's principal reflection of the society-at-large. Because of the peculiar institution of tenure, the younger writer tends to publish too quickly and the older one too little. It's no wonder that steady academic employment has done strange things to a number of literary careers and, to my mind, has devitalized the relationship between literature, particularly fiction, and society.

For a young writer, the graduate writing program is a mixed blessing: while it starts him out under conditions that are extremely favourable, they are also extremely unreal. At a university or college like Johns Hopkins or Houston or Sarah Lawrence or the twenty or thirty others with prestigious programs, the chances are that several highly accomplished, even famous, writers will be reading one's work—John Barth, perhaps, or Donald Barthelme, or Grace Paley. His work will be taken very seriously, and also read by a responsive and usually supportive audience—the other writers in the program: a small, intense milieu that envisages the good life as a literary career. And, of course, he will have a structure of work habits provided by the workshops, degree requirements, and deadlines.

While I think graduate writing programs are mostly wasted on the young, I can also see these programs as a kind of greenhouse that enables certain talents to bloom, particularly those that produce straightforward well-made stories, the kind that teach well in class, and, depending on the teacher, even certain eccentric ones, particularly those patterned on a prevailing fashion of post-modernism. Nevertheless, the graduate writing program makes the next stage—being out there by oneself in the cold—particularly chilling. Here, she receives not personal and enlightened responses to her writing, but mostly rejection slips. Instead of standing out, she is among the anonymous masses. Without a literary community, she now has to rely on herself for stimulation, support, and discipline. And writing itself has to be fitted into the interstices left by a full-time job or parenthood. In short, her character as a writer will now be tested—and not for a year or two but much more likely for five or ten.

That's how long it generally takes for the gifted young fiction writer to find his way, to come into her own. The two fiction writers whose work appears to be the most admired and influential in the graduate writing programs just now are Bobbie Ann Mason and Raymond Carver. Mason spent some seven years writing an unpublished novel, and then story after story, sending each one to Roger Angell, an editor at the *New Yorker*, getting it back, writing another until finally the twentieth one was accepted. In his essay 'Fires', Carver tells about the decade of struggle to write the stories that grew out of his heavily burdened life of 'working at crap jobs' and raising two children until an editor, Gordon Lish, began to beckon from the tower of *Esquire*. It would be another seven years before Carver's first book appeared. Three novelists whose recent 'arrival' I attended—Lynne Sharon

Schwartz, Joan Chase and Douglas Unger—were by then in their thirties and each had already written at least one unpublished novel. My most recent find, Alan Hewat, whose novel *Lady's Time* will be published this summer, is in his early forties and has written two unpublished novels.

Why this long delay? These writers no longer regard it as one. All of them say that the unpublished novels shouldn't have been published, and that they were mainly part of a protracted effort to find a voice, a more or less individual and stable style that best uncovers and delivers the writer's material. And this effort simply requires time. The writer in his middle twenties is not that far removed from adolescence and its insecurities; indeed, the high level sensitivity he is trying to develop comes precisely from that side of himself that he probably tried to deny only a few years ago as freakish, unmanly and unpopular. Hence the painful paradoxes of his new vocation: that his most vulnerable side is now his working one—the one that goes forth into the world and represents him; and that through this vulnerable side he must now find his subject: *his* understanding about how and why he and others live, and *his* conviction about what is morally significant in their lives as well as his own. And all of this from a self that is likely to be rejected each time it looks for confirmation by sending out a manuscript.

The typical student in creative writing has spent eighteen of his, say, twenty-five years in school and university. His grasp of how people live and feel and look at things is still fairly limited to books and films—sources he still needs to sift out—and to his family and its particular culture, from which he is probably rebelling in predictable ways. Throw in a few love-affairs and friendships, a year or two of scattered work experience, perhaps a trip abroad, and his consciousness is still playing a very limited hand. (There appears to be a long term psycho-social trend over the past fifty years or so in which each generation takes several years longer to mature than the preceding one: many of the post-war generation of fiction writers such as Mailer, Bellow, Styron, Baldwin, Bowles, Flannery O'Connor, Truman Capote, Updike, Roth, Reynolds Prices were highly developed by their mid- to late twenties.) The writer's gift itself may keep him from understanding his true situation by producing a few exceptional stories, or even a novel from the most deeply held experiences of his life. But except for these he has only his share of the common life of his age that he must learn to see and write about in a complex and uncommon way.

A young writer I know won a national award a few years ago for the best short story submitted by the various writing programs. It was one of a group of several remarkable stories that she published, almost all of them about members of her family, grey-collar people finely viewed in their contemporary perplexities by her as the kid sister and the one who would leave. But almost nothing she wrote later came near their standard; the new fiction was mostly about a difficult love affair to which she was still too close to write about with the same circumspection and touch as her family stories. After they were turned down, she went to work reading for a film company. Recently she sold an adaptation of one of her early stories, is now writing another script, and is looking to take up fiction again. By the time she publishes her first collection, if she does, she'll be well into her thirties.

What she has been going through as a fiction writer is the crisis of rejection from without and, more importantly, from within. All writers are always sending themselves rejection letters, as the late George P. Elliot observed, to this sentence and paragraph and turn of the story, or—heartbreak time—to the story that has eluded months of tracking, or the hundred pages of a novel that has come to a dead stop. Through adversity the writer learns to separate rejection of her work from self-rejection, and self-criticism from self-distrust. For the inexperienced writer a year or two of rejection or a major rejection of, say, a novel, can lead all too easily to self-distrust, and from there to a disabling distrust of the writing process itself. Anxious, depressed, defensive, the writer gives up her most fundamental and enabling right: the right to write uncertainly, roughly, even badly. A garden in the early stage is not a compelling place: it's a lot of arduous, messy, noisome work—digging up the hard ground, putting in the fertilizer, then the seeds and seedlings. So with beginning a story or novel. But the self-rejecting writer goes not from task to task, as in a garden, but from creating to judging: from her mind to the typewriter to the waste-paper basket, and in time, her mind becomes a ruthless system of self-cancellation.

The longer this goes on, the more writing becomes not a process but an issue of entitlement and prohibition. Even if she hits upon an exciting first sentence or paragraph or even a whole opening development, the dull stuff returns, her uncertainty follows, and soon she is back in court again, testifying against herself. To stay in this state too long is to reach the dead-end of narcissistic despair known as writer's block in which vanity and guilt have so persecuted craft and imagination and so deprived them of their allies—heart, curiosity, will—that they have gone into exile and into the sanctuary of silence.

It is not too much to say that how well a writer copes with rejection determines whether he has a genuine literary vocation or just a literary flair. Rejection along with uncertainty are as much a part of a writer's life as snow and cold are of an Eskimo's: they are conditions one has not only to learn to live with but also learn to make use of.

Most youthful first novels lack complexity, the evidence of prolonged struggle with uncertainty. They typically keep as much as possible to the lived lines of the author's life, providing the security of a certain factuality but at the expense of depriving the imagination of its authority. Too insistent here, too vague there, the novel is often overstuffed and overwritten: the doubt of what belongs and what doesn't being too easily resolved by leaving it in. If he has some literary sophistication, the writer may try to quell uncertainty by allying himself with some current literary fashion. Of course, the struggle with uncertainty may intermittently be strongly engaged and won: the material rings true, the narrative grows intense and unpredictable. If there is enough earned truth and power the manuscript is viable and its deadnesses are relatively detectable. The rest is mostly a matter of the writer's willingness to persist in his gift and its process and to put his ego aside.

Douglas Unger, whose first novel, *Leaving the Land*, was received with considerable acclaim last year, began writing it in 1976. He had already had a previous novel optioned by a major publisher, had rewritten it three times to meet his editor's reservations, only to have it finally rejected. 'He literally threw the manuscript at me and told me to get out of his office. Since I didn't know what to do next—I didn't have an agent or anything—I enrolled at the Iowa Writers' Workshop.' I met him there the following year when I used the opening section of his next novel to teach a workshop. It begins with a young woman, Marge, walking along the street of a farm town in the Dakotas, on her way to be fitted for a wedding dress by her prospective mother-in-law. It is just after World War II, in which her two brothers have been killed, and she has chosen the best of a bad lot. The writing was remarkably sensitive to the coarse and delicate weave of a farm girl's childhood and adolescence and to the pathos of her love life. At the same time, Unger wrote vividly about crops and farm machinery and the plight of farmers, driven by wartime policy into the clutches of a giant food trust that had driven down the farmers' prices and wanted their land. Marge's thoughts are interrupted when a convoy of trucks transporting factory equipment rolls into town, in the midst of which is an attractive man in a snappy roadster. She senses that her luck may have suddenly changed, and she sets out to pick him up. All in all, it was a terrific beginning.

About eighteen months later Unger sent me the final manuscript. It was some 700 pages long. About a fifth was taken up by a separate story of German prisoners-of-war working for the food trust; the final third jumped ahead thirty years to tell of the return of Marge's son to Nowell, now a ghost town. Along with its disconnected narrative, the writing had grown strangely mock-allegorical and surreal in places, as though Unger's imagination had been invaded by an alien force, perhaps Thomas Pynchon's. Most disappointing of all, he seemed to have turned away from a story with a great deal of prospective meaning—the eradication of farmers and agrarian values by agribusiness—to make instead the post-modernist point of pointlessness. I wrote him a long letter along these lines, and ended by saying that I still sensed there was a genuine novel buried inside this swollen one and hoped he would have the courage to find it. When he read the letter, Unger was so enraged he threw down the manuscript and began to jump on it, shouting, 'But I've spent so much time on it already.'

He didn't write anything for a year and a half. By then he was living on an unworked farm and had become a commercial fisherman. One night he woke up with the people he had written about on his mind, pulled out the manuscript and began to reread it. He was struck by the distortions: 'I was running up against people every day who gave the lie to what I'd done to my characters. Then one day my wife's older sister turned up with one of her sons to try to get the farm going again: he wanted nothing to do with it. Their struggle made me see that the original version was wrong. It should have been about Marge all along and her efforts—by staying in that forsaken community—to hold on to the land with the same tenacity her father had shown and pass it on to her son. Much of this material was already there. In order to feel easy again, I had to rework it.'

It took another three years. After he had left Iowa City, Unger spent some time with Raymond Carver. 'Anyone who knows Ray knows that you have to believe that if you write well you'll eventually get published. Ray kept saying that "a good book is an honest one." I knew that his whole career had been an effort to write honestly, so those words really sunk in. At Iowa I was desperate to get published, and I thought it would help if I put in a lot of post-modernist effects. Barth and Barthelme and Pynchon were all the rage.'

Ungar ended up with three novellas: Marge's early life culminating in her affair and marriage to the man in the roadster, a lawyer for the food trust; the prisoners-of-war story; Marge and her son twenty-five years later, her marriage long over, the farm and most of the area abandoned. A brave, sad, increasingly bleak wind of feeling blew through the final novella, joining it tonally as well as narratively to the first. Were they the buried novel? The prose of all three maintained the straightforward realism of the original opening but Unger's style had grown diamond-hard, with glints of light whichever way it turned. The three were eminently publishable as they were. Unger decided to go for the novel and set to work revising the first and last to join them more securely together.

What enabled him to persist through all of his rewriting and also to let 150 pages of very good writing go by the board? 'By now I'd lost any egotistical involvement in the work, and was watching—almost impersonally—a process occurring. The book wanted to come together and I was the last person to stand in its way.'

Unger needed a period of adversity and silence not only to recover from 'my litany of flaws', as he put it, but also to reorient himself as a writer and to undo the damage that the fashionable and false writer, wanting to be published as soon as possible, had done to the uncertain true one who had started the project. Then the characters, like rejected family or abused friends, began to return.

I t is precisely this struggle with rejection that helps the young writer develop his main defence against the narcissism that prompts him to speak out in the first place. Writing to a friend, Pushkin tells of reading a canto of *Eugene Onegin* which he had just composed, jumping from his chair, and proudly shouting, 'Hey you, Pushkin! Hey you, son of a bitch!' Every writer knows that feeling, but every writer also knows how easily it can turn over into self-hatred, when the writing or the blank page reflects back one's limitations, failure, deadness. The writer's defence is his power of self-objectivity, his interest in otherness, and his faith in the process itself which enables him to write on into the teeth of his doubts and then to improve it. In the scars of the struggle between the odd, sensitive side of the self that wants to write and the practical, socialized one that wants results, the gifted young writer is likely to find his signature. Writing itself, if not misunderstood and abused, becomes a way of empowering the writing self. It converts diffuse anger and disappointment into deliberate and durable aggression, the writer's main source of energy. It converts sorrow and self-pity into empathy, the writer's main means of relating to otherness. His wounded innocence turns into irony, his silliness into wit, his guilt into judgement, his oddness into originality, his perverseness into his stinger.

Because all of this takes time, indeed most of a lifetime to complete itself, the gifted young writer has to learn that his main task is to persist. This means he must be tough-minded about his fantasies of wealth, fame and the love of beautiful men or women. However stimulating these may be for the social self, for the writing one who perforce needs to stay home and be alone, they are enacted mostly as fantasies that maintain the adolescent romance of the magically empowered ego that the writer must outgrow if he is to survive. And this is so even if the fantasies come true, and often enough, particularly if they come true. No writer rode these fantasies further or more damagingly than Scott Fitzgerald, but it was Fitzgerald who said that inside a novelist there has to be a lot of the peasant.

Rejection and uncertainty teach the writer the value and fragility of his gift—a gift that is both a skill, better at some tasks than others, and a power that comes and goes. Even when it comes, it is often only partly functioning and its directives are only partly understood. Writing a first draft is like groping one's way into a pitch dark room, or overhearing a faint conversation, or telling a joke whose punchline you've forgotten. As someone said, one writes mainly to rewrite, for rewriting and revising are how one's mind comes to inhabit the material fully.

In its benign form, rewriting is a second, third, and *n*th chance to make something come right, to 'fall graciously into place', in Lewis Hyde's phrase. But it is also the test: one has to learn to respect the misgiving that says, This still doesn't ring true, still hasn't touched bottom. And this means to go back down into the mine again and poke around for the missing ore and find a place for it and let it work its will. Revision is another process: turning loose the editor in oneself, a caretaker who straightens out and tidies up.

At the same time, one must come to the truth of Conrad's remark that no work is ever finished, only at a certain point abandoned. Beyond that point, rewriting and revising can turn compulsive and malignant, devouring the vitality and integrity of what one has to tell.

There appear to be better and worse ways to get through this long period of self-apprenticeship. Of the first novelists and story writers I've recently been involved with, virtually none of them were teaching writing, at least not full-time. Teaching offers the lure of relatively pleasant work and significant free time, but it comes with the snare of using and distorting much of the same energy that goes into writing and tends to fills the mind with the high examples of the models one teaches and the low ones of student work. It is insulating and predictable during the period when the young fiction writer should be as open as possible to a range of experience, for the sake of his characters as well as his material. A job that makes use of another skill or talent and doesn't come home with one seems to work best over the long haul. It's also well, of course, to give as few hostages as possible to fortune.

W hat the young writer most needs is 'patient time'. Bobbie Ann Mason says that, when asked by students how to get published, she feels like saying, 'Don't worry about it for twenty years or so. It takes that long before you really know what you're doing.' She began writing fiction in 1971 after she got out of graduate school, and for the next five years or so wrote in a desultory way, finding it hard to get focused—until 1976, when she finished a novel about a girl, like herself addicted to Nancy Drew novels. 'It took another two years before I began to find my true subject, which was to write about my roots and the kinds of people I'd known, but from my own point of view. It mainly took a lot of living to get to that point. I'd come from such a sheltered and isolated background that I had to go through culture-shock by living for years in the North to see the world of Mayfield, Kentucky, in a way I could write about as I was now—as an exile of sorts. It wasn't until I was in my thirties that I got enough detachment and objectivity to see that many of those people back home were going through culture-shock too.'

My own sense is that young fiction writers should separate the necessity to write fiction from what it is often confused with, the desire to publish it. This helps to keep the writer's mind where it belongs—on his own work—and where it doesn't—on the market, which is next to useless, and on writers who are succeeding, which is discouraging. Comparisons with other writers should be inspiring; otherwise they're invidious. Bobbie Ann Mason says that 'the writer I was most involved with was Nabokov. It was because he was a stylist and had a peculiar sensibility. In some ways, comparing myself to him is like comparing Willy Nelson to an opera singer, but I felt connected to him because he had the sensibility of an exile, was working with two opposing cultures which made him peculiar, the same way I felt myself.'

T hirty years ago there was a great fear of 'selling out', and 'prostituting your talent'. Literary mores no longer place as much stock in the hieratic model of the writer, which is just as well. Unless one is good at self-sacrifice, endowed with an iron will and a genius-sized gift, it's likely to be a defeating thing to insist on producing Art or nothing.

If one of the primary projects of the gifted young writer is to begin to create a 'demilitarized zone' between his social side and his literary one, so that the latter can live in peace for a while, it is also true that both need exercise and some degree of satisfaction and toughening. Many novelists-in-progress find it helpful to take their talent, at least some of the time, out of the rarefied and tenuous realm of literature and put it to work in the market-place to try to earn part of its keep. Even hackwriting has the benefit of putting serious writing into its proper perspective as a privilege rather than a burden. At a respectable professional level, writing for publication makes one into someone who writes rather than, in Robert Louis Stevenson's distinction, someone who wants to have written. Writing without publishing gets to be like loving someone from afar—delicious for fantasies but thin gruel for living. That is why, to my mind, a strongly written review, profile, piece of reportage in a regional magazine—the *Village Voice*, or the *Texas Monthly* or *Seattle Magazine*—is worth three 'Try us again's' from the *New Yorker*.

The first years on your own are a good time to let the imagination off the leash and let it sniff and paw into other fields of writing. From journal writing it's only a small Kierkegaardian leap into the personal essay. There is also the possibility of discovering that criticism or reportage or some other mode is for the time being more congenial than fiction. A young fiction writer I'd been working with for years had about come to the end of his line when he had the wit to turn one of his stories into a one-act play, and has been writing as a playwright ever since. One of the most deforming aspects of American literary culture is the cult of the novel and—with it—the decline of the concept of the man of letters, which less specialized times and less academicized literary cultures than ours took for granted. And still do in Europe, where a Graham Greene, a Robbe-Grillet, a Grass, a Kundera write in three or four modes, depending upon the subject, occasion and the disposition of his well-balanced Muse. Experimenting with other modes, in any case, releases energy and helps to demystify the writer's vocation which, like any other, is an ongoing practice rather than a higher state of being. This is particularly so for a prospective novelist. Auden puts it very well when he says that the novelist

Must struggle out of his boyish gift and learn
How to be plain and awkward, how to be
One after whom none think it worth to turn.

For to achieve his lightest wish, he must
Become the whole of boredom, subject to
Vulgar complaints like love, among the Just
Be just, among the Filthy filthy too.

Virtually all of the fiction writers I've mentioned fix the turning point in their writing lives at the stage when the intrinsic interest of what they were doing began to take over and generate a sense of necessity. This seems to be particularly true of women writers. As Lynne Sharon Schwartz explained, 'Most women don't give themselves the freedom to pursue their dream. Being brought up a girl has meant just that.' She began to write stories when she was seven and did so again during and after college, but without taking the enterprise very seriously. 'I'd get a letter from the *Paris Review* inviting me to submit other work and I'd think, "That's nice," and then put it away in a drawer. Writing fiction was one of several dreams that probably wouldn't be realized.' She married, had children, went back to graduate school which somehow seemed okay to do, perhaps because no one does much dreaming in graduate school. 'I found, though, that I didn't want to write a dissertation when I got to that point. I just couldn't face the library part of it. Going down into the stacks seemed so alien to my real sources. About that time a childhood friend who also was married and had children told me she had resolved to give herself five years to become a dance critic. It was the way she did it, putting everything else to the side. It was her fierce tenacity that inspired me. I gave up graduate school and started to write fiction again.'

Over the next few years she worked on a first novel which went unpublished. 'Just as well, but it got me an agent and some nice rejection letters, which was encouraging.' In time she developed a small network of women fiction writers, published two stories in little magazines, and then a satire on Watergate in the *New Republic*. 'Doris Grumbach, then the literary editor, called me up to tell me and asked me who I was, where I'd been all this time. I realized I might be someone after all.'

Shortly after that, she received a rejection letter from me which so offended her that she burned it in a little ceremony of exorcism. A year or two later I chose another of her stories, about a professional couple trying to have a baby and then to cope with the changes it brings, for the *Best American Short Stories of 1977*. I sent her a blithe letter asking if she had anything else I could see or talk with her about. Her outrage was still on tap. 'I had been learning from my husband how one went about developing a career, and when I told him I'd be damned if I'd have lunch with you, he told me to be sensible and see what you had to say—"He probably doesn't even remember writing to you." So I decided to be very professional about it.' Which she was. One meeting led to another in which we began to plan a collection of stories about the professional couple, which instead turned into the novel *Rough Strife*.

Now, four books later, Lynne Schwartz looks back at these years and sees mainly herself at work. 'I had to learn to write completely alone. There was no help, no other writer to emulate, no one's influence. It was too private for that. Once I got started I wanted the life of a writer so fiercely that nothing could stop me. I wanted the intensity, the sense of aliveness that came from writing fiction. I'm still that way. My life is worth living when I've completed a good paragraph.'

The development of this sense of necessity seems to be the rock bottom basis for a career as a novelist. Whatever may feed it, whatever may impede it finally comes to be subsidiary to the simple imperative of being at work. At this point, writing fiction has become one's way, in the religious sense of the term. Not that there are any guarantees that it will continue to be for good or that it will make your inner life easier to bear. The life of published fiction writers is most often the exchange of one level of rejection, uncertainty and disappointment for another, and throughout, they need the same durable, patient conviction that got them published in the first place.

LETTERS

CR (a?) P

To the Editor

Your Editorial (*Granta* 13) is the intellectual equivalent of a knitting basket after the cat has finished with it—a woolly muddle.

Insofar as I can disentangle a main thread, you argue:

1. That Conor Cruise O'Brien wrote a column to disabuse some wimpy liberals of their soft notions about post-colonial black Africa.

2. That 'Tiny' Rowland, the proprietor of the *Observer*, in which O'Brien's piece appeared, also owns a mine in (colonial, white-ruled) South Africa, where black Africans are horribly exploited. *Ergo*,

3. Dr O'Brien, by writing what he did where he did, was exercising 'unpardonable licence'.

Leaving aside the obvious non-sequiturs, you seem to be propounding an interesting new doctrine of your own, which might be called, in the O'Brien Acronymic Mode, CRP: Columnist Responsible for Proprietor. Because Tiny Rowland exploits black miners in South Africa, you imply, Dr O'Brien has no moral right to say anything critical about black Africa. Thus, according to the Buford Doctrine (CRP), before sitting down to write for, say, *The Times* about the exploitation of workers in communist Poland, I should first make exhaustive inquiries to establish that Rupert Murdoch does not anywhere own a capitalist company which exploits white Europeans. This is fatuous.

You reinforce your argument by recalling the conflict between the *Observer* and Rowland about reporting the atrocities in Zimbabwe. But doesn't the fact of those atrocities in a post-colonial black African country suggest that Dr O'Brien may just have a point? If I were Dr O'Brien I would be tempted once again to quote *Granta*—the very number in which your editorial appears—to illustrate what can happen, what almost always does happen, after the revolution. Because Americans committed atrocities against Cambodians, it did not follow that Cambodians could not commit atrocities against Cambodians. On the contrary. Similarly, because Europeans committed (and in South Africa still commit) atrocities against Africans, this doesn't mean that Africans can't commit atrocities against Africans.

In a parting shot, you note triumphantly that Dr O'Brien was sacked at Rowland's insistence. I suppose this shows just how far he was responsible for his proprietor's actions.

Timothy Garton Ash
Oxford

The Editor replies:

Timothy Garton Ash's letter is written with great confidence. It would be even stronger, I suspect, if before writing it, he actually read properly the editorial his letter criticizes. The editorial objects not to Conor Cruise O'Brien's claim in itself—that Western liberals refuse to admit the injustice in Africa perpetuated by blacks—but to the far more ludicrous assumption underlying it: that today injustice in and no longer by European

Africa is perpetuated only by blacks countries. This struck me as a rather peculiar way to think, especially when it is so vividly undermined by the very paper in which these views are published: the South African interests of the *Observer*'s publisher are not, as the editorial clearly establishes, limited to one mine; similarly, the terrible injustice seen in those mines is not that different from the injustices found in his other mines in other parts of Africa. To elaborate on Timothy Garton Ash's own example, O'Brien's myopic assertions expressed in the *Observer* would be analogous to a piece in *The Times* arguing, say, that proprietors play a negligible role in what British papers publish: there are occasions when it's awkward not taking your outlet into account, especially when the nature of the outlet contradicts what you want to say in it.

Finally, I am not suggesting that columnists be responsible for their proprietors, but simply that they, like letter writers, not allow their prejudices and hobby-horses to govern their vision.

SHOCK! HORROR!

To the Editor

I don't know what shocked me more: that Peter Preston, the editor of the only readable paper in Britain, should write a letter of such mindless, self-implicating and reckless slander; or, that *Granta* would actually publish it [*Granta* 13]. Preston's portrait of David Caute is cheap, sensational and tawdry, and was used merely to obscure the fact that he had

absolutely no defence against the charge David Caute makes: Peter Preston betrayed his source. But in publishing his letter, *Granta* has, in turn, betrayed one of its authors: David Caute should sue both of you for everything he can get.

Philip Chapman
London

Commies

To the Editor:

Granta has always been distinguished for its international flavour, remaining open to literary developments in Latin America and, most recently, Eastern Europe. And some wonderful issues have been the result. Lately, however, the work you've published is starting to seem all too predictable. Do we really need to 'learn' that yet another communist poet is arrested, telling the same story that we hear in the same issue from another Russian novelist, which is, even down to some of its smallest details, the same story we hear from yet another Czech? We already know the horrors of Soviet society—do you need to tell us that communism is bad?—and there are more than enough outlets to keep us up to date. But I expect something different from *Granta*. I still expect the internationalism. But it would be a shame if the politics became predictable.

A. David Jones
London

All letters are welcome and should be addressed to the Editor, Granta, 44a Hobson Street, Cambridge CB1 1NL, England.

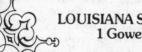

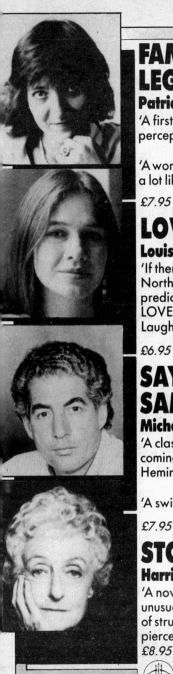

FAMILY MYTHS AND LEGENDS
Patricia Ferguson
'A first novel of great funniness and perception and stunning originality'
Daily Telegraph
'A wonderfully spare first novel – in places a lot like early Beryl Bainbridge'
The Observer
£7.95

LOVE MEDICINE
Louise Erdrich
'If there has been a better novel about the North American Indian and his predicament between two worlds than LOVE MEDICINE in all the years since Laughing Boy it has not come my way'
The Guardian
£6.95

SAY GOODBYE TO SAM
Michael J. Arlen
'A classic tale of filial confrontation and coming to terms . . . spare, controlled with Hemingwayesque overtones'
Publishers Weekly
'A swift sure-handed performance'
Newsweek
£7.95

STONES FOR IBARRA
Harriet Doerr
'A novel of extraordinary beauty, of unusual finish, and, though free of any sort of strutting, of striking originality . . . it pierces the heart'
New Yorker
£8.95

ANDRE DEUTSCH

Notes on Contributors

Richard Ford is the author of two novels, *A Piece of my Heart* and *The Ultimate Good Luck*, and is currently finishing a third. His work has appeared in *Granta* 8 and 12. **Philip Norman**'s collection of profiles and portraits, *Tilt the Hourglass and begin again*, is published in England in June. He contributed to *Granta* 7, 'Best of Young British Novelists'. **James Fenton** spent a total of eighteen months in Vietnam, Cambodia, Laos and Thailand between 1973 and 1975. 'Road to Cambodia', another memoir of his time in Indochina, was published in *Granta* 10, 'Travel Writing'. He is the author of *The Memory of War and Children in Exile* , a collection of poetry. **Frank Snepp**'s *Decent Interval: the American Debacle in Vietnam and the Fall of Saigon* is published by Penguin Books. He now lives in Los Angeles. **Noam Chomsky**'s most recent book is *The Fateful Triangle: Israel, the United States and the Palestinians*. **Norman Podhoretz** is the editor of *Commentary* and author of *Why We were in Vietnam*. **Nadine Gordimer** is the author of seven novels and four collections of short stories, the most recent of which is *Something Out There*, published last year. She lives in Johannesburg. **George Steiner**'s most recent book is *Antigones*. His novella *The Portage to San Cristobal of A.H.* was published in *Granta* 2. **Salman Rushdie** is the author of *Grimus, Midnight's Children*, and *Shame*. His essay 'Outside the Whale' was published in *Granta* 11. Both his piece and **Günter Grass**'s '*The Tin Drum* in Retrospect' will be included in Grass's second collection of essays, *On Writing and Politics,* to be published in the United States in June by Harcourt Brace Jovanovich and in Britain in July by Secker and Warburg. **John Berger**'s work has appeared in *Granta* 13, 'After the Revolution', and *Granta* 9 which featured his novella, 'Boris'. 'Go ask the Time' is included in the collection of essays *About Time* published in Britain in May by Jonathan Cape. **Marilynne Robinson** is the author of one novel, *Housekeeping*. She lives in Northampton, Massachusetts. **Michael Crick** is a reporter and producer on ITN's Channel Four News, and the author of *Scargill and the Miners*. **Ted Solotaroff** edited the New American Review from 1967 to 1977. He is an editor at Harper and Row in New York.

Photocredits (in order): Popperfoto; Ian Berry/Magnum; Popperfoto; Bryn Campbell/Magnum; Jean-Claude Francolon/Gamma; Popperfoto; C. Leroy/Photo Researchers, Inc; Associated Press; Popperfoto; Associated Press; Herve Cloaguen/Viva; Embassy of the People's Republic of Vietnam; Keystone; C. Leroy/Photo Researchers, Inc; William Campbell/Sygma; Sygma; 'Self Portrait with Snail' from *Günter Grass: Drawings and Words, 1954–1977* courtesy of Herman Luchterhand Verlag; National Galleries of Scotland; Burt Glinn/Magnum.

KING PENGUIN

1982 JANINE
Alasdair Gray
'A remarkable black humorist . . . a painful, almost flawless tour-de-force' – George Melly in the *Sunday Times* 'Books of the Year' £3.95.

THE PORK BUTCHER
David Hughes
Winner of the W. H. Smith Literary Award 1985
'An unforgettable experience, a fable which touches many unexpected nerves' – *Observer* £2.95

ANGELS
Denis Johnson
'Prose of amazing power and stylishness . . . a small masterpiece' – Philip Roth in the *Sunday Times* 'Books of the Year' £2.95

DANGEROUS PLAY
Poems 1974-1984
Andrew Motion
One of the most original voices of his generation – winner of the 1984 John *Llewelyn Rhys Memorial Prize*. £2.95

THE HAWTHORN GODDESS
Glyn Hughes
'Triumphantly individual, mingling the eerie, the sombre and the rhapsodic in writing of inexorable power' – *Observer* £2.95

PARALLEL LIVES
Five Victorian Marriages
Phyllis Rose
'Outstanding . . . brilliantly evokes those inky-fingered unions before the bright coal fires' – Norman St John-Stevas in the *Sunday Times* 'Books of the Year' £3.95

You'll be surprised.